The Empowered Condo Board

by Matthew Snyder

DISCLAIMER

The information contained in this book is intended to provide general guidance on condominium association management. It is not a substitute for legal advice specific to your jurisdiction or your association's governing documents. Laws and regulations governing condominiums can be complex and change frequently. Please consult a qualified attorney for all legal matters related to your condominium association. The author and publisher disclaim any liability for actions taken based on the information in this book.

FOREWORD

Condominium communities are dynamic – it's about more than just buildings and rules, it's about the people and how they interact. Volunteer boards face tough decisions they're often unprepared for. That's why this book exists. We're not offering those simplistic, one-size-fits-all answers you often hear. To succeed, boards need flexible tools and strategies. We'll cover the nitty-gritty, the stuff you only learn from experience, and go beyond the basics.

Whether you're a seasoned board member or a newbie, you'll find value here. We'll strike a balance – never too simplistic or too overwhelming. This isn't just about following rules, it's about creating a thriving community: legal stuff, resident happiness, strong finances, and a vision for the future.

What makes this book different? We go beyond basic survival mode. We'll cover conflict resolution, communication, building community, even the psychology behind group interactions. These are the keys to turning a bunch of condos into a place people truly love calling home.

We'll break down complex topics (like reserve funds, dealing with vendors) in plain English, so you can make the best decisions for your community.

Having seen good communities fall apart from bad choices and petty squabbles, I'm driven to create a guide that shares what I've learned. Let's tackle this together!

Sincerely,

Matthew Snyder

https://managemax.properties/

TABLE OF CONTENTS

Disclaimer
Foreword
Table of Contents
Introduction: Setting the Stage for Effective Condominium Management
    Welcome and Acknowledgement
    The Heart of the Condominium
    The Board of Directors: Stewards of the Community
    The Power of Effective Management
    Common Challenges & Exciting Opportunities
    The Guide Ahead
Chapter 1: Understanding Your Community's Foundation
    Introduction
    Governing Documents
    State and Local Laws Affecting Condominiums
    The History of Your Community
    Putting Knowledge into Action
    Chapter Summary: Understanding Your Community's Foundation
    Test Your Knowledge!
    Case Study: The Bylaw Battle
    Case Study: Navigating the Zoning Maze
    Case Study: Overcoming Obstacles to Accessibility
    Case Study: The Reserve Fund Rescue
    Case Study: From Conflict to Collaboration
    Case Study: Fair Housing – More Than Just a Law
    Test Your Knowledge! Answers
Chapter 2: Financial Health and Planning
    Introduction

- Creating and Adhering to an Annual Budget
- Understanding Reserve Funds
- Setting Appropriate Assessment Fees
- Financial Reporting and Transparency
- Expansion: Reserve Studies and Communication
- Conclusion
- Test Your Knowledge!
- Case Study: The Dues Dilemma
- Case Study: The Case of the Missing Reserve Fund
- Case Study: Reserve Study Revelations
- Case Study: The Zero-Based Budget Success
- Case Study: Financial Reporting Facelift
- Case Study: Proactive Planning Pays Off
- Test Your Knowledge! Answers

Chapter 3: Maintenance and Operations
- Introduction
- Developing Maintenance Plans
- Vendor Selection and Contract Management
- Proactive Maintenance vs. Reactive Repairs
- Emergency Preparedness
- Sustainable Maintenance: Good for the Planet, Good for Your Wallet
- Conclusion
- Test Your Knowledge!
- Case Study: The Leaky Roof (Proactive vs. Reactive)
- Case Study: The Reserve Study Savior (Long-Term Planning)
- Case Study: Beyond the Bottom Line (Vendor Selection)
- Case Study: Communication is Key (Resident Involvement)
- Case Study: Going Green (Sustainability)
- Case Study: Evolving with the Times (Continuous Improvement)
- Test Your Knowledge! Answers

Chapter 4: Resident Communication and Engagement
- Introduction
- Setting Clear Communication Expectations
- Encouraging Resident Involvement
- Effective Dispute Resolution

    Nurturing a Sense of Community
    Additional Considerations for Board Members: Beyond the Basics
    Conclusion: Communication – The Heart of a Thriving Community
    Test Your Knowledge!
    Case Study: The Newsletter That Wasn't
    Case Study: The Listening Board
    Case Study: When Social Media Bites
    Case Study: The Squeaky Wheel
    Case Study: The Phantom Decision
    Case Study: From Blame Game to Brainstorm
    Case Study: The Overloaded Manager
    Test Your Knowledge! Answers
Chapter 5: Board Governance and Leadership
    Introduction
    Roles and Responsibilities of Board Members
    Effective Board Meetings
    Board Member Training and Education
    Fiduciary Duty and Acting in the Best Interests of the Community
    Building a Strong and Sustainable Board
    Conclusion
    Test Your Knowledge!
    Case Study: The Self-Serving Vendor (Conflict of Interest)
    Case Study: The Missing Minutes (Importance of Documentation)
    Case Study: Orientation Overload (Effective Onboarding)
    Case Study: The Tiebreaker (Decision Making)
    Case Study: Bridging the Skills Gap (Training and Education)
    Case Study: The Succession Success (Board Recruitment)
    Test Your Knowledge! Answers
Chapter 6: Assessing Your Community's Health
    Introduction
    Recognizing a Community in Crisis
    Hallmarks of a Stable Community
    A Well-Functioning Community: Going Above and Beyond
    Call to Action
    Test Your Knowledge!

Case Study: Financial Foresight – A Cautionary Tale
Case Study: The Power of Proactive Maintenance
Case Study: Decline Due to Neglect – The Downward Spiral of Whispering Pines
Case Study: From Conflict to Collaboration at Maplewood
Case Study: Help from the Professionals
Case Study: Curb Appeal's Impact
Test Your Knowledge! Answers

Chapter 7: Strategies for Improvement
Introduction
Prioritizing Actions for Distressed Communities
Enhancing a Stable Community: Focus and Strategies
Taking a Well-Functioning Community to the Next Level
Conclusion: The Journey of Continuous Improvement
Test Your Knowledge!
Case Study: From Crisis to Stability (Distressed Community)
Case Study: Small Change, Big Impact (Stable Community)
Case Study: Tech Upgrade - Winning Over the Skeptics (Well-Functioning Community)
Case Study: When Bylaws Get Dusty (All Communities)
Case Study: The Power of Planning (Long-Term Finance)
Case Study: Building a Future Board (Succession Planning)
Test Your Knowledge! Answers

Chapter 8: Working with Professionals
Introduction
The Role of a Management Company
Selecting and Managing Attorneys, Accountants, and Other Specialists
Defining Expectations and Ensuring Effective Collaboration
Conclusion: The Power of Professional Partnerships
Test Your Knowledge!
Case Study: The Bylaw Blunder
Case Study: The Missing Money Mystery
Case Study: Communication Breakdown
Case Study: The Power of Proactive Planning
Case Study: Seeking a Second Opinion – When "Good Enough"

    Isn't Good Enough
    Case Study: The Power of Finding the Right Cultural Fit
    Test Your Knowledge! Answers

Chapter 9: Legal and Regulatory Compliance
    Introduction
    Key Federal Laws
    State and Local Regulations: A Navigational Guide for Boards
    Understanding Insurance Fundamentals
    Staying Informed and Proactive
    Staying Ahead of the Curve: Addressing New Legal and Social Trends
    Conclusion: Compliance as a Continuous Journey
    Test Your Knowledge!
    Case Study: The Pet Policy Problem
    Case Study: Insurance Nightmare – When Coverage Isn't Enough
    Case Study: The Bylaws Backfire
    Case Study: The Reserve Fund Crisis
    Case Study: The Short-Term Rental Showdown
    Case Study: The Power of Proactive Compliance
    Test Your Knowledge! Answers

Chapter 10: Amenities and Lifestyle Management
    Introduction
    Understanding Your Current Amenities
    Amenity Evaluation for Beginners
    Strategic Planning for New Amenities: A Must-Do
    Amenity Management Best Practices
    Enhancing the Lifestyle Experience
    Beyond the Amenities: Planning for Long-Term Success
    Test Your Knowledge!
    Case Study: The "Small But Mighty" Condo (Rewritten)
    Case Study: The Revitalized Fitness Center (Rewritten)
    Case Study: Embracing Accessibility in Luxury Living (Rewritten)
    Case Study: The Community Coffeehouse (Rewritten)
    Case Study: The Tech-Forward Amenity Upgrade
    Case Study: Partnering for Perks
    Test Your Knowledge! Answers

Chapter 11: The Board-Manager Partnership
   Introduction
   The Foundation of a Successful Partnership
   Performance Evaluations: A Tool for Excellence
   Contract Negotiation
   Conflict Resolution
   Optimizing the Board-Manager Partnership
   Test Your Knowledge!
   Case Study: The Value of Open Communication
   Case Study: Mediation Makes the Difference
   Case Study: Trouble at the Top
   Case Study: The Power of a Point Person
   Case Study: Why Documentation Matters
   Case Study: Investing in the Manager – The Power of Professional Growth
   Test Your Knowledge! Answers
Chapter 12: Data-Driven Decision Making
   Introduction
   Data: The Key to Informed Decisions
   Tools for Smart Data Collection
   Analyzing Data for Smart Decision-Making
   Using Data to Make Smart Decisions
   Data: Your Roadmap to a Thriving Community
   Test Your Knowledge!
   Case Study: The Case of the Unexpected Expense
   Case Study: Pool or Playground? The Power of Resident Feedback
   Case Study: The Curious Case of the Rising Expenses
   Case Study: The Parking Policy Problem
   Case Study: Ice Cream vs. Sunburns: When Data Saves the Day
   Case Study: The Power of Visualization
   Test Your Knowledge! Answers
Chapter 13: Community Psychology
   Introduction
   Beyond Formal Roles – Understanding Group Dynamics
   Understanding What Drives Residents (And How to Respond)
   Building a Positive Community Mindset: Together

- Conclusion: The Heart of a Thriving Condo Community
- Discover Your Communication Style – Key to a Harmonious Condo Board
- Test Your Knowledge!
- Case Study: When a Muffin Becomes a Mountain
- Case Study: When a Passion Project Becomes a Battleground
- Case Study: The Phantom Barking Dog
- Case Study: Great Idea, But How? When Community Funds Spark Conflict
- Case Study: When Personalities Clash – Transforming Dysfunction into Dialogue
- Case Study: From Apathy to Action – Revitalizing a Disengaged Community
- Test Your Knowledge! Answers

Conclusion
- The Launchpad: Embracing Your Role as a Leader
- Beyond Problem-Solving: The Board's Strategic Role
- Stay Ahead of the Curve: Prioritize Board Education
- Dynamic Leadership for Dynamic Communities

About the Author

INTRODUCTION: SETTING THE STAGE FOR EFFECTIVE CONDOMINIUM MANAGEMENT

Welcome And Acknowledgement

Let's work together to improve your experience as a board member! This book is for everyone, from newcomers to seasoned veterans. You'll find tools and support to help you navigate challenges and create a thriving community.

Having been both a property management professional and a board member myself, I understand that every decision, big or small, shapes your community's future. My goal is to give you the knowledge and confidence to make the best choices for your residents.

The Heart Of The Condominium

Condominiums are more than just buildings – they're legal agreements where owners share spaces and responsibilities. There are areas everyone uses (think lobbies, elevators) and spaces attached to specific units. Understanding this is key for good decision-making.

Living in a condo means being closer to your neighbors. This changes how you interact compared to single-family homes, where you have more privacy. To maintain property values, you have to plan and pay for shared upkeep. Well-maintained common areas make everyone's life better! On the flip side, even a few neglected properties bring the whole community down.

One owner's actions can impact everyone. Think about things like noise, pet policies, and how shared amenities are used. Even your community's reputation is a shared asset! All this shared living comes at a cost – your dues fund maintenance and management so your investment stays strong.

Let me give you an example: In one community I managed, some folks wanted to keep the pool open later. Sounds harmless, right? But it disrupted the sleep of neighbors. This shows how well-intended actions can backfire. Always think about how decisions will ripple out and affect everyone.

That's where the board comes in, and that's what this book will help you with. Let's dive deeper into how condominium communities work!

The Board Of Directors: Stewards Of The Community

Boards have some serious jobs! One of the toughest is balancing different resident needs. You hear the most vocal complaints, but do they really represent everyone in the community? Another major job is making smart decisions for the entire community. Finally, boards must uphold the community's rules and values.

Here's what that looks like in practice:

- Budgeting wisely
- Maintaining shared spaces
- Enforcing rules fairly
- Dealing with resident issues
- Hiring the right companies to help run things

Think of the board as the community's caretakers. You're not just checking legal boxes – you must always plan ahead to avoid problems. As the community's leaders, the board is legally required to act in the community's best interest. This trust is essential!

Plus, the board sets the tone for everyone else. A calm, fair, and focused board inspires those same qualities in residents. Boards should be role models: respectful, professional, following the spirit of the rules, and committed to the community's success. A trustworthy board builds a trustworthy community.

Think about this example: A roof project goes bad when the board puts its own interests first instead of being fair. The mess destroys trust and harms the community. This shows how the board's choices shape the whole community's experience.

So, ask yourself – are you setting a good example, or do you see yourself as above the rules?

The Power Of Effective Management

Being a board member isn't just about paperwork – it makes a huge difference in everyone's lives! Here's how effective management directly impacts residents:

Boosting Everyone's Investment:

- A well-maintained community is a desirable one, keeping property values strong.
- Smart budgeting and spending reassure buyers and keep prices stable.
- Good management attracts great residents and keeps the ones you have, increasing demand and driving up property values.

Happier Residents:

- When problems are addressed quickly, and residents get clear updates, they feel valued and trust grows.
- Open communication cuts down on misunderstandings and helps everyone feel heard.
- A welcoming community with fun events, nice amenities, and fair rules makes people feel good about where they live.

Protecting the Community's Future:

- Proactive maintenance saves everyone money in the long run by preventing big repair bills.
- Planning ahead protects your buildings, your finances, and helps you weather any storms.

All these things add up to a thriving community where everyone wants to live! So, as a board member, take pride in shaping a better present and future for your residents.

Common Challenges & Exciting Opportunities

Board life has its ups and downs. Here are some common hurdles you'll face:

- **Squabbles:** Neighbor disputes happen. Dealing with them fairly is key to keeping the peace and protecting property values.
- **Tight Budgets:** Finding the right balance between needed repairs and what residents can afford is always a challenge. If you neglect things, it costs more later. But overspending makes people angry.
- **Low Interest:** It can be hard to get residents involved in meetings, surveys, or votes.

This is just a taste of the challenges you'll face as a board member – there are plenty more!

But wait, there's a bright side! Here's where being a board member gets exciting:

- **Community Builder:** Throw fun events, volunteer together... these connections make your community stronger.
- **Fix-It Hero:** Sprucing up common areas, even with small stuff like fresh paint, makes everyone feel proud.
- **Planner Extraordinaire:** Taking steps today (like budgeting for future repairs) protects your community for years to come.

We'll dive deeper into both the challenges and opportunities of board life throughout the book. My goal is to help you make the most of this experience and create a community you love!

The Guide Ahead

This book is your roadmap for being an effective board member! I'll give you the tools for everyday tasks and long-term planning. Plus, we'll cover building a strong community and creating a clear vision for where you're headed.

You'll learn how to handle typical problems: disputes, budgets, understanding the rules, choosing vendors, keeping an eye on your management company, and running meetings that actually get things done! I aim for a mix of practical tips and big-picture strategy.

This book covers it all: legal stuff, communication, maintenance, and how to be a strong leader. I'll share real-life examples to bring the ideas to life and help you apply them to your own community.

Get ready to step into your full potential and create a community you can be proud of! We'll start with the must-knows (financial health, upkeep, communication), then get into deeper waters: assessing how well your community is really doing, improvement strategies, and working with the pros. I've even saved a few special surprises for the end!

I'm excited to have you here. Let's use my experience to make your board service a success!

CHAPTER 1: UNDERSTANDING YOUR COMMUNITY'S FOUNDATION

Introduction

Think of your condominium community as a building. Just like any building needs a solid foundation, good community management relies on a strong understanding of rules and laws. Think of this knowledge as your blueprint! It might seem a bit dry at first, but it's absolutely crucial for making smart decisions, keeping things fair, and solving any problems that pop up.

With everyone on the same page about rules – both board members and residents – your community becomes a much smoother-running machine. Fewer misunderstandings, less conflict, and a shared focus on creating a great place to live. Of course, some disagreements are inevitable, but having this solid foundation makes resolving them much easier.

Yes, this chapter dives into some less-than-thrilling details. But trust me, it's the groundwork for everything else we'll cover in the book. Power through this, and you'll be equipped to tackle all the fun and challenging parts of condominium management that come up in the book chapters ahead.

Governing Documents

Understanding Your Community's Foundation

A community's foundation lies in its governing documents. The most important of these is the Declaration (or Master Deed). This document officially establishes the condominium project, defining essential elements like:

- Legal description of the land
- Unit boundaries and ownership percentages
- Common areas (pools, hallways, parking, etc.)
- Restrictions on how units can be used
- General outline of maintenance responsibilities

The bylaws serve as your community's operational manual. They provide the detailed guidance that residents and new board members often reference regarding:

- **Board of Directors:** Structure, elections, powers, and duties
- **Meetings:** Frequency, notice requirements, and voting procedures
- **Finances:** Budgeting, assessments, and financial reporting
- **Maintenance:** Responsibilities of the association vs. individual owners
- **Amendments:** How the bylaws themselves can be changed

Over time, communities may amend their governing documents. These amendments often address rule changes directly impacting the bylaws or provide greater clarity on maintenance responsibilities outlined in the Master Deed.

Rules & Regulations set further standards for everyday community life, covering areas like noise restrictions, parking, pets, and use of common areas. The Board of Directors can implement these rules, and they must align with existing governing documents. That means rules can further define the bylaws, but cannot conflict with them. Boards cannot make new rules that are not reasonably put forth in the governing documents. It is a fine line that boards have to walk on rules - reach out to your legal counsel if you find yourself in a potential grey area. Rules typically become enforceable with a simple majority vote of the board and generally don't require resident input.

Remember: The Master Deed and Bylaws are foundational, recorded when the condominium is established. The Board of Directors can more easily update Rules & Regulations to address the community's changing needs.

Fast Fact: Your community's declaration might outline pet restrictions like breed, size, or the number of pets per unit.

Pro Tip: Review your governing documents annually. Even if no major changes are needed, it refreshes the board's knowledge.

Checklist:
- **Obtain Copies:** Ensure you have updated versions of the following:
    - Declaration/Master Deed
    - Bylaws
    - Rules and Regulations
- **Board Member Familiarization:** Schedule mandatory reading and comprehension sessions.
- **Resident Accessibility:**
    - Post documents online (if allowed).
    - Provide copies in the community office on request.

Timeline:

- **Within 30 days of election:** Board members complete a thorough reading of governing documents.
- **Within 60 days:** Hold a "Know Your Rules" resident orientation.
- **Ongoing:** Review documents annually for needed updates.

Action Steps:

- **Identify Ambiguities:** Highlight areas of the documents that are unclear or open to interpretation. Consult legal counsel for clarification.
- **Create a Summary:** Prepare a simplified guide to the key rules for resident distribution.

State And Local Laws Affecting Condominiums

Understanding the Impact of State and Local Laws

Understanding the legal framework is crucial for effective condominium management. Educational seminars highlight the significant impact of state and local laws on community operations. Attorneys specializing in condominium associations offer invaluable insights by discussing new regulations and clarifying common areas of misinterpretation within existing rules.

Here's an overview of key legal areas to consider:

- **Condominium-Specific Statutes:** These form the primary legal backbone for your community, outlining reserve account minimums, board powers and duties, and election procedures. Remember, these statutes can vary from state to state.

- **Fair Housing Rules:** These laws protect residents from discrimination based on factors like race, ethnicity, religion, national origin, sex, familial status, and disability.

- **Americans with Disabilities Act (ADA):** Communities may need to make accommodations in common areas (clubhouses, pools, fitness centers, etc.) for accessibility.

- **Landlord-Tenant Regulations:** While primarily impacting individual unit owners who rent out their property, these laws can indirectly influence community dynamics.

- **Building Codes:** Regulations designed to ensure the safety and quality of construction projects. Permits and inspections are a vital part of this process.

- **Zoning Ordinances:** Local zoning rules may place limitations on what types of improvements or replacements your community can undertake.

Staying Informed: Utilize resources like industry organizations, government websites, and your community's legal counsel to stay updated on legal changes and best practices.

We'll discuss these legal areas in more detail throughout the book, giving you a solid understanding of this important aspect of condominium management.

Fast Fact: Did you know that your building code might dictate the color you can paint your front door?

Fast Fact: Many states have specific laws about how often condominium associations must hold elections.

Fast Fact: Fair housing laws protect more than just race and religion – they also cover factors like familial status and national origin.

Pro Tip: Don't just react to legal changes – subscribe to industry or government newsletters for proactive updates.

Checklist:

- **Legal Counsel:** Verify that your community attorney specializes in condominium law and relevant local regulations.
- **Resource List:** Compile the following:
    - State agency overseeing condominiums

- Local government websites (zoning, building codes, etc.)
- Industry organization websites

Timeline:

- **Quarterly:** Check resource websites for updates or announcements.
- **Annually:** Request a briefing from the community attorney on any significant legal changes.

Action Steps

- **Subscribe to Newsletters:** Sign up for updates from relevant government agencies or industry organizations.
- **Proactive Compliance:** Identify potential areas where your community might be out of compliance with current laws (e.g., outdated accessibility requirements).

The History Of Your Community

Understanding Your Community's History: A Roadmap for Decision-Making

Your community's present state is a direct result of its past decisions. By studying its history, you'll gain insights into how past boards shaped the community, helping you make informed choices for the future. This understanding allows you to avoid repeating past mistakes and build on previous successes.

Where to Find Historical Information:

- **Development Documents:** While not always easily accessible, these offer insights into the community's original design and intent.
- **Meeting Minutes:** A valuable record of challenges, solutions, and decision-making processes faced by previous boards.
- **Architectural Plans:** These can reveal the evolution of the community's physical structure, but may be challenging to obtain.
- **Legal Records:** While best accessed through your attorney, legal records can highlight past disputes and their resolutions.
- **Longtime Residents:** These individuals offer a unique perspective and may be the only source for certain historical details. Open communication between boards and residents is crucial for accessing this knowledge.

Fast Fact: Longtime residents are often a treasure trove of community knowledge - don't overlook their potential insights!

Important Historical Events:

Pay attention to significant milestones in the community's history, such as:

- **Development Phases:** Understanding how the community grew over time provides context for current conditions.
- **Major Renovations/Repairs:** Knowledge of past repairs helps anticipate future maintenance needs.
- **Legal Disputes:** Learning from past disputes with residents, developers, or vendors will aid in conflict prevention and resolution.
- **Key Transitions:** Knowing when developer control ended and major board changes occurred offers a timeline for the community's evolution.

Remember, your community's history is a valuable resource. Utilize it to make informed decisions and guide your community towards a successful future.

Pro Tip: Archive meeting minutes diligently – they're an invaluable historical resource for future boards.

Checklist

- **Sources:** Identify potential repositories of information:
    - Management company archives
    - Long-time residents
    - Local historical society
    - Public records searches (for major legal disputes)
- **Organization:** Designate a secure way to store historical documents, both physical and digital.

Timeline:

- **Ongoing:** Actively collect information as it becomes available.

- **Milestone Anniversaries:** Use historical events to create community celebrations.

Action Steps:

- **"History Corner":** Share a historical tidbit in the community newsletter or bulletin board.
- **Resident Input:** Solicit resident stories and photos from past eras.

Putting Knowledge Into Action

A board of directors must have a thorough understanding of the foundational elements discussed in this chapter. This knowledge empowers informed decision-making, ensuring actions align with community rules and governing laws. Additionally, the board should take the following steps:

- **Educate Residents:** Keep residents informed about the community's rules to promote compliance and a sense of shared understanding.
- **Orient New Board Members:** Provide incoming board members with a solid understanding of the governing documents and applicable laws, ensuring continuity in decision-making practices.

How the Foundation Supports Conflict Resolution

Governing documents and relevant laws provide a clear framework for handling disputes within the community. Understanding this framework offers boards a structured path toward fair and consistent conflict resolution.

Proactive Management

A strong grasp of the community's foundation allows the board to anticipate potential challenges and address issues before they escalate. This proactive approach fosters a harmonious and well-managed community.

Checklist:

- **Board Education:** Is there a knowledge gap among board members? If so:
    - Plan specific training sessions
    - Provide clear written guides
- **Communication Plan:** How will you keep residents well-informed?
    - Regular newsletters
    - Community website updates
    - Educational workshops

Timeline:

- **Immediate:** Ensure new board members receive a comprehensive orientation packet.
- **Annually:** Assess the effectiveness of resident communication and make adjustments as needed.

Action Steps:

- **Conflict Resolution:** Clearly outline the process for residents and the board to follow.
- **Proactive Problem-Solving:** Use the knowledge you've gained to anticipate potential issues and create preventative plans.

Chapter Summary: Understanding Your Community's Foundation

In this chapter, we've explored the essential building blocks that shape your condominium community:

- **Governing Documents:** We've delved into the specific components of your governing documents (declaration/master deed, bylaws, rules and regulations), explaining their roles in defining community structure and expectations.

- **State, Municipal, and Federal Laws:** We've highlighted how laws related to fair housing, building codes, zoning, and other regulations influence decision-making within your community.

- **The Importance of History:** We discussed the value of understanding your community's past and where to find historical information (meeting minutes, architectural plans, legal records, longtime residents). This knowledge helps explain your community's current state and informs future strategies.

- **Board Responsibility:** We emphasized the board's duty to understand these foundational elements and ensure that residents and new board members have the knowledge to make aligned decisions. This understanding is crucial for proactive management and effective conflict resolution.

Remember, a strong foundation is key to successful condominium governance!

Pro Tip: Hold a "Know Your Community" resident orientation session– better understanding leads to fewer conflicts.

Pro Tip: Consider regular training sessions for board members to reinforce foundational knowledge and discuss new challenges.

Test Your Knowledge!

1. What are the three primary components of a condominium community's governing documents?
2. Name two ways in which the Americans with Disabilities Act (ADA) might impact a condominium community.
3. What is the difference between a condominium's bylaws and its rules and regulations?
4. Briefly describe the concept of "reserve account minimums," often found in condominium statutes.
5. Why is it important to stay updated on changes to state and local laws affecting condominiums?
6. List two sources where you might find information about your community's history.
7. What is one key benefit of boards of directors understanding a community's history?
8. Why is it important for boards to educate both residents and new board members about the community's governing documents?
9. How do governing documents and laws work together to support conflict resolution in a condominium?
10. What is one example of a proactive management step a board can take, informed by their knowledge of the community's foundation?

The answers are at the end of this chapter

Case Study: The Bylaw Battle

Rosewood Condominiums had always prided itself on its peaceful atmosphere. But when a wave of younger professionals moved in, a generational divide emerged. At the heart of the growing tension was a seemingly innocuous bylaw: "No unreasonable noise after 10 PM." The long-standing board, comprised mostly of retirees, felt strongly about maintaining tranquility in the evenings. The new residents, often working late, saw the rule as unnecessarily stifling their ability to socialize and unwind on weekends.

What began as minor complaints escalated into heated debates at community meetings. The board, citing the bylaws, felt powerless to change the rule. The new residents, feeling ignored, grew resentful. Animosity began to fester. Realizing the situation was spiraling, a long-time board member, respected by both sides, made a suggestion: create a resident committee tasked with drafting bylaw revisions that could achieve a compromise.

This committee became a battleground of its own. There were passionate arguments over decibel levels, designated "quiet hours" vs. "courtesy hours", and the process for handling violations. Yet, the necessity of finding middle ground drove them forward. After weeks of tense negotiations, a revised policy emerged: "Noise should be kept at reasonable levels after 11 PM on weekdays, and after midnight on weekends." A detailed complaint procedure was added, ensuring fair enforcement. Put to a community-wide vote, the revisions passed with a comfortable majority. The experience underscored the bylaws' role as a living document, adaptable to community needs while maintaining the core purpose of ensuring a harmonious environment for all.

What Could They Have Done Differently? The board could have preempted this conflict by periodically reviewing bylaws with the changing community in mind. Open dialogue with new residents early on could have revealed potential friction points.

Board Member Voice: "Honestly, I was frustrated. These young folks didn't understand what we'd built at Rosewood. But as Sarah said, 'would you rather be in court, or find a way to live together?' That hit me hard."

Question for the Reader: Are there areas in your bylaws that might inadvertently favor one group of residents over another?

Key Takeaways:
- Bylaws should evolve with the community they serve.
- Proactive communication prevents small issues from turning into major divisions.
- Seeking compromise demonstrates the board's commitment to the well-being of ALL residents.

Case Study: Navigating The Zoning Maze

For years, the board of Sunnyview Condos had fielded resident requests for a community pool. They finally had the budget and a plan: a gleaming pool nestled in a corner of unused common space, complete with a shaded cabana and bathhouse facilities. With enthusiastic resident backing, they proudly submitted their meticulously crafted permit application. Weeks later, the response wasn't celebration, but a rejection letter citing a local zoning ordinance strictly regulating structure heights.

Initially, the board was demoralized. They had meticulously reviewed the community's governing documents, but town zoning rules were an unexpected hurdle. However, a board member with experience in construction mentioned the possibility of a variance. This sparked a flurry of research. They learned that variances existed for unique circumstances, but required strong justification. They began gathering ammunition. Real estate listings from neighboring towns demonstrated similar pools were common. They enlisted an architect to revise the plans, lowering the pool house roofline slightly while maintaining functionality. Finally, they prepared a presentation for the zoning board.

The presentation was both practical and emotional. They outlined safety regulations, potential property value increases, and the overwhelming resident support. But it was the stories that swayed the board: kids longing for summer fun, seniors seeking gentle water exercise, families craving a place to connect. The board stressed that the minimal height difference wouldn't obstruct views or violate the spirit of the ordinance. After careful deliberation, the zoning board granted the variance with minor stipulations. A few months later, the sound of children splashing and laughing echoed through Sunnyview Condos, a testament to the board's persistence and their understanding that even seemingly rigid zoning laws often have pathways for communities to achieve their goals.

What Could They Have Done Differently?

The board could have saved time and heartache by researching zoning ordinances BEFORE finalizing their pool design. Early consultation with the town planning department might have revealed the height restrictions, allowing them to adjust plans proactively.

Board Member Voice: "We were so focused on our dream pool, we completely overlooked town regulations. It felt like a punch in the gut! But then we realized, rules are there for a reason, and we had to find a way to work within them."

Question for the Reader: Do you have a clear understanding of the zoning ordinances that might affect potential projects in your community?

Key Takeaways

- Zoning compliance is crucial. Research thoroughly BEFORE investing time and resources into a project.
- Don't view ordinances purely as obstacles. They can provide a framework for finding creative solutions.
- A compelling presentation to zoning boards should balance practical arguments with the community benefits of a project.

Case Study: Overcoming Obstacles To Accessibility

Mrs. Johnson was an Oakwood Condos fixture. She'd raised her children there, served on the board twice, and was known for her legendary potluck casseroles. But as aging knees made the stairs to the community room more daunting, she felt increasingly isolated. Events she once cherished became sources of frustration. Determined, she wrote a letter to the board requesting a chairlift.

The board was sympathetic but had concerns. Installation costs were high, potentially impacting everyone's maintenance fees. Some worried that one accommodation would open the floodgates to endless requests. Feeling unsure, they sought legal counsel. The attorney's explanation was stark: under the Americans with Disabilities Act (ADA) and similar state laws, the community was likely obligated to make reasonable accommodations for residents with disabilities. Failure to comply could result in legal action and fines.

This was a turning point. The board shifted their mindset from a "burden" to a "responsibility." They researched chairlift options, learning about different models and safety features. An internet search revealed grants specifically for condo communities to improve accessibility. With financial help, the project suddenly was much more feasible. Installation day was a community event. Neighbors cheered as Mrs. Johnson took her inaugural ride, waving regally. The experience wasn't just about the chairlift. It had sparked community-wide conversations about inclusivity. The board now proactively considered accessibility in future projects, realizing the ADA wasn't just a set of rules, but a pathway for all residents to feel valued and participate fully in the community they called home.

What Could They Have Done Differently?

- The board could have educated themselves on the ADA and disability inclusion earlier, potentially avoiding the feeling of being caught off guard by Mrs. Johnson's request.
- Proactively budgeting for potential accessibility needs would have eased the financial concerns.

Board Member Voice: "In the beginning, we saw the cost, the hassle... all the reasons to say 'no'. But then we learned about the law, and more importantly, started thinking about Mrs. Johnson as more than just a name on a letter. That changed everything."

Question for the Reader: Does your community have a plan in place to address potential accessibility requests in a timely and proactive manner?

Key Takeaways:

- Understanding the ADA isn't just about avoiding fines, it's about creating an inclusive community where everyone feels welcome.
- Proactive planning for accessibility (budgeting, researching options) smoothes the process when needs arise.
- A single accommodation can spark a broader conversation about creating a welcoming environment for all residents, regardless of ability.

Case Study: The Reserve Fund Rescue

Sunset Pines Condos had always prided itself on its well-maintained grounds and amenities. But a recent storm revealed a harsh reality: the community was facing a financial crisis. A major roof leak caused by years of deferred maintenance had eaten away a large chunk of their reserve funds. To make matters worse, an inspection revealed that the aging HVAC system was teetering on the brink of failure. Special assessments loomed – a surefire way to ignite resident anger.

The board felt overwhelmed. They inherited a problem that had been silently brewing for years. A newly elected board member, Sarah, had a background in accounting. Unwilling to simply pass the buck, she dove into the community's financial history. Old budgets and audit reports told a story of neglect. Successive boards, hesitant to raise maintenance fees, had consistently underfunded the reserves, barely meeting the bare minimums required by state law. Now, the chickens had come home to roost.

Sarah knew they couldn't sugarcoat the situation. The board scheduled a special town hall meeting. They presented the stark facts: the costs of immediate repairs, the long-term projected expenses for major replacements, and the potential financial disaster if they did nothing. Residents were shocked, some irate, but the transparency was crucial. The board outlined their plan: a phased fee increase over several years to replenish the reserves, coupled with strict budgeting for ongoing maintenance. It wasn't an easy sell, but by showing the community how they got into this mess, and the consequences of inaction, the board gained enough support to pass the plan. Sunset Pines learned a painful lesson, but the experience transformed their financial approach, prioritizing long-term stability over short-term comfort.

What Could They Have Done Differently?

- Past boards could have implemented smaller, gradual fee increases to avoid a sudden financial shock.
- Reserve studies would have provided long-term projections, allowing for better budgeting.
- Educating residents consistently about the purpose of reserve funds would have created greater understanding.

Board Member Voice: "At first, I was tempted to blame the old board. But then I realized... we're all owners here. If we don't face up to the hard choices, no one else will."

Question for the Reader: Does your community conduct regular reserve studies and factor those long-term costs into your budget planning?

Key Takeaways:

- Reserve funds are not optional – they are vital for the long-term health of the community.
- Proactive financial management avoids knee-jerk decisions that can alienate residents.
- Transparency builds trust, even when the news is bad. Residents are more likely to accept tough solutions when they understand the why.

Case Study: From Conflict To Collaboration

Whispering Creek Condos had a problem that was anything

but quiet. For years, a bitter feud raged between the Smiths, proud owners of an exuberant Labrador named Buddy, and the Millers, who cherished their tranquility. Buddy's barking became a daily soundtrack, countered by the Millers' escalating noise complaints to the board. The board felt trapped. Their governing documents had a general "nuisance noise" policy, but it lacked teeth. Citing the rules achieved nothing but further animosity between the neighbors. Realizing that inaction could poison the whole community, the board took a bold step.

They researched professional mediators specializing in condominium disputes. A seasoned mediator explained that animosity often stems from feeling unheard and powerless. The board, acting as a neutral party, invited both families to a mediation session. Initially awkward, the structured process allowed each side to vent frustrations and to truly listen to the other's perspective. The mediator guided them away from blame and toward practical solutions. Compromises emerged: the Smiths agreed to designated "barking breaks" during less disruptive hours and invested in obedience training. The Millers contributed to the cost of sound-absorbing hedges along their shared property line.

The outcome went beyond just resolving a barking dog issue. The neighbors, forced to collaborate, found common ground. Inspired, the board worked with the mediator to update their rules & regulations, adding a step-by-step dispute resolution process. They also hosted a community workshop on conflict resolution, teaching residents how to communicate effectively and de-escalate tensions before they reached a boiling point. Whispering Creek discovered that well-structured mediation can be a powerful tool, transforming feuding neighbors into participants in the greater community good.

What Could They Have Done Differently?

- A detailed noise policy in the governing documents could

have included proactive solutions (barking hours, buffer zones). This would have given the board more power to act early.
- The board could have engaged sooner, facilitating a conversation between the neighbors before the situation became hostile.

Board Member Voice: "At first, I figured, 'Let them work it out.' But this was an issue that impacted the whole community's atmosphere. It was our job to step in."

Question for the Reader: Do you have a clear process for handling recurring resident-to-resident disputes, or is your approach more reactive?

Key Takeaways:

- Detailed rules on common issues like noise save headaches in the long run.
- Don't assume conflicts will resolve themselves. Boards have a duty to create a harmonious environment for all.
- Mediation isn't just about the current problem, it's about teaching the community the skills of conflict resolution.

Case Study: Fair Housing – More Than Just A Law

Willowbrook Condos had a reputation as a peaceful haven for retirees. Its well-manicured lawns and quiet social events attracted a specific demographic. When a young family with two toddlers applied to rent a vacant unit, a ripple of unease spread through the board. Some members voiced concerns: Would noisy children disrupt the tranquility? Could the playground equipment handle the extra wear and tear? There was an unspoken desire to maintain the community's "senior-friendly" atmosphere. Wanting to protect themselves, the board consulted their attorney... and received a wake-up call.

The attorney gave them a crash course in the Fair Housing Act (FHA). Denying housing based on familial status wasn't just unethical, it was illegal. They couldn't advertise "adult-only" or target certain age groups in their marketing. The board felt chastened and a bit defensive. Yes, they were used to a certain type of resident, but did that mean excluding others? Their attorney steered the conversation towards practicalities. They had to screen this family like any other applicant. Financial checks, references, and past rental history were the only legal criteria to consider.

With renewed focus, they processed the application. The family was well-qualified: stable income, good credit, and positive landlord references. Reluctantly, the board gave their approval. The first few weeks brought some minor adjustments – a few more giggles at the pool than usual, the occasional crying child at bedtime. But what surprised the board was the infusion of energy. The young parents volunteered on committees, organized a children's book drive, and their smiles were contagious. Willowbrook didn't lose its identity; it expanded it. The experience taught the board that fair housing wasn't just about avoiding lawsuits, it was about creating a welcoming community for people of all ages, enriching the experience for everyone.

What Could They Have Done Differently?

The board could have benefited from proactive education about the Fair Housing Act. Understanding the law's protections would have prevented initial anxieties and the need for an emergency legal consultation.

Board Member Voice: "We honestly thought a 'seniors-focused' vibe was okay. Not about excluding people, but attracting like-minded residents. Turns out, our mindset was out of step with the law."

Question for the Reader: Does your community have any marketing materials or practices, even informal ones, that could be interpreted as discouraging certain groups protected by fair housing laws?

Key Takeaways

- Ignorance of fair housing laws is no excuse for violating them.
- Boards should seek regular updates on legal issues impacting their community.
- Diversity can enhance, not threaten, the positive atmosphere of a condominium.

Test Your Knowledge! Answers

1. **The three primary components of governing documents are:**

   - The Declaration (or Master Deed)
   - The Bylaws
   - Rules and Regulations

2. **The ADA may impact a condominium community by requiring:**

   - Modifications to common areas to ensure accessibility (ramps, wider doorways, etc.)
   - Allowances for service animals or emotional support animals
   - Accommodations for residents with disabilities in individual units (with limitations)

3. **Key differences between bylaws and rules & regulations:**

   - Bylaws: Operational rules for the community, covering board structure, meetings, finances, etc. More difficult to change.
   - Rules & Regulations: Day-to-day living guidelines (noise, parking, pets, etc.) Generally easier to update through board action.
4. **Reserve account minimums:** State laws might mandate that condominiums maintain a minimum financial reserve fund. This money is intended for major repairs or replacements (roofs, siding, infrastructure).

5. **Staying updated on laws is important because:**

   - Changes can impact community operations, resident rights, and board responsibilities.
   - Non-compliance can lead to legal issues and fines.
6. **Sources of community history:**

   - Meeting minutes
   - Architectural plans
   - Legal records
   - Longtime residents
7. **Benefits of understanding history:**

   - Informs current decision-making, avoiding repeating past mistakes.
   - Provides context for the community's current state.
8. **Educating residents and new board members is crucial because:**

   - Promotes consistency and fairness in applying rules.
   - Minimizes conflicts due to misunderstandings.

9. **How governing documents and laws support conflict resolution:**

   o They provide a framework of rights, responsibilities, and processes for resolving disputes.

10. **Example of proactive management:**

    o Knowing the community's repair history can inform budgeting and scheduling for future maintenance needs.

CHAPTER 2: FINANCIAL HEALTH AND PLANNING

Introduction

Okay, I know governing documents and laws in the last chapter weren't exactly a page-turner, but you made it through! Now we're onto the financials – a bit more exciting, right? Trust me, this book gets much better as we go along. But first, we've got to cover the basics before getting into the really good stuff.

Financial health is absolutely vital for a successful community. It builds on those legal foundations we covered in the last chapter. In the condo world, financial health means you can pay the bills now (utilities, maintenance, vendors) while also saving for those big future repairs. Think of your reserve fund like a long-term savings account – it's for major fixes, not everyday upkeep. Another key piece is a balanced budget, ideally a zero-based one. That means your income from assessments and such covers operating costs and transfers to the reserve account.

Of course, responsible spending is also essential. This means prioritizing needs, making smart contract decisions, and knowing when to say a respectful 'no' or 'not now, maybe later' to resident requests if the budget doesn't allow it.

Pro Tip: "Sweat equity" has limits. Volunteer labor can be great, but major repairs usually require licensed professionals.

So why bother with all this? Strong financial management

leads to:

- **Protected Property Values:** Well-maintained communities keep residents happy and attract buyers.
- **Cost Stability:** Predictable fees mean no nasty surprise assessments.
- **Quality Amenities:** Your clubhouse, pool, and other shared spaces stay in top shape.
- **Community Harmony:** Openness about finances builds trust and minimizes conflict.

Fast Fact: Condo boards have a fiduciary duty. This means acting in the best interests of the community, especially with finances.

Pro Tip: Board member financial literacy is essential. Invest in board training or seek out members with relevant skills.

Creating And Adhering To An Annual Budget

Budget Time: Your Board's Big Task

Crafting a budget is one of your board's most important jobs each year. You can tackle this as a team (with your management company as a sounding board) or have the management company prepare a draft that you then revise to fit your community's needs. Remember, the final decision is always yours – no exceptions!

The 3 Parts of a Condo/HOA Budget

1. **Operating Expenses:** These are your everyday costs – maintenance, repairs, utilities, administration, etc.
2. **Reserve Fund Contributions:** This isn't money *spent* from reserves, but the regular deposits from your operating account into your savings for big future repairs.
3. **Income:** This covers assessment fees (regular and special), investment earnings, late fees, amenity charges – basically, any money your community brings in.

Pro Tip: Look for hidden costs in management contracts. Scrutinize billing practices to avoid unexpected fees.

The Right (and Wrong) Way to Budget

- **The Right Way:**
    o   Review past operating expenses to predict the upcoming year's costs.
    o   Calculate what your reserve deposits need to be, meeting legal requirements *and* your future repair

needs.
    - Set your resident fees so income minus expenses and reserve contributions equals zero.
- **The Wrong Way:**
    - Decide what you want fees to be and work backward, squeezing operating costs to fit.
    - Deposit only the bare minimum into reserves without a long-term plan.
    - Base your projections on *just* the most recent year.

Doing it the wrong way might seem easier, but it leads to big trouble! Good budgeting means no nasty surprises.

Budget Check-Ins: A Year-Round Job

Your board should review financial statements at each meeting, comparing actual spending with the budget. If things are off track, your management company should provide detailed breakdowns so you can spot the cause. Some companies even offer fully transparent online tools for this.

Once you know where the money's going, figure out how to fix any overspending. Otherwise, you'll run into cash flow problems, missed reserve deposits, or even have to go back to your residents for an additional assessment on short notice – nobody wants that!

Keep Your Residents in the Loop!

Share a monthly update on the budget, not just dry numbers. Include a short summary: Where is spending higher than expected? What does this mean for residents? Transparency builds trust and helps folks understand if changes are needed.

Pro Tip: Involve residents early in the budget process. Get their input on priorities to foster understanding and buy-in.

Checklist

- **Review Historical Expenses:**

- Gather the last 3-5 years of financial statements.
  - Identify recurring costs and any unusual fluctuations.
- **Project Future Costs:**
  - Account for inflation and anticipated increases (utilities, contracts).
  - Obtain quotes/estimates for major planned projects.
- **Input from Committees/Management:**
  - Collect budget requests from committees (social, landscaping, etc.).
  - Consult with your management company for their insights.
- **Draft the Budget:**
  - Use a clear template, separating operating expenses and reserve contributions.
  - Include notes explaining changes or significant expenses.
- **Board Review and Approval**
- **Communicate to Residents**

Timeline

- **3-4 Months Before Fiscal Year End:** Start review and projections.
- **2 Months Before:** Get input and draft the budget.
- **1 Month Before:** Board approval, resident distribution.

Action Steps

- **Assign Tasks:** Delegate parts of the process (gathering data, contacting vendors).
- **Use Budgeting Software:** Tools streamline calculations and formatting.

Understanding Reserve Funds

Reserve Funds: Your Emergency Savings, Not Everyday Cash

Remember, reserve funds are for those major repairs and replacements. If you find yourself dipping into them to cover everyday operating expenses, that's a red flag! Your budget is seriously out of whack, and you need to take action. Those reserves are there for emergencies – tapping them for regular bills likely means you need to ask residents for additional funds.

The Purpose and Importance of Reserve Funds

Reserve funds exist to prevent those dreaded special or additional assessments. They help keep property values strong by ensuring your community can keep up with maintenance. Don't treat your reserve fund target like a mystery number! Get a reserve study done. Yes, it costs money, but it's a worthwhile investment compared to the headaches of underfunding.

Reserve studies aren't crystal balls; they provide estimates by professionals to give a good picture of your community's long-term needs. Since those needs can change, refresh your study every few years. Your management company can advise on the best timing.

Tracking Your Progress

Your reserve study outlines your funding goals. It's your board's duty to track your community's progress against those goals. Think of it like saving for a new car – if you're behind schedule, you need to adjust. Pushing back repair timelines might seem like a quick fix, but it'll backfire in the long run. Be realistic and adjust your contributions, not your assumptions about when those repairs will be needed.

Best Practices for Reserve Funds:

- **Adequate Funding:** Make sure you're saving enough!
- **Smart Investments:** Stick to safe, liquid investments suitable for reserves. Check your state laws and consult your legal counsel and management company on allowed options.
- **Regular Updates:** Refresh that reserve study every few years to stay on track.

Fast Fact: State laws on reserve funds vary. Always consult your governing documents and legal counsel to ensure compliance.

Decoding Reserve Fund Jargon

To fully understand your reserve funds and explain them to residents, these two concepts are key:

Percentage Funded

- **What is it?** How much money you have in reserves NOW compared to what your reserve study says you'll need for future repairs.
- **Calculation:** Current Reserve Balance / Total Projected Need = Percent Funded
- **Example:** $50,000 in reserves, $100,000 needed = 50% funded.
- **Why it matters:** Tracks your progress. Lower percentages often mean a higher chance of surprise assessments.

Baseline Funding

- **What is it?** The bare minimum your reserve study recommends saving to avoid major problems.
- **How it's figured out:** Experts in your reserve study look at:

- How long things in your community last (roofs, roads, etc.)
  - Replacement costs (factoring in inflation)
  - Minimum needed to keep things afloat
- **Why it matters:** Fall below this, and you're in serious trouble – big assessments or crumbling infrastructure might be the result.

Key Points

- 100% funded is great, but not always realistic. Baseline funding gives you a safer target.
- Even "fully funded" is temporary. Costs change, so update your reserve study regularly!

Fast Fact: Underfunded reserves are a widespread problem. Many communities don't save enough, leading to surprise assessments or deteriorating infrastructure.

Checklist

- **Get a Reserve Study (if none exists):**
  - Find qualified companies through referrals or professional organizations.
- **Review Reserve Study (if you have one):**
  - Is it less than 3 years old?
  - Understand % funded and baseline funding recommendations.
- **Calculate Reserve Contributions:**
  - Ensure your budget aligns with reserve study goals.
  - Use calculators/tools provided by your management company.
- **Investment Strategy:**
  - Consult with legal counsel on restrictions.
  - Prioritize safe, liquid options.

Timeline

- **New Communities:** Get a reserve study ASAP.

- **Existing Communities:** Refresh your reserve study every 3-5 years.
- **Ongoing:** Review reserve funding at each budget cycle.

Action Steps

- **Educate Your Board:** Not everyone will have financial expertise.
- **Communicate to Residents:** Explain what reserves are for, and how they impact dues.

Setting Appropriate Assessment Fees

The Challenge of Setting Dues

Once you have a realistic operating budget and reserve fund plan (based on your reserve study), it's time to figure out those dues. This is tough! Here's what to consider:

- **Market Appeal:** Too high regular dues make your community less attractive to buyers. Using additional/special assessments might be received better, even if the total cost is the same.
- **Affordability:** Balance community needs with what residents can realistically pay. Don't leave your community with extremes – happy residents who live in a deteriorating complex or unhappy residents paying through the nose.
- **Long-term Stability:** A good budget isn't just about today's costs; it protects the community's future.

How Dues Are Decided

Your governing documents usually dictate this:

- **Equal Share:** Everyone pays the same.
- **Variable:** Based on usage or square footage, with different units paying different percentages. Your board can't change these allocations at will.

Communicating the 'Why'

Be transparent about the budget! Explain the challenges, the opportunities, and the real needs of your community. Share your reserve study to show you're planning responsibly, not just guessing.

When big projects are essential, break it down for residents: "The leaky roofs will cost X to fix. We have Y saved. To get there by Z year, we need to increase dues by this amount."

The Hard Truth

You'll never please everyone. Your job is to make the best, most responsible decisions, even if those are unpopular or fixing past boards' mistakes.

Pro Tip: Don't just compare dues to similar communities. Look at the whole picture – reserve funding, amenities, etc.

Checklist

- **Determine Total Need:** Start with your budgeted expenses + reserve contributions.
- **Factor in Other Income:** Investment earnings, late fees, etc.
- **Market Research:** Compare dues to similar communities in your area.
- **Consider Affordability:** Can residents realistically handle the proposed fees?
- **Allocation Method:** Check your governing documents (equal shares or usage-based)

Timeline

- **Conducted alongside the budget process.**
- **Allow Time for Resident Feedback:** Especially if increases are significant.

Action Steps

- **Gradual vs. Sudden:** If a big increase is needed, can it be phased in over time?
- **Be Transparent:** Explain the necessity of increases, don't just announce them.

Financial Reporting And Transparency

Financial Transparency: The Reports You Need

To be open with residents and other stakeholders, your community needs comprehensive financial reports. Management companies usually present these from most to least detailed:

- **Balance Sheet:** A snapshot of your community's assets (what's owned), liabilities (what's owed), and owner equity at a specific moment in time. Compare balance sheets over months, quarters, or years to see how your community's financial health is changing.
- **Income Statement:** Tracks income and expenses over a period (usually a month). This is your main tool to see if spending and collections are on track with your budget. Compare against past months, quarters, or years for insight.
- **Statement of Cash Flows:** Measures actual cash in and out, stripping away some accounting adjustments found in the income statement. Think of this as a more "real-world" view of money movement. Like the others, you can get these monthly, quarterly, etc.

Modern Management: Access and Understanding

Many management companies use board portals for financial transparency. You can often access and analyze reports as needed, not just during meetings.

Management companies use different accounting methods (cash, accrual, modified). There's no single right way – it's about finding what presents the clearest picture for your board *and* residents. Aim for financial statements that even non-accountants can grasp.

Fast Fact: "Cash basis" vs. "accrual basis" accounting matters. Understanding which your association uses helps you interpret financial statements accurately.

Board Engagement is Key

During meetings, all board members should actively discuss the financials. If only one or two members seem to understand, there's work to do! This might mean:

- Revising how your statements are presented and tracked
- Educating board members who are struggling

Remember, if the board finds the statements confusing, residents definitely will. Regularly sharing financials with residents builds trust and understanding of your community's decisions.

Fast Fact: Financial reports aren't just for accountants. Modern software makes statements easy to understand – a sign of a well-managed community.

Checklist

- **Reporting Frequency:** Monthly statements are ideal, at minimum quarterly.
- **Statement Format:** Are they easy to understand, even for non-accountants?
- **Distribution Method:** Mailed, online portal, or both?
- **Board Training:** Ensure all board members can read and interpret reports.

Timeline

- **Ongoing:** Residents should have regular, predictable access to financials.

Action Steps

- **Audit Annually:** Use an independent accountant.
- **Resident Q&A:** Hold budget sessions or allow questions at meetings.

Expansion: Reserve Studies And Communication

Understanding Reserve Studies

A reserve study is a deep dive into your community's infrastructure. Here's how it works:

1. **Consultation:** Engineers or specialists meet with your board/management to discuss priorities and concerns.
2. **Walkthrough:** They physically inspect the community, noting the condition of infrastructure components (roofs, roads, etc.).
3. **Analysis:** They estimate:
   - Useful life remaining for each component.
   - Repair or replacement costs, factoring in inflation.
   - Projected cash your community will need over the study period (often 15-20 years).

The Report

You'll get a long, detailed report with photos and breakdowns. It's designed to be understandable for non-experts. This aligns with the goal of reserve studies nationwide – clear information for boards and residents.

Explaining It To Residents

If residents need extra help understanding:

- Provide your own summary alongside the full report.
- Focus on the long-term benefits of a well-maintained community that avoids surprise assessments.

- Emphasize that ignoring infrastructure isn't an option – eventually those costs hit, and you want to be prepared.

Visual Aids

Reserve studies often have charts, graphs, and photos. These are great tools for explaining the community's needs to residents in a compelling way. Sharing the full study builds trust, as residents can see the basis for your decisions and debate facts from a neutral 3rd party, not just board opinions.

Checklist

- **Explain the Reserve Study:** Share a summary (not just the full report).
- **Visual Aids:** Charts and graphs can make the data more impactful.
- **Emphasize Long-Term Benefits:** Focus on avoiding future assessments.

Timeline

- **Share the Study:** When it's completed.
- **Ongoing Reminder:** Bring it up at budget time, reference it when discussing projects.

Action Steps

- **Resident Input:** Seek feedback on priorities *before* the reserve study if possible.

Conclusion

Okay, congrats! You survived another important, yet slightly dry, topic – financial planning. It's the foundation for a healthy community, the difference between a thriving neighborhood and one headed for a point of no return.

Think of those communities that bury their heads in the sand, dodging tough decisions. They end up trapped, unable to dig out from under bad choices. Don't be that community!

Here's the key: do your budget right, get a reserve study, fund those reserves properly, and keep that study updated. Communicate openly with residents, and don't let a few loud voices derail you from doing the right thing.

Results might not be instant, especially if you inherit a community with years of bad financial decisions. You might need to raise dues for a time, and residents will see those old problems even as you save for the fix. But don't lose heart – responsible choices now will turn things around in the long run. It'll make an already good community even better, or pull a struggling one out of the slump.

It's all about the board making those decisions, working together with management and residents. Getting everyone rowing in the same direction is essential. Imagine a rowboat with everyone paddling a different way – you'd just spin in circles! Keep everyone on the same page, heading towards that healthy, beautiful island of a community you all dream of.

Test Your Knowledge!

1. What are the three main components of a typical HOA/condo association budget?
2. Why is a reserve fund different from your regular operating budget?
3. What is the recommended way to determine your association's dues?
4. Name two benefits of having a current reserve study.

5. What's the difference between a balance sheet and an income statement?
6. Why is regular financial reporting to residents important?
7. What does "zero-based budgeting" mean in the context of an HOA?
8. Who ultimately decides how dues are allocated – divided equally or based on other factors?
9. If your community has to dip into reserve funds to cover regular expenses, what does that indicate?
10. What is "baseline funding" for reserve accounts?

The answers are at the end of this chapter

Case Study: The Dues Dilemma

The board meeting at Seaview Condos was buzzing with a tension thicker than the coastal fog. On the agenda: dues. For years, they'd kept them artificially low – a point of pride and a major selling point for potential buyers.

But the cost was starting to show. Patched-up walkways, a pool with peeling paint, and worst of all, that roof... whispers of leaks grew louder with every rainstorm. Mr. Jenkins, on the board for a decade, was the voice of reason: "We need a market-rate dues increase. It's long overdue." He laid out the reserve study numbers – bleak projections and eye-watering replacement costs.

Mrs. Peterson, a newer resident, balked. "We'll lose buyers with higher dues! Nobody cares about fancy reserves, they want a low monthly payment." A chorus of agreement rumbled through the room.

Susan, a newer board member, cleared her throat. "It's about more than getting buyers in the door," she began. "What happens when those buyers are stuck with a huge bill a year later because the roof finally caves in? That's not attractive." She explained how underfunded reserves led to surprise assessments, scaring off potential buyers long-term.

The arguments swirled. Some residents saw the value in long-term planning, others clung to short-term affordability. It was uncomfortable, messy... but it was progress. The board agreed to hold a community-wide meeting, not just to vote on dues, but to walk residents through the 'why'. The reserve study would be their guide, but they'd need to translate numbers into the real-world impact on the community they all loved.

In the end, a modest increase passed – the bare minimum to start rebuilding their savings. It wasn't a perfect victory, but Seaview Condos was on the path to avoiding a major financial crisis. And most importantly, they'd opened a dialogue that would hopefully bridge the gap between sticker price and long-term stability.

What Could They Have Done Differently?

- **Proactive Education:** Waiting until a crisis looms breeds defensiveness on both sides. Ongoing education about reserves, market comparisons, and the true cost of delayed maintenance is key.
- **Gradual vs. Shocking:** A series of smaller dues increases can be easier to accept than one huge hike.

Board Member Voice: Mr. Jenkins: "We thought keeping dues low was doing residents a favor. Instead, we were unknowingly setting them up for a rude awakening."

Question for the Reader: Does your community prioritize immediate affordability over the potential for costly surprises down the line?

Key Takeaways

- Dues comparisons with similar properties MUST factor in reserve health and amenities.
- It's never too late to start educating residents, but the earlier, the better.
- Sometimes the best solution is a compromise – enough to get moving in the right direction, even if not at the ideal pace.

Case Study: The Case Of The Missing Reserve Fund

The Maplewood HOA board meeting was tense. Residents packed the small meeting room, anger buzzing in the air. It wasn't just the cracked, pothole-riddled parking lot that had them riled up, it was the bombshell the board had just dropped.

"We have...an issue," admitted Board President Mrs. Henderson, her voice wavering slightly. "You see, several years back, reserves were tapped for the clubhouse renovation. We're now nearly empty."

A roar of disbelief went through the crowd.

"How is that even possible?" shouted Mr. Jacobs, a resident known for his booming voice. "We pay dues for those reserves, so things like this don't become a crisis!"

The board shuffled uncomfortably. Turns out, the snazzy clubhouse *had* been popular, but at a hidden cost. The previous board reasoned the community would rather have a nice place to gather than deal with a crumbling parking lot. But no plan was put in place to refill the reserves.

Now, estimates for the lot repaving project exceeded the remaining balance. Mrs. Henderson presented the options: a hefty special assessment payable immediately, or a significant dues increase for years to come.

The mood turned ugly. Residents felt betrayed, accusing the board of mismanagement. Some argued that fancy clubhouse events should now be fundraisers to fix the parking lot. Others threatened to sell, predicting property values would plummet.

It took hours, but eventually, a grim compromise was reached. A smaller assessment to get the work started, followed by moderate dues increases. The Maplewood board learned the hard way: when you tap into those emergency savings, you don't just need to replace the money – you need a plan to make sure it doesn't become a crisis all over again. Honesty now, even about bad news, would've saved them a world of pain.

What Could They Have Done Differently?

- **Be Proactive with Reserve Studies:** Regular studies prevent nasty surprises.
- **Treat the Reserve Fund as Sacred:** Only used for true emergencies or planned replacements outlined in your reserve study.
- **Don't Confuse Wants with Needs:** A clubhouse renovation is a choice, not a necessity. Prioritize core infrastructure.
- **Communicate Honestly:** If reserves are used, explain why, AND present a plan for replenishment immediately.

Board Member Mindset: "We figured, a nicer clubhouse will attract more buyers, that's good for everyone, right? Turns out…not necessarily if it means you can't drive to your own house." – Anonymous Maplewood board member, reflecting years later

Reader Question: Does your community have clear rules on when reserve funds can be used? What's the process for deciding if it's justified?

Key Takeaways:

- Reserve funds are for your community's survival, not its social life.
- Delaying maintenance means higher costs AND resident anger.
- It's better to ask for a small increase for a good reason than a massive one out of desperation.

Case Study: Reserve Study Revelations

The monthly board meeting at Old Town Villas was buzzing. It had been years – decades, really – since the residents were this engaged. Unfortunately, it wasn't excitement, but seething anger.

"Double? You're saying our reserve funds need to be DOUBLE what we've been saving?" Mrs. Peterson, known for her immaculate flowerbeds and sharp tongue, glared at the board.

Board President Tom sighed. "I wish I had better news. But this new reserve study…it's a wake-up call." The reserve study, the first in 15 years, lay on the table. Its projections were grim. Costs had soared, inflation gnawing away at their savings. Worse yet, it factored in things the old study had missed – the aging pool equipment, the cracked tennis courts…

"But this is outrageous!" Mr. Johnson shouted. "We'll never be able to sell here! Who'd buy into this mess?"

Tom felt a headache brewing. "Look, ignoring problems didn't make them go away. That roof isn't getting younger. And these numbers…" he gestured at the study, "these are what contractors charge NOW. In five more years? It'll be worse."

A young couple, new homeowners, spoke up timidly. "But we just bought in based on the dues we were told…"

Tom nodded grimly. "That's the worst part. We should've had smaller increases years ago, kept that study updated. Now, we're either looking at a massive jump or…" He didn't want to say it, but everyone knew the alternative: deteriorating buildings and plummeting property values.

The meeting dragged on, a whirlwind of accusations and despair. Tom felt the weight of those 15 years of neglect. They had tried to keep dues low, to be 'resident-friendly'. In the end, it was the cruelest decision of all.

What Could They Have Done Differently?

- **Regular Reserve Study Updates:** Costs fluctuate, components age – a reserve study done in the stone age won't be accurate. Update it every few years for the most realistic picture.
- **Gradual Dues Increases:** Big jumps shock residents. Smaller, consistent increases tied to reserve study projections are easier to swallow.
- **Early Resident Communication:** Don't wait until a crisis. Educate owners on *why* reserves matter, long before the bad news hits.

Board Member Voice: Tom: "We thought keeping dues low was doing residents a favor. Now, I see it was the opposite. You can't put off fixing a leaky roof forever... eventually, the whole house falls apart."

Reader Question: Has your community had a reserve study updated recently? If not, could you be facing a similar surprise?

Key Takeaways

- Reserve studies aren't forever – treat them like a checkup, not a cure.
- "Cheap" now can mean *astronomically* expensive later.
- Transparency avoids blindsiding residents when the bill comes due.

Case Study: The Zero-Based Budget Success

Lakeview Condominium Association had a reputation – the bad kind. Every year seemed to bring another surprise: a busted water main, a crumbling pool deck, a leaky roof...and another end-of-the-year special assessment hitting residents' mailboxes right before the holidays. The grumbling was constant, the turnover rate high, and every board meeting felt like wading into a battlefield.

Sarah, who joined the board out of a mix of desperation and stubborn optimism, had heard about zero-based budgeting. It sounded brutal but also like the shock to the system Lakeview desperately needed. Instead of starting the budget with last year's spending and tweaking the numbers, they'd start from zero, justifying every dollar as if they were a brand new community.

The first meeting was rough. Department heads were offended, board members squirmed, and Sarah found herself repeatedly saying, "It's not personal! We're safeguarding residents' money." They scrutinized landscaping contracts, negotiated bulk rates on utilities, even debated the necessity of the monthly lobby flower arrangement.

Miracles didn't happen overnight, but some surprising things did. They found an insurance policy no one knew they had, saving thousands. A resident with HVAC experience offered to train the maintenance guy on basic repairs, cutting contractor calls. They even discovered the "essential" security patrol was mostly napping in their car.

The final budget wasn't just lower – it was targeted. Residents saw new playground equipment instead of hiked fees. Common areas got a fresh coat of paint within budget. The next board meeting? People volunteered ideas instead of airing grievances. Lakeview still had problems, but for the first time in years, they also had a real plan to solve them.

What Could They Have Done Differently?

- **Started Sooner:** Proactive budgeting avoids crisis-driven cuts down the line.
- **Involved Residents Earlier:** Explaining the crisis and getting input builds support for tough choices.
- **Regular Budget Reviews:** Catching overspends early allows mid-course corrections vs. a year-end surprise.

Voice of a Board Member: "We thought we were doing okay, just winging it a bit. Turns out, those little leaks add up to one big sinking ship."

Question for the Reader: Could regular budget check-ins (even informal ones) reveal potential savings in your community?

Key Takeaways:

- "Budget as usual" often breeds hidden inefficiencies that cripple you later.
- Zero-based budgeting isn't comfortable, but neither is facing angry residents with another assessment.
- A well-justified budget builds trust, making future hard decisions easier to accept.

Case Study: Financial Reporting Facelift

Emily, treasurer of the Greenbrier Estates HOA Board, sighed as she clicked "print" on yet another accusatory email. The financial reports were out, and the complaints were flooding in. Wasn't anyone happy? The community was in decent financial shape!

But the truth was, Emily wasn't so sure anymore. The reports were a mess. Dense spreadsheets, accounting jargon... she barely understood them herself, and she'd taken college-level bookkeeping. How could Mrs. Peterson, with her limited eyesight, or the Johnsons, new to the community, make heads or tails of it?

"Hiding something..." that accusation stung. All those late nights, volunteer hours...for this? Worse, it was starting to feel like they might actually have things to hide. Not intentional, just a lack of clarity that could look suspicious.

At the next board meeting, Emily put her foot down. "We need new software," she insisted. "Something that gives plain English summaries, maybe even charts."

Mark, the president, was skeptical. "More expense?" But Emily had done her research. Modern HOA software didn't just make bookkeeping easier; it was designed for communication.

A few weeks later, the new reports landed in mailboxes. Gasps of surprise replaced the usual grumbling. "I can actually understand this!" Mrs. Peterson exclaimed. The Johnsons sent a thank-you note – the clear financials had reassured them about buying here.

That budget meeting? Easiest one ever. Residents focused on priorities, not deciphering numbers. Turns out, when you speak their language, trust comes naturally. Emily learned a valuable lesson: It wasn't enough to be honest; you had to look honest too.

What Could They Have Done Differently?

- **Proactive Communication:** Instead of waiting for complaints, the board could have presented the

financial reports alongside a simple explainer. This proactive approach builds understanding and preempts misconceptions.
- **Resident Feedback:** A quick survey asking residents about the report's clarity could have identified the problem much earlier.

Board Member Voice: "Honestly, we thought as long as the numbers were right, that was enough. We never considered how the reports actually looked or felt to read for the average resident." – Emily, Treasurer

Question for the Reader: Are your community's financial communications an afterthought, or do you treat them as a vital way to build trust and understanding?

Key Takeaways

- **Clarity is Key:** Even with good intentions, complex reports breed distrust.
- **Communication is Not One-Way:** Don't just send reports, actively explain them and invite feedback.
- **Perception Matters:** Being honest isn't enough, your financial processes need to *look* transparent to residents.

Case Study: Proactive Planning Pays Off

Clara, president of the Sunny Acres HOA board, couldn't help but relax slightly as she listened to the pounding rain. Usually, a storm like this made her anxious. Roofs leaked, basements flooded, and the barrage of emergency resident calls began. But not tonight.

See, Sunny Acres wasn't like other communities Clara knew. A few years back, under a prior board, things had been shaky. Neglected maintenance, underfunded reserves... it was the classic recipe for disaster. Clara took over determined to change things.

It hadn't been easy. Getting a reserve study done took convincing – some residents didn't see the point. Even after it revealed the true state of the infrastructure, increasing dues was a hard sell. But Clara held firm, explaining *why* it mattered.

Then came the hailstorm. Reports of damage trickled in. Clara steeled herself...and instead, found an email from their management company. Subject: Roof Replacements. Turns out, the reserve fund was more than enough to cover everything. Quotes were already being gathered.

Walking outside later, some neighbors were nervously surveying their roofs for damage. She met their worry with a grin. "Don't worry," Clara reassured them, "we've got this covered."

News spread fast. At first, disbelief, and then relief. Even the residents who'd grumbled about dues increases came by to thank her. The next week, an agent called. A prospective buyer loved Sunny Acres, but with the storm...they were hesitant. Clara confidently showed them the approved repair plans, fully funded. The house sold the next day.

It was a small victory, but Clara knew it was just the beginning. A well-run HOA wasn't just about avoiding crises; it was about building a community where people felt secure, where their investment was protected. Storms would keep coming, figuratively and literally, but Sunny Acres was in good shape to weather them.

What Could They Have Done Differently?

Nothing! This is the ideal scenario. Sunny Acres is a model for how responsible budgeting and reserve planning should work.

Board Member Mindset: Clara: "At first, changing things was tough. But I knew if we didn't act, we'd end up paying way more later, with angry residents on top of it. Prevention beats panic anytime."

Question for the Reader: Does your community have a "prevention beats panic" mindset? Or are you constantly playing catch-up, facing one crisis after another?

Key Takeaways

- Well-funded reserves aren't just protection, they're peace of mind.
- Reserve studies provide the roadmap for responsible planning.
- Educating residents about the 'why' behind decisions fosters support, even for tough choices.
- Good financial management boosts property values and community pride.

Test Your Knowledge! Answers

1. **Components of a Budget:**
   - Operating Expenses (maintenance, repairs, utilities, etc.)
   - Reserve Fund Contributions
   - Income (assessments, investment earnings, etc.)
2. **Reserve vs. Operating:**
   - Reserve funds are for major, long-term repairs/replacements (roofs, siding).
   - Operating budget covers day-to-day expenses.
3. **Determining Dues:**
   - Start with your budgeted operating expenses and reserve needs.
   - Subtract other income sources.
   - The remaining amount needs to be covered by dues.
4. **Reserve Study Benefits:**
   - Provides a roadmap for saving, preventing sudden assessments.
   - Demonstrates responsible planning to residents and potential buyers.
5. **Balance Sheet vs. Income Statement:**
   - Balance Sheet: A snapshot of financial health at one moment (assets, liabilities, equity).
   - Income Statement: Tracks income and expenses over a period of time (usually monthly).
6. **Importance of Reporting:**
   - Builds trust and transparency.
   - Helps residents understand community finances and support decisions.
7. **Zero-Based Budgeting:**

- Starting from scratch each year, justifying every expense.
- Prevents automatic increases, ensuring money is spent wisely.

8. **Who Decides Dues Allocation:**
   - Your community's governing documents (CC&Rs, bylaws) dictate this.

9. **Using Reserve Funds for Operating Costs:**
   - Indicates a budget shortfall or underfunded reserves.
   - Usually requires an additional assessment from residents.

10. **Baseline Funding:**
    - The minimum amount your reserve study recommends saving to meet future needs without severe underfunding.

CHAPTER 3: MAINTENANCE AND OPERATIONS

Introduction

A Case Study in Deferred Maintenance

A community I once managed faced hundreds of deteriorating wood fences. Rather than addressing the root of the problem, the Board opted for a short-sighted, cash-conserving approach: they directed maintenance to paint over the rotten wood. This failed to hold for even six months, resulting in wasted labor and resources. This situation underscores the critical need for effective maintenance and operations within any condominium association. Here are two main solutions to avoid such a problem:

- **Proactive Replacement:** Instead of temporary fixes, plan for the proactive replacement of aging or compromised fencing. This might mean budgeting for a phased replacement strategy.
- **Alternative Materials:** If repeated wood fence replacement proves costly, explore alternative fencing materials with longer lifespans or lower maintenance requirements.

A well-maintained community upholds property values, resulting in higher resale prices. Conversely, deferred maintenance leads to costly repairs, property devaluation, and resident dissatisfaction. Safety concerns and disruptions further erode resident morale.

As discussed in the finance chapter, boards must balance proactive maintenance with realistic budgets to avoid both excessive dues and property neglect. This involves finding a sustainable approach that protects the long-term interests of the association and its residents.

The board's role is primarily oversight – setting policies, approving budgets, and monitoring maintenance activities. While not involved in daily operations, they ensure that those responsible (managers, vendors) are held accountable for maintaining the community's standards.

Fast Fact: Resident satisfaction is often linked to a community's upkeep and the perceived value of their investment.

Pro Tip: Don't neglect common areas – they play a significant role in resident satisfaction and property value.

Developing Maintenance Plans

Developing Short- and Long-Term Maintenance Plans

When developing maintenance plans, boards must consider two key categories:

1. Short-Term Plans

- **Purpose:** Address day-to-day upkeep to ensure the functionality and aesthetic appeal of the community.
- **Examples:**
  - Cleaning common areas (lobbies, hallways, pool areas, etc.)
  - Trash and recycling management
  - Groundskeeping (mowing, weeding, fertilization, snow/leaf removal, planting)
  - Minor repairs (leaky faucets, replacing light bulbs, door repairs)
  - Safety and security checks (lighting, fire extinguishers, pet waste stations)
- **Scheduling:**
  - Typical schedules include daily cleaning, weekly landscaping, and monthly safety checks.
  - Crucially, short-term plans need built-in flexibility to accommodate unexpected repairs and weather-related events (e.g., downed tree limbs, emergency roof tarping).

2. Long-Term Plans

- **Purpose:** Forecast major expenses and ensure the community's financial preparedness.

- **Reserve Studies:**
    - As covered previously, reserve studies are crucial. They analyze the lifespan of major building components, predict replacement costs, and recommend funding strategies to ensure timely, like-for-like replacements.
    - They prevent assessment surprises and ensure smooth transitions from project need to financing availability.
- **Component Lifespans and Schedules:**
    - Reserve studies inform a replacement timeline for typical components: roof, siding, HVAC, plumbing, elevators, pool furniture, concrete, asphalt, signage, etc.
    - Engineers use industry averages, inflation estimates, and local climate/usage patterns to provide reasonably accurate projections.
- **Capital Improvement Projects:**
    - These enhancements go beyond standard maintenance (e.g., pool renovation, lobby upgrade).
    - They differ from repairs, focusing on improvement rather than restoration of original condition.
    - Budgeting strategies include inclusion in reserves, special assessments, or financing.

Fast Fact: Many states now require condominium associations to conduct regular reserve studies.

Pro Tip: Document everything! Keep detailed records of maintenance activities, vendor contracts, and resident complaints.

Checklist:

- **Short-Term Plan**
    - Identify daily, weekly, monthly, and seasonal maintenance tasks.
    - Create schedules and assign responsibility.

- o Plan for unexpected repairs and emergency situations.
- **Long-Term Plan**
  - o Have a reserve study conducted or updated.
  - o Predict major component lifespans (use study and industry standards).
  - o Create a prioritized, long-term replacement schedule.

Timeline:

- **Within 30 Days:** Draft initial short-term plan.
- **Within 90 Days:** Commission or update a reserve study.
- **Within 6 Months:** Finalize short-term plan. Develop a multi-year long-term outlook.

Action Steps:

1. Gather input from management, maintenance staff, and residents on current practices.
2. Research industry standards for task frequency and reserve planning.
3. Present plans to the board and residents for feedback and approval.

Vendor Selection And Contract Management

Finding the Right Vendor: Bidding and Contracts

Selecting and managing vendors is crucial for any community. A fair and transparent bidding process ensures you find the best fit at a competitive price.

1. Defining the Scope of Work

The foundation of a good bid is a detailed scope of work. This outlines the project, including materials, labor, timeline, and expectations. A well-written scope:

- Prevents future disagreements with vendors.
- Ensures accurate bids.
- Provides legal protection for the community.
- Guarantees timely project completion.

2. The Request for Proposal (RFP)

An RFP is a formal document sent to potential vendors. It details the project requirements and includes:

- Scope of work
- Timeline and deadlines
- Bid submission instructions
- Required vendor information (experience, references, insurance)

3. Evaluating Bids: Beyond Just Price

Price is important, but it's not the only factor. Consider:

- **Experience:** Has the vendor handled similar projects successfully?
- **References:** Check references to confirm quality work.
- **Insurance:** Does the vendor have adequate coverage to protect the community?
- **Reputation and Responsiveness:** Does the vendor have a good track record and communicate effectively?

The Goal: Best Value, Not Lowest Price

Strive for the vendor who offers the best overall value, which may not always be the lowest initial bid, but stay in alignment with the guidelines immediately below.

4. Ethical Bidding Practices

Respecting vendors' time and effort builds a positive

reputation for your community and management company, attracting higher-quality contractors for future projects. Here's how to ensure ethical practices:

- **Purposeful RFPs:** Only issue RFPs for projects the community is financially prepared to undertake. Don't waste vendors' time if you can't realistically afford the work.
- **Serious Consideration:** Be open to hiring *any* vendor who submits a competitive and professionally prepared bid. Don't issue RFPs to simply fulfill a formality.
- **Fair Competition:** Avoid practices that give unfair advantage to "preferred" vendors, such as price matching. This undermines the bidding process and discourages participation.

Why Ethics Matter

Unethical bidding practices damage the reputations of both the community and the management company. Developing a reputation for fairness attracts higher-quality vendors and leads to better outcomes for everyone involved.

Building Trust is Key

Respectful interactions with vendors foster trust. Unethical practices damage the community's reputation and limit future vendor options.

5. Contract Essentials

A well-written contract protects both the association and the vendor. It should include:

- Clear scope of work
- Payment terms and timelines
- Workmanship requirements
- Project timelines (start, completion, milestones)
- Performance expectations (communication protocols)
- Dispute resolution mechanisms (mediation, arbitration)

- Termination clauses for non-performance

By following these steps, your community can find qualified vendors and establish strong working relationships through effective contract management.

Pro Tip: When evaluating bids, prioritize experience and references over solely focusing on price.

Checklist:
- **Bid Process**
    - Define a clear scope of work.
    - Prepare a detailed RFP.
    - Solicit bids from multiple reputable vendors.
- **Evaluation**
    - Check references and credentials.
    - Compare costs, experience, and communication style.
    - Select vendor based on best value, not just price.
- **Contract**
    - Include clear work scope, timelines, payment terms, performance expectations, and termination clauses.
    - Have the contract reviewed by an attorney.

Timeline: Varies depending on project size. Allow ample time for RFP, bid review, and contract negotiation.

Action Steps:
1. Identify the need for a vendor and define the project.
2. Create draft RFP, seek board input for revisions.
3. Finalize contract template with legal guidance for future use.

Proactive Maintenance Vs. Reactive Repairs

Proactive Maintenance: The Cost-Effective Long-Term Strategy

While proactive maintenance requires upfront investment, it often offers better long-term value than relying solely on reactive repairs. Here's why:

Benefits of Proactive Maintenance:

- **Extends Asset Lifespans:** Regular attention prevents minor issues from becoming major, costlier problems.
    - Examples:
        - Replacing HVAC filters extends system life.
        - Muddy crocks and backed-up drains can greatly shorten the life of a sump pump; regular maintenance prevents this.
- **Minimizes Disruptions:** Prevents equipment failures during peak use (e.g., pool pump in summer). Reduces the need for expensive emergency repairs.
- **Improves Safety and Resident Satisfaction:**
    - Addresses hazards proactively (e.g., fixing loose railings, uneven concrete).
    - Well-maintained properties contribute to community pride and resident retention.

Pro Tip: Regularly walk the property with board members and/or the property manager to spot potential maintenance issues early on.

When Reactive Repairs Become Necessary:

Sometimes, reactive maintenance is unavoidable due to:

- **Unexpected Failures:** Even with good care, components can fail unexpectedly.
- **Budget Constraints:** Limited funds may force reactive responses to emergencies.
- **Cost-Benefit Analysis:** At times, replacing an aging component might be more cost-effective than repeated repairs (e.g., a frequently patched roof).

Finding the Balance

Boards must balance proactivity with financial realities. Here's how:

- **Risk-Based Approach:** Prioritize maintenance where failures would be most disruptive or costly. Consider asset condition, criticality, resident impact, and the potential cost of failure.
- **Financial Practicality:** Ideal maintenance sometimes clashes with budget limits. Boards must make the most of available resources.
- **Transparency:** Open communication with residents about maintenance choices builds trust and understanding.

Key Takeaway: Think of proactive maintenance as a long-term investment. While the upfront cost may be higher, it often leads to greater savings and community well-being over time.

Fast Fact: Insurance premiums can be lower for communities that demonstrate proactive maintenance practices.

Checklist:

- **Risk Assessment**
    - Identify critical assets (roof, HVAC, etc.)
    - Estimate the impact and cost of failure.
    - Prioritize proactive maintenance for high-risk items.
- **Budgeting**

- - Balance proactive spending with financial realities.
  - Explore phased projects or alternative financing for major costs.
- **Communication**
  - Explain the benefits of proactive maintenance to residents.
  - Highlight successes to build support for the approach.

Timeline: Ongoing. Regular risk assessment and budget review are essential.

Action Steps

1. Start a log of past failures, noting the costs and disruption.
2. Educate the board on the long-term value of proactive maintenance.
3. Share success stories with residents (ex: catching a minor roof leak prevents major damage).

Emergency Preparedness

Emergency Preparedness: Protecting Your Community

Many communities underestimate the importance of emergency planning. Don't be one of them! Proactive preparation can save lives, minimize damage, and aid in quick recovery.

Types of Emergencies

1. **Natural Disasters:**
   - Tailor this to your location (flooding, storms, earthquakes, etc.).

o   Consider how these would specifically impact your community.
2. **Fire:**
   o   Emphasize fire safety protocols in units and common areas.
   o   Have clear evacuation plans, especially for high-rise buildings.
3. **Plumbing/Electrical Failures:**
   o   Address scenarios like large-scale leaks, power outages, and related hazards.
4. **Security Incidents:**
   o   Plan for intruders, break-ins, and active threats.
   o   Coordinate with law enforcement and establish communication protocols.

Develop a Response Plan

- **Chain of Command:** Clearly define who's in charge during an emergency (board member, manager, designated personnel). Maintain an updated contact list for all parties.
- **Evacuation Procedures (if applicable):** Designate safe routes, assembly points, and include assistance plans for residents with disabilities.
- **Communication Channels:** Establish how the board/management will communicate with residents. Have backup plans if primary methods fail (phone trees, social media).
- **Emergency Vendor List:** Have pre-approved vendors (plumbers, electricians, restoration companies) and insurance carrier contact information ready.

Annual Review and Practice

- **Update Regularly:** Contact info, procedures, and vendor agreements change. Keep your plan current.
- **Practice Drills:** Fire drills are essential in multi-story buildings. Test communication systems with smaller-

scale drills.
- **Educate Residents:** Share key parts of the plan to ensure everyone is informed and prepared.

Community-Specific Considerations

- Communities with sump pumps prone to failure should plan for extended power outages.
- Consult your local fire marshal regarding fire safety procedures and the process for building board-ups if a fire occurs.
- Regularly evaluate your plan against evolving best practices and learn from other communities.

Key Takeaway: Emergency preparedness isn't just a plan; it's an ongoing process. By being proactive, your community can better weather any crisis.

Checklist:

- **Emergency Plan Development**
  - Establish a chain of command and communication protocol.
  - Create evacuation procedures (if applicable).
  - Maintain vendor contact list for emergency services.
- **Resident Communication**
  - Distribute key parts of the plan to residents.
  - Share contact information for reporting emergencies.
- **Review and Practice**
  - Update the plan and contact lists annually.
  - Conduct fire drills and practice communication systems.

Timeline:

- **Within 60 days:** Draft initial plan.
- **Ongoing:** Annual review, updates, and drills.

Action Steps:

1. Assign responsibility for plan development (manager, board committee, etc.)
2. Consult with local fire/emergency services for guidance.
3. Provide resident education in multiple formats (meetings, newsletters).

Sustainable Maintenance: Good For The Planet, Good For Your Wallet

Choose sustainability for a healthier environment and potential financial benefits for your community. While not every strategy in this section might fully apply, use it as inspiration to find ones that do.

Even communities with limited maintenance responsibilities can still promote sustainability. Consider ways your community might:

- Subsidize or fully fund resident upgrades like water-saving toilets or LED bulbs.
- Offer support for low-cost, high-impact conservation projects that residents might need encouragement to tackle.

Remember, there's no single right way to do this. Use the list as a springboard for ideas that align with your community's needs and maintenance plan. Sustainable practices reduce your environmental impact, improve resident well-being, and can even boost property values.

Why It Matters

- Electricity and fossil fuel use worsen climate change.
- Overusing water puts a strain on vital resources.
- Excessive waste adds to overflowing landfills.

Fast Fact: LED bulbs can last 10-20 times longer than traditional incandescent bulbs.

Sustainable Solutions

- **Energy Efficiency**
    - **Lighting:** Switch to LEDs for longer life, big energy savings. Use motion sensors for smarter lighting.
    - **HVAC:** Programmable thermostats mean better efficiency. Regular maintenance keeps systems working at their best. Long-term, explore high-efficiency HVAC upgrades.
    - **Building Improvements:** Better insulation means less heating/cooling. Seal leaks for energy savings. Consider replacing old windows if needed.
- **Water Conservation**
    - **Low-Flow Fixtures:** WaterSense-labeled options save water.
    - **Leak Prevention:** Proactive maintenance saves water. Educate residents to report leaks quickly.
    - **Smart Landscaping:** Native plants need less watering.
- **Reduce, Reuse, Recycle**
    - **Easy Recycling:** Clear signage encourages participation.
    - **Composting:** Divert food/yard waste where possible.

Fast Fact: A single leaky toilet can waste hundreds of gallons of water per day.

Beyond the Basics

- **Renewable Energy:** Look into solar if it makes sense.
- **Resident Involvement:** Educate residents on sustainable choices.
- **Utility Incentives:** Explore rebates or cost-saving programs.

By going green, your community fosters a healthier environment while potentially saving money in the long term!

Pro Tip: Encourage resident involvement in sustainability initiatives; even small changes can add up!

Checklist

- **Energy Efficiency**
    - Assess potential for lighting upgrades, HVAC optimization, etc.
    - Explore long-term investments in renewables (if feasible).
- **Water Conservation**
    - Evaluate fixtures, landscaping, and potential for leak detection.
- **Waste & Recycling**
    - Optimize recycling programs and consider composting.
- **Education**
    - Empower residents with sustainable practice tips.

Timeline: Can be staggered. Low-cost changes can have an immediate impact; some upgrades may be longer-term.

Action Steps

1. Initiate an energy audit to identify efficiency opportunities.
2. Consult with utility companies for rebates or incentives.
3. Launch a resident awareness campaign on conservation practices.

Conclusion

This chapter has highlighted the advantages of proactive maintenance for your community. Let's recap the key takeaways:

- **Proactive Pays Off:** Yes, it may cost more initially, but proactive maintenance often saves money long-term and prevents major headaches.
- **Board's Role:** Focus on the big picture—policies, budgets, and oversight. Leave the daily tasks to professionals.
- **Vendor Partners:** Reliable vendors are crucial for handling everything from routine fixes to emergencies.
- **Be Open:** Clear communication builds community trust when it comes to maintenance choices.
- **Go Green:** Sustainable practices help the environment, make residents feel good, and can even save money over time.

Think Long-Term

- **Reserve Studies are a Must:** Protect your community's finances and avoid nasty surprises. Get one done now if yours is not current.
- **Maintenance is Smart Investing:** Well-cared-for properties hold their value and keep residents happy.
- **Budget Wisely:** Balance proactive maintenance with the reality of what residents can afford.

Keep Improving

- **Be Flexible:** Needs change, so should your plans. Don't get stuck in the past.

- **Listen to Residents:** Their input makes maintenance work better for everyone.
- **Stay Updated:** Boards and managers, keep learning about the latest trends and regulations.

Remember: Maintenance is an ongoing process for a thriving community. Commit to continuous improvement!

Test Your Knowledge!

1. Why is proactive maintenance generally a better long-term strategy than reactive repairs?
2. List three key components of a well-developed short-term maintenance plan.
3. What is the purpose of a reserve study, and why is it essential for community associations?
4. Describe two ways a community board can effectively find and select reliable vendors.
5. How can a community balance proactive maintenance with potential budget constraints?
6. List two specific examples of how a community can reduce its water consumption.
7. Give one example of how sustainable maintenance practices can have financial benefits for the community.
8. What is the board's primary role in overseeing community maintenance operations?
9. Why is resident communication important in a successful maintenance plan
10. Why is continuous improvement a crucial mindset for community maintenance?

The answers are at the end of this chapter

Case Study: The Leaky Roof (Proactive Vs. Reactive)

Hidden Valley Condominiums prided themselves on their "low-cost" approach. For years, minor roof leaks were met with quick patches – a philosophy of "out of sight, out of mind." Residents occasionally complained about water stains on ceilings, but the board dismissed them as isolated incidents. They were confident their budget was better spent elsewhere.

Then came the storm season. Weeks of relentless downpours turned those minor leaks into major problems. Water cascaded into multiple top-floor units. Drywall bubbled and collapsed. Carpets were soaked, and mold became a serious threat. Residents' furniture and belongings were damaged. A call for an emergency roof replacement yielded shocking results:

- Limited Contractor Availability: Most reputable companies were booked solid with crisis repairs.
- Sky-High Pricing: The few available contractors charged exorbitant rates, knowing the community was desperate.
- Insurance Woes: The insurance adjuster determined the damage was due to long-term neglect, not a sudden event, reducing coverage.

Displaced residents were angry and frustrated, forced into temporary housing. The board faced a massive special assessment, causing a wave of resentment throughout the community. Some owners put their condos up for sale at a reduced price just to escape the financial mess. Property values plummeted. The reputation of Hidden Valley was tarnished, making it difficult to attract new buyers.

What Could They Have Done Differently?

- A regular roof inspection and maintenance program would have caught deteriorating areas early, allowing for smaller, more cost-effective repairs to prevent major failures.
- Including roof replacement in the reserve study would have prepared them financially, preventing the need for

large special assessments.

Board Member Mindset: "We thought we were saving money by avoiding big-ticket replacements... turns out, we just kicked the can down the road and ended up paying far more in the end."

Question to Ponder: Are there any areas in your community where a "patch it and forget it" mentality could lead to a much bigger problem down the line?

Key Takeaways

- Proactive maintenance is almost always cheaper than emergency repairs in the long run.
- Neglecting major components can significantly damage finances and property values.
- Reserve studies are essential tools to prevent unpleasant surprises and maintain financial stability.

Case Study: The Reserve Study Savior (Long-Term Planning)

Oakwood Village was once a beacon of pride for residents. Its sprawling grounds and well-kept homes were the envy of neighboring communities. The board touted their commitment to low association fees as a key selling point. Yet, behind this facade of affordability, a crisis was brewing.

Unbeknownst to many residents, Oakwood Village had never conducted a reserve study. They lacked a long-term financial roadmap for the inevitable replacement of major community assets. When the 20-year-old pool started showing major structural cracks, the board was caught off guard. Desperate repairs proved to be a temporary bandage. Then, the unthinkable happened – the clubhouse HVAC system, also reaching the end of its lifespan, failed during a scorching heatwave.

Panic set in. The board found themselves between a rock and a hard place. The cost of replacing both the pool and HVAC soared into hundreds of thousands of dollars. Emergency special assessments landed like bombshells on residents' doorsteps. Many long-time homeowners, particularly those on fixed incomes, couldn't bear the sudden financial burden. Frustration turned to anger, and several residents chose to sell their homes at a loss, further destabilizing property values.

A new board finally took control and made the tough decision to commission a reserve study. The results were sobering. It revealed a pattern of chronic underfunding, leaving the community woefully unprepared for major expenses. The board had no choice but to implement gradual dues increases to catch up. While these increases were necessary, they added financial strain to residents already reeling from the earlier assessments.

Oakwood Village is slowly recovering, but the scars of financial mismanagement remain. The community lost valuable long-term residents, and attracting new buyers is difficult due to the higher fees and the lingering perception of instability. Trust between residents and the board remains fragile.

What Could They Have Done Differently?

Oakwood Village could have avoided this financial disaster with a proactive long-term approach. A reserve study would have identified the looming replacement costs and allowed for gradual funding over time, avoiding the shock of emergency assessments.

Board Member Mindset: "We believed keeping monthly dues as low as possible was the best way to serve residents. In hindsight, it was incredibly short-sighted. We didn't fully understand the importance of reserve studies back then."

Question for the Reader: Is your community willing to pay slightly more now in monthly dues to avoid the risk of massive assessments later?

Key Takeaways

- Reserve studies are essential tools for protecting a community's financial health; they are NOT a luxury.
- Focusing solely on low dues without a long-term financial plan is a recipe for disaster.
- The cost of inaction is often far greater than the cost of proactive planning.
- Communicating the value of reserve funding to residents from the outset is crucial for building understanding and avoiding future conflicts.

Case Study: Beyond The Bottom Line (Vendor Selection)

Sunset Hills HOA prided itself on its attractive landscaping. But their long-time landscaping company had become unreliable – missed appointments, patchy work, and a dwindling crew. It was time for a change. The board meticulously crafted a detailed Request for Proposal (RFP), outlining the exact scope of work: lawn care, seasonal plantings, shrub trimming, irrigation maintenance, and a dedicated account manager.

The bids rolled in, and the price gap was staggering. "Fly-By-Night Landscaping" offered a rock-bottom price, but their online reviews were dismal, filled with complaints about disappearing crews and neglected properties. On the higher end was "Green Gardens," a well-established firm with numerous glowing reviews and a portfolio of HOA properties remarkably similar to Sunset Hills.

The board faced a dilemma. Stretching the budget was tempting, but doubts about "Fly-By-Night" lingered. Several board members contacted other communities serviced by "Green Gardens." The feedback was overwhelmingly positive: responsive, reliable, and going the extra mile. After weighing the pros and cons, the Sunset Hills board decided on "Green Gardens."

The transformation was remarkable. Flower beds were vibrant, lawns were meticulously manicured, and the dedicated account manager even offered suggestions to enhance the landscape design. Resident compliments poured in, and inquiries from prospective buyers increased. The higher landscaping cost proved to be an investment, not just an expense.

What Could They Have Done Differently?

The tempting low bid from "Fly-By-Night Landscaping" might have been the path of least resistance. However, skimping on landscaping would have reflected poorly on the community's image, potentially harming property values and resident satisfaction in the long run.

Board Member Voice: "We knew we couldn't just chase the lowest number. We had to consider the value for our money. A neglected property is no bargain, and it sends the wrong message to our residents." – Sarah, Sunset Hills HOA Board President

Question for the Reader: When seeking vendors, are you tempted to prioritize short-term savings over long-term quality and reliability? Consider the potential hidden costs of poorly executed services.

Key Takeaways

- Price is important, but it's not the only factor. Experience, reputation, and responsiveness are crucial for successful vendor partnerships.
- Don't neglect due diligence. Thorough research and reference checks can save you from future headaches.
- Remember, sometimes the lowest bid is the most expensive option in the long run. Investing in quality reflects on the value of your community.

Case Study: Communication Is Key (Resident Involvement)

Lakeview Apartments, a bustling complex with a 10-story high-rise as its centerpiece, had always enjoyed a sense of community. Then, the unexpected happened — the building's only elevator stopped working. Panic could have ensued, particularly among elderly residents and those with limited mobility on the upper floors.

Instead, the Lakeview Apartments board took swift, decisive action focused on communication:

- **Immediate Notice:** Within hours, every resident received a detailed message via email, text, and a physical notice posted in common areas. It acknowledged the breakdown, outlined the vendor's initial assessment, and provided a realistic (if tentative) timeline for repairs.
- **Addressing Anxieties:** The notice empathetically addressed the hardship this posed, especially for those with mobility issues. It offered a temporary solution – a designated volunteer "carry-up" service to help residents with groceries and other items.
- **Regular Updates:** As the situation evolved, the board provided consistent progress reports, even when the news was about delays caused by parts availability. Residents felt informed, minimizing frustration.
- **Gratitude & Celebration:** When the elevator was finally fixed, the board didn't just breathe a sigh of relief. They sent out a thank-you to the entire community for their patience, highlighted the residents who volunteered as "carriers," and even hosted a small ice cream social in the

lobby to celebrate getting back to normal.

What Could They Have Done Differently?

While Lakeview's response was excellent, they could've potentially prevented the elevator failure. Regular maintenance and inspections might have caught early signs of wear, allowing for preemptive repairs and avoiding a complete shutdown.

Board Member Voice: "At first, we were as surprised as anyone about the elevator. But we knew panicking wouldn't help. Clear, honest communication would reassure people that we were on top of the situation."

Question for the Reader: Does your community have a plan for unexpected disruptions (power outages, plumbing emergencies, etc.)? How will you quickly communicate with residents and offer support if needed?

Key Takeaways

- Proactive communication builds trust even in crisis situations.
- Transparency about challenges, timelines, and solutions minimizes anxiety and fosters understanding.
- Empathy matters! Acknowledging resident hardship goes a long way.
- Celebrate the return to normal – it reinforces a sense of community resilience.

Case Study: Going Green (Sustainability)

Pine Creek HOA had a growing concern about rising water costs and the community's environmental impact. The board wasn't sure where to start but knew they wanted to make a difference. A bit of research revealed that inefficient showerheads were a major culprit in water waste. After consulting with a plumber and researching products, they settled on high-efficiency, WaterSense-labeled showerheads for all community units.

The upfront cost was substantial, raising concerns among some residents. To address this, the board spearheaded an educational campaign. They sent out newsletters highlighting the average water savings per household and the projected reduction in the community's overall water bill. To make it personal, they included a calculator so residents could estimate their potential individual savings long-term.

The board also partnered with the local utility company to offer conservation workshops. These workshops covered topics like fixing leaky faucets, smart landscaping choices, and energy-efficient appliances. Residents shared tips and learned from each other, generating a sense of collective action.

The impact was remarkable. Pine Creek's water usage dropped significantly, exceeding the initial projections. This led to both immediate and ongoing savings on water bills. Beyond the finances, a sense of pride swept over the community. Residents felt empowered to make a positive environmental impact. Children in the community got involved as "water waste detectives," reporting leaky faucets to the management office, further amplifying conservation efforts.

Inspired by the success, Pine Creek began exploring other sustainability initiatives. They installed recycling bins in common areas, composted yard waste, and investigated solar panel options for the clubhouse. These projects fostered community spirit and engagement while creating a greener and more cost-effective future for Pine Creek HOA.

What Could They Have Done Differently?

- **Pilot Program:** Consider initially installing the new showerheads in a few sample units to gather resident feedback before committing to the full rollout. This could help generate buy-in and address any unforeseen concerns.

- **Resident Incentives:** Explore offering a small rebate or discount to residents who purchase the same water-efficient showerheads for their own bathrooms, further amplifying the conservation efforts.

Board Member's Voice: "At first, we were nervous about the expense. But we realized that true cost isn't just about the upfront price tag. Protecting our resources and creating a positive legacy for our community was the right investment."

Question for the Reader: Are there areas in your community where a relatively small investment could create a ripple effect of cost savings and environmental impact?

Key Takeaways

- **Small Changes Add Up:** Sustainable initiatives don't have to be grand. Incremental changes can yield significant results.
- **Education is Powerful:** Informing residents about the benefits of conservation builds support and encourages

participation.
- **Momentum Matters:** The success of one green project can inspire further action, creating a continuous cycle of improvement.

Case Study: Evolving With The Times (Continuous Improvement)

Willow Creek was a classic example of a well-maintained but aging community. Built in the 1980s, its clubhouse sported worn carpets and outdated furniture. The pool area was basic, and the lack of modern amenities like a fitness center or dedicated gathering spaces put it at a disadvantage compared to newer developments. Residents were mostly long-term owners, and while they loved the location and sense of community, they voiced a desire for a refresh.

The board faced a dilemma. Significant upgrades required substantial investment. They sought resident input through surveys and town hall meetings. The overwhelming sentiment was that people were willing to pay slightly higher dues for a revitalized Willow Creek that would appeal to new buyers and keep property values strong.

The board prioritized a phased modernization plan based on feedback:

- **Phase 1: Common Areas** The clubhouse received new flooring, paint, updated furniture, and improved lighting. This created a welcoming space for events and informal gatherings.
- **Phase 2: Fitness Focus** An underutilized storage room was converted into a fitness center with basic cardio and weight equipment, catering to resident preferences without the expense of a full-scale gym.
- **Phase 3: Outdoor Oasis** The pool area got a facelift with new lounge chairs and updated landscaping. A fenced-in

dog park was added, recognizing the growing number of pet owners in the community.

The results were transformative. Willow Creek shed its dated image and became an attractive option for younger buyers and families. Existing residents expressed high satisfaction, feeling their investment was paying off. Property values increased, justifying the upgrades. The success spurred additional improvements over time, like enhanced security and eco-friendly initiatives.

What Could They Have Done Differently?

While Willow Creek's approach was successful, some communities might benefit from smaller-scale test projects before major investments. For instance, updating a small common area or adding a few pieces of fitness equipment can gauge resident enthusiasm and refine the long-term modernization plan.

Board Member Voice: "We knew things couldn't stay the same forever. But change can be risky. By listening closely to our residents, we were able to make smart improvements that truly benefited the entire community." – Susan Miller, Board President, Willow Creek.

Question for the Reader: Are there any small changes your community could implement that would signal a shift toward modernization and test resident receptiveness to larger updates?

Key Takeaways

- Don't let "well enough" become the enemy of progress. Even well-maintained communities need to evolve with resident needs and expectations.
- Resident input is crucial. Surveys and open dialogue inform the best modernization strategies.
- Phased plans ease financial burdens and allow

communities to adjust their approach based on results.
- Successful modernization creates a win-win scenario, boosting resident satisfaction and strengthening property values.

Test Your Knowledge! Answers

1. **Why is proactive maintenance generally a better long-term strategy than reactive repairs?**

    - Proactive maintenance prevents minor issues from escalating into major, costly problems.
    - It extends the lifespan of expensive assets (roofs, HVAC, etc.), saving money in the long run.
    - It minimizes disruptions and inconveniences for residents by addressing problems before they become emergencies.

2. **List three key components of a well-developed short-term maintenance plan.**

    - Routine Tasks: Daily, weekly, monthly cleaning, landscaping, minor repairs, etc.
    - Addressing Immediate Problems: Responding to breakdowns, leaks, and resident requests.
    - Seasonal Requirements: HVAC changeovers, snow removal, pool maintenance, etc.

3. **What is the purpose of a reserve study, and why is it essential for community associations?**

    - Purpose: A reserve study professionally assesses the condition of major building components and estimates their remaining lifespans and projected replacement costs.

- Essentiality:
    - Prevents "assessment surprises" by forecasting major expenses.
    - Ensures the community is financially prepared for replacements.
    - Guides the board in setting appropriate reserve funding levels.
4. **Describe two ways a community board can effectively find and select reliable vendors.**

    - Seek Referrals: Ask management companies, other communities, or realtors for recommendations.
    - Verify Credentials: Check licensing, insurance, and references from past clients.
5. **How can a community balance proactive maintenance with potential budget constraints?**

    - Risk-Based Prioritization: Focus on the components most likely to cause major disruption or expense if they fail.
    - Phased Repairs: Consider spreading out large projects over multiple budget cycles to ease the financial burden.
    - Resident Communication: Transparency about the pros and cons of proactive vs. reactive spending builds understanding.
6. **List two specific examples of how a community can reduce its water consumption.**

    - Install low-flow fixtures (showerheads, faucets, toilets).
    - Implement a leak detection and repair program.
7. **Give one example of how sustainable maintenance practices can have financial benefits for the community.**

- Energy-efficient upgrades (like LED lighting) can significantly reduce utility bills.

8. **What is the board's primary role in overseeing community maintenance operations?**

- Setting Policies: The board establishes the overall maintenance philosophy and standards.
- Approving Budgets: The board ensures sufficient funding for maintenance needs.
- Monitoring Activities: The board oversees the work of management and vendors, not the day-to-day tasks.

9. **Why is resident communication important in a successful maintenance plan?**

- Builds Trust: Open communication about maintenance decisions fosters resident support.
- Encourages Participation: Residents are more likely to adopt sustainable practices or report issues if they feel informed.
- Reduces Conflict: Transparency minimizes misunderstandings and disputes about maintenance.

10. **Why is continuous improvement a crucial mindset for community maintenance?**

- Needs Evolve: Community needs and best practices change over time.
- Technology Advances: New solutions and products offer improvements in efficiency and sustainability.
- Resident Expectations: Residents expect a well-maintained community that reflects modern standards.

CHAPTER 4: RESIDENT COMMUNICATION AND ENGAGEMENT

Introduction

One challenge condominium boards often face is getting residents on board with their vision. Finding resident champions who will support the board's decisions, explain the reasoning behind them, and rally the community is vital for a successful association.

A healthy communication flow – both from the board to residents and among residents themselves – is essential in any condominium setting. Effective communication within a condominium serves several key purposes:

- **Building Trust:** Residents need to feel confident that decisions are made with their best interests in mind.
- **Promoting Transparency:** The community should have a clear understanding of how their association operates, both in terms of finances and its social network.
- **Creating a Sense of Community:** Residents should feel connected, invested, and proud to be part of their home.

Fast Fact: Studies show that communities with strong communication enjoy higher resident satisfaction and lower turnover rates.

Pro Tip: Don't let perfect be the enemy of good. Even a simple resident newsletter is better than no communication at all.

Setting Clear Communication Expectations

Communities should establish designated communication channels for different purposes. Here's a breakdown of effective options and their uses:

- **Email:** Ideal for regular updates, announcements, and targeted communication that doesn't require extensive back-and-forth.
- **Newsletters/Bulletins:** Provide in-depth summaries, community highlights, and less time-sensitive information.
- **Website/Portal:** Serves as a central source for governing documents, event calendars, payment options, and resident information.
- **Meetings (formal/informal, in-person/virtual):** Facilitate open dialogue, major decision-making, and resident input.
- **Emergency Protocols:** Include clear contact points (management, board members, third parties) and thresholds for when to activate these channels. We covered the design of emergency protocol systems in a previous chapter; this is where we detail the specific communication methods supporting that system.

A communication policy ensures consistency, professionalism, and clarity. Key elements include:

- **Response Times:** Realistic goals for how quickly the board aims to respond to inquiries. Consider the workload of both the board and management company when setting these.

- **Appropriate Channel Use:** Educate residents on when to use email vs. the portal, etc. The board and management need to enforce these guidelines and redirect residents when they attempt to use channels for inappropriate purposes.
- **Respectful Communication:** Establish standards for resident-board/resident-management interactions, emphasizing professional and courteous language. Emotionally charged, lengthy communications that violate the policy should not receive a response or should be returned to the sender for revision.

Key Takeaway: Avoid overpromising and underdelivering. Design a system that doesn't place 24/7 reliance on a single person.

Systems fail when the community manager becomes a communication bottleneck. To prevent this, boards must ensure their management company distributes responsibilities across a scalable support team. Simply forwarding all resident communications to the manager is unacceptable. Boards must hold the management firm's senior leadership accountable for providing adequate manager support. This will prevent delays, burnout, and compromised service to residents.

The board plays a crucial role in designing robust communication protocols and processes. They must clearly communicate these to the management company, along with the expectation that residents will be held accountable for violating those policies. This includes returning inappropriate communications for revision or declining to respond when violations occur. All resident communications should be stored digitally for future reference in case of disputes.

Fast Fact: Email is often the primary communication channel, but response times can vary. Set clear expectations with residents.

Checklist:

- **Identify Official Channels:** List all approved methods (email, website, portal, newsletter, etc.)
- **Define Channel Purpose:** State what each channel is best used for (announcements, questions, maintenance requests, etc.)
- **Set Response Time Goals:** How quickly should the board/management respond to inquiries on each channel?
- **Create a Communication Policy:** Outline rules of conduct, respect, and what happens if guidelines are violated.
- **Communicate Widely:** Share the policy on all official channels and make it easily accessible.

Timeline (Example):

- **Week 1-2:** Draft policy, get input from management company and legal counsel.
- **Week 3:** Board reviews and approves the policy.
- **Week 4:** Launch! Share the policy widely, hold a brief resident Q&A session.

Action Steps:

- Train staff on the policy.
- Regularly review resident communications to spot trends and address pain points

Encouraging Resident Involvement

Resident involvement is crucial for several reasons we've discussed: better decision-making, identifying potential problems early, and creating a sense of community ownership.

Here's why resident feedback matters:

- **Improves decision-making:** Boards gain valuable insights to align decisions with residents' needs.
- **Proactive problem-solving:** Feedback can flag potential issues before they escalate, saving time and preventing the need to revise policies.
- **Encourages ownership:** Residents feel invested and represented, dissolving the perception of "board vs. residents".

Methods for Gathering Feedback

- **Resident surveys:** Offer general satisfaction surveys or targeted topic surveys. Consider best practices for design and distribution (web portals, 3rd parties, dropboxes, etc.).
- **Dedicated feedback channels:** Use your website, newsletter, or a 3rd-party form. Make forms easy to use and set clear expectations for review and response times.
- **Open forums at meetings:** Use facilitation techniques, like time limits per speaker, to manage discussions and ensure everyone has a voice. Take detailed notes for follow-up.
- **Focus Groups:** Go in-depth on specific issues (landscaping, etc.) with engaged residents.

Beyond Feedback: Creating Participation Opportunities

- **Resident Committees:** Form committees for landscaping, social events, rule review, etc. To ensure full board ownership and accountability, elect a committee leader to report directly to the entire board during meetings. This distributes administrative load, prevents a single board member from becoming a bottleneck, and gives more weight to the committee's recommendations.
- **Volunteering for events/initiatives:** Create diverse opportunities to fit various interests and schedules. Publicly recognize and thank your volunteers – everyone appreciates genuine gratitude!

Key Takeaway: Resident involvement builds strong communities where everyone feels heard and valued.

Fast Fact: Resident surveys are a valuable tool, but keep them short and focused to get the best participation rates.

Checklist

- **Survey Residents:** Find out their interests, skills, and availability for volunteering.
- **Identify Committee Needs:** List areas where resident input would be valuable (landscaping, social, etc.)
- **Match Residents to Roles:** Connect interested residents with suitable committees.
- **Provide Support:** Offer meeting space, small budgets if needed, and board liaison.
- **Recognize Contributions:** Publicly thank volunteers to promote a culture of appreciation.

Timeline (Example):

- **Month 1:** Develop interest survey, distribute, and collect responses.
- **Month 2:** Form committees, board assigns liaisons to each one.

- **Month 3:** First committee meetings, develop goals.
- **Ongoing:** Regular check-ins with committees, public recognition of their work.

Action Steps:

- Start small! A few successful committees are better than many that fizzle out.
- Empower committee leaders to drive their group's agenda.

Effective Dispute Resolution

Disputes are inevitable in any community, where residents have diverse needs. Implement a structured complaint process to ensure fairness, consistency, and clear escalation paths.

A strong complaint policy should include:

- **Steps for filing complaints:** Make it easy and accessible for residents.
- **Board review process:** The board, not the management company, should handle resident complaints about community decisions or policies.
- **Timeframes for resolution:** Set realistic expectations for residents.
- **Escalation and appeal options:** Outline the process if a resident is unhappy with the initial response.

This proactive approach benefits the board by:

- **Protecting the management company:** They're responsible for operations, not policy disputes.
- **Demonstrating fairness:** Residents know their concerns will be heard and addressed systematically.

Consider Mediation and Alternative Dispute Resolution (ADR):

- Consult your governing documents regarding ADR options (mediation, arbitration).
- Discuss these options with your attorney *before* rolling out the complaint policy.
- ADR can be a cost-effective alternative to litigation, if

used appropriately.

Key Takeaways: Residents deserve timely, professional responses, but not necessarily their desired outcome. A robust complaint policy streamlines the process, increases resident satisfaction, and can prevent costly legal battles.

Pro Tip: Train board members on conflict resolution techniques early in their tenure

Checklist:

- **Formal Complaint Process:** Have a multi-step process that includes timelines for resolution.
- **Neutral Documentation:** Train those involved in complaint resolution on impartial, factual record-keeping.
- **Consider Mediation/ADR:** Discuss with an attorney if these options are right for your community.
- **Fairness and Transparency:** Ensure residents understand the process and feel heard throughout.

Timeline (Example - Complaint):

- **Day 1:** Resident submits formal complaint.
- **Days 2-5:** Board reviews, may request additional info if needed.
- **Within 2 Weeks:** Hearing / decision-making meeting.
- **Within 1 Week of Meeting:** Decision communicated to the resident.

Action Steps:

- Communicate the complaint process clearly to residents.
- Don't let legal fears prevent action on legitimate complaints.

Nurturing A Sense Of Community

This book emphasizes building a sense of community – the heart of a board's role in ensuring resident peace of mind, satisfaction, and strong social networks. Community combats isolation, fosters belonging, and boosts resident satisfaction.

Create opportunities for connection:

- **Social events & gatherings:** Welcome new residents with speed-friending events and community tours. Host seasonal celebrations like trunk-or-treat, volunteer days, or pool opening parties. Consider interest groups like book clubs, walking groups, or volunteer initiatives.
- **Resident-led initiatives:** Support resident-organized activities with space, promotion, even small budgets. Clubs like movie buffs, gardening, cooking, fitness, game nights, or pet groups are all excellent options.
- **Community-building events:** Welcome committees, block parties (great for smaller communities), holiday celebrations, skill-sharing workshops, or charity drives build a stronger sense of place.

Board Tips:

- **Survey residents:** Discover their interests before launching initiatives.
- **Offer support:** Provide space, promotion, and consider small budgets.
- **Empower leaders:** Let passionate residents own the planning and execution.
- **Variety is key:** Cater to different ages, interests, and

schedules.

Communication beyond announcements:

- **Resident spotlights:** Feature residents in newsletters or on the website.
- **Community news & resources:** Share local events, tips, or classifieds.

Success Story: A community board I worked with struggled with low resident involvement and lackluster board elections. By actively seeking resident input on various decisions, they gained the support of dozens of residents, improving communication, idea generation, and building a strong pool of future board candidates.

Pro Tip: A "resident spotlight" in your newsletter is a great way to build community and recognize positive contributions.

Checklist:

- **Target Diverse Interests:** Plan events that appeal to different ages, families, new residents, etc.
- **Welcome Newcomers:** Create a welcome packet or host a newcomer social.
- **Beyond Announcements:** Use newsletters/website to share resident spotlights, community stories, local resources.
- **Online AND Offline:** Have both in-person events *and* ways for residents to connect digitally.

Timeline (Example):

- **Quarterly Planning:** Brainstorm a range of events for the upcoming quarter.
- **Monthly Events:** At least one gathering per month, varying in scale/focus.
- **Ongoing:** Regular newsletter/website updates with community-focused content.

Action Steps:

- Delegate! Resident committees can own event planning.
- Get feedback after each event to improve future ones.

Additional Considerations For Board Members: Beyond The Basics

While the core responsibilities of a board member may seem straightforward, the most effective boards master certain skills and adopt a strategic mindset. Here's how to elevate your board's impact:

Effective Communication Skills

- **Active Listening:** Even when you disagree with a resident, demonstrate genuine empathy and attempt to understand their perspective. This builds trust, even in difficult situations, and opens the way for finding solutions.
- **De-escalation:** Tense situations require a calm approach. Avoid getting drawn into debates that only worsen the problem. Focus on lowering the emotional temperature and finding common ground for a productive resolution.
- **Neutrality:** Remaining impartial is essential. Decisions should always align with established community policies, not personal feelings about a resident or situation. This ensures fairness and consistency for all.

Handling Difficult Residents

- **Setting Boundaries: Respect is a Two-Way Street:** Board members are volunteers dedicating time and effort for the benefit of the community. While communication should be respectful, board members should never tolerate being treated with disrespect. Establish and uphold clear boundaries for interaction – this protects both the board and encourages a harmonious environment. Residents who refuse to de-escalate or engage in a civil manner should be asked to leave and informed that their current communication will receive no response. They may re-engage at a later time if they can present their issue respectfully and objectively.

- **Documenting Interactions: Your Shield Against Misinformation:** Meticulous documentation is essential when dealing with recurring issues or residents who might misrepresent interactions. Accurate records protect the community in several ways:
  - **Maintaining Consistency:** Detailed notes prevent misunderstandings and ensure everyone is working from the same set of facts.
  - **Deterring Escalation:** Residents are less likely to distort the truth when they know their interactions are documented.
  - **Legal Defense:** Should a dispute escalate, clear documentation becomes a powerful tool for the community.

Fast Fact: Many states have laws protecting volunteer board members from personal liability in certain situations. Consult an attorney for details in your area.

Pro Tip: If a resident interaction gets heated, document what happened immediately afterward while it's fresh in your mind.

- **Solution-Focus: The Path to Progress:** Boards must resist the temptation to dwell on past decisions or assign blame to individual board members. Shift conversations away from venting and complaining towards constructive problem-solving. Accept the current situation and ask, "How can we move forward from here?" Getting caught in a cycle of blame is not only unproductive but also erodes the trust and teamwork essential for a well-functioning board. Remember, the community looks to the board for solutions, not excuses. Focus on the facts as they are and collaborate to chart the best path forward.

Pro Tip: When handling complaints, focus on "What can we do now?" instead of dwelling on the past.

Navigating Social Media & Technology: Tools with Tradeoffs

- **Private Groups: Proceed with Caution** Private groups can foster connection but also risk negativity. Establish clear rules and active moderation to prevent them from becoming echo chambers that drive residents away.

- **Apps: Efficiency Needs Oversight** Communication and maintenance apps offer benefits, but the board MUST define guidelines and provide oversight. Enforce proper channel use, consistently pushing back on residents who try to misuse emergency systems for non-urgent matters.

Fast Fact: Social media can be a boon or a burden for communities. Have clear guidelines in place before launching any private groups.

Best Practices: Set the Standard for Online Interaction

Develop a comprehensive policy outlining how the board will engage with residents online. Here are the essentials:

Communication Best Practices

- **Official Voice:** Designate specific representatives for online communication to ensure consistency.
- **Be Accountable:** Set and meet clear expectations for response times to resident inquiries.
- **Professional Tone:** Maintain a formal, respectful tone at all times.
- **Issue-Focused:** Keep discussions centered on policies, not personal attacks.
- **Active Oversight:** Monitor online activity and address violations swiftly.

Transparency Best Practices

- **Define the Space:** Clearly outline the intended use of each online platform and any off-limits topics.
- **Open Records:** Share meeting minutes and key decisions in an easily accessible online location.
- **No Digital Divide:** Ensure inclusivity by offering support to residents who may need help accessing online tools.

Building Respect

- **Validation Matters:** Acknowledge concerns even when saying "no," and explain your reasoning.
- **Stay Objective:** Respond to criticism with facts, not emotion.
- **Rules of Engagement:** Set and enforce clear guidelines for respectful online conduct.

Additional Tips

- **Adapt and Evolve:** Regularly review the policy as your community's use of online platforms changes.
- **Protect Yourself:** Consult an attorney to ensure the policy is legally sound.

Remember: Successfully navigating these areas not only reduces board member stress but fosters positive relationships with residents, leading to a truly thriving community.

Checklist:

- **Skills Training:** Offer opportunities on conflict resolution, de-escalation, neutrality.
- **"Difficult Resident" Strategy:** Have a plan for how the board will handle repeated unreasonable behavior, in consultation with legal counsel.
- **Social Media Oversight:** Rules on board interaction with residents online, focusing on professionalism.
- **Documentation Matters:** Emphasize the importance of

clear, factual records of interactions.

Timeline (Example):

- **With Each New Board:** Onboarding training covering communication skills and policy reminders.
- **Annually:** Review social media guidelines, adjust as needed.
- **As Needed:** Targeted training on specific issues the board is facing.

Action Steps:

- Proactive is better! Don't wait for a crisis to train on handling difficult situations.
- Lead by example: The board's own behavior sets the standard.

Conclusion: Communication – The Heart Of A Thriving Community

Think of proactive, transparent communication as the foundation of your community – not an optional extra. When everyone is informed, moving in the same direction, and focused on shared goals, even the toughest challenges become surmountable. Building these connections takes time and dedication.

The Board's Essential Role

Communication isn't just about reacting to problems – it's about boards setting a positive standard that shapes the entire community. By actively promoting honest dialogue, mutual respect, and a solution-focused mindset, you create an environment where challenges are met with collaboration instead of conflict. Make communication a central topic in your meetings and lead by example.

Your Blueprint for Success

This chapter has been packed with powerful strategies:

- **Clear Expectations:** Define how communication channels should work and create a strong policy.
- **Support, Not Roadblocks:** Empower your management company with the right infrastructure, preventing bottlenecks.
- **Resident Voices Matter:** Encourage involvement, offer support, and build a pipeline of future leaders.
- **Fairness and Efficiency:** Establish a strong dispute resolution process that protects everyone, including your management team.
- **Community is Human:** Use social gatherings to break down digital barriers and put faces to names.

- **Boundaries for Well-being:** Protect your board members with respect guidelines and document interactions to prevent misrepresentation.

Continuous Improvement

Revisit these best practices often. Adapt them to your community's unique needs. Actively seek resident feedback – it shows you care and helps you refine your processes even further. Champion transparency by proactively sharing information, building trust, and preventing misunderstandings.

The Rewards of Commitment

Challenges will inevitably arise, but a community united by strong communication is a resilient one. Your dedication will create a sense of shared purpose and strengthen the bonds between residents and their board. This is how truly successful, fulfilling communities are built.

Test Your Knowledge!

1. Why is establishing a structured communication policy important for a condominium community?
2. List three essential elements of active listening.
3. How can social gatherings and events foster a sense of community?
4. What is one key benefit of resident committees?
5. What should a board member do if a resident becomes verbally abusive or disrespectful during a meeting?
6. Why is documenting resident interactions important?
7. Describe one way to encourage resident feedback.
8. How can a board promote transparency in their communication?
9. Why are private resident groups a double-edged sword for a community?
10. What's the difference between "de-escalation" and "defensiveness" when handling difficult residents?

The answers are at the end of this chapter

Case Study: The Newsletter That Wasn't

Willow Creek Condominiums had always prided itself on a sense of tranquility. Life moved at a leisurely pace, reflected in the community's time-honored traditions – the summer barbecue, the holiday caroling group, and, of course, the monthly newsletter. It was far from fancy: typed updates from the board, reminders about lawn care, maybe a recipe swap section. But residents like Mrs. Peterson relied on it. She didn't have a computer, and the newsletter was her connection to the community.

Then, a new board swept in, full of energy and promises to "modernize" Willow Creek. The newsletter was the first casualty. "No one reads those anymore," the board president declared, touting plans for a shiny new website and resident portal. "Website?" Mrs. Peterson scoffed to her neighbor, "What use is that to me?" The board, focused on their vision, dismissed these concerns as old-fashioned resistance to change.

Months passed. The website was mired in development delays, the portal confusing to those unfamiliar with technology. Residents, once casually informed, felt out of the loop. Minor issues, easily addressed in a newsletter notice, escalated into tense confrontations at meetings. The board felt besieged, their efforts met with grumbles instead of gratitude. It took a surprisingly heated argument over the flower color for the entrance planters to make them realize their mistake. They'd disrupted the community's rhythm without providing a viable alternative. The newsletter was hastily reinstated, with a new appreciation for its simple ability to keep everyone on the same page.

What Could They Have Done Differently?

- **Surveyed Residents:** Before scrapping the newsletter, a survey could have identified potential technology gaps among residents and assessed their true level of interest in a website.
- **Phased Approach:** Introducing new communication methods alongside the existing newsletter would have eased the transition and allowed for gathering feedback.

Board Member Voice: "We truly believed a website would be better for everyone. We never considered that something so simple, even outdated, could be so important to some residents."

Question for the Reader: Does our communication assume a level of access and tech-savviness that might not apply to all residents in your community?

Key Takeaways

- Never disregard established communication channels without thorough assessment and a transition plan.
- Simple solutions can hold surprising value - don't fix what isn't broken in the pursuit of "progress".
- Inclusivity means considering the needs of all residents, not just the most tech-forward.

Case Study: The Listening Board

Sunset Hills prided itself on being a family-friendly condominium. However, its amenities were showing their age. The pool's cracked liner was an eyesore, and the playground equipment was outdated and lacked safety features. The decision was clear: something needed to be done. But what? The community was sharply divided. Younger families clamored for a modern playspace, while older residents felt the pool was the higher priority. Board meetings became battlegrounds, with each faction pushing their agenda.

Realizing this approach was getting them nowhere, the board decided to hit pause. Instead of arguing amongst themselves, they turned to the community. A carefully designed survey went out, not just asking 'pool or playground,' but having residents rank their priorities: safety, aesthetics, inclusivity for different age groups, and overall value for their dues. The results were eye-opening. While a clear preference emerged, safety concerns about both the pool and playground topped the list.

This changed the conversation. Suddenly, it wasn't an either-or choice. The board, armed with this data, worked with contractors. They negotiated a phased plan: urgent safety upgrades to both facilities in year one, followed by a full playground renovation in year two. The pool would still need major work, but that was a battle for another budget cycle. Did everyone get exactly what they wanted? No. But the process felt fair, residents understood the compromise, and, most importantly, felt their voices had been heard. This built trust and made future difficult decisions easier to navigate.

What Could They Have Done Differently?

The board could have avoided a great deal of conflict by seeking resident input earlier in the process. Preconceived notions of what the community wanted led to wasted time and strained relationships.

Board Member Voice: "Honestly, we thought we knew what was best. It was a bit of a shock to realize how divided the community actually was. Humbling, too."

Question for the Reader: When was the last time your board actively sought resident feedback on a major decision? Are there tools you could be using to do this more effectively?

Key Takeaways

- Assumptions about resident priorities can be dangerously wrong.
- Seeking input isn't about getting everyone their way; it's about understanding needs and finding the most equitable solution.
- A fair process builds trust, even when the outcome isn't universally loved.

Case Study: When Social Media Bites

Whispering Pines prided itself on being a forward-thinking community. Their website was modern, email blasts kept residents informed, and their private Facebook group was a hub of activity... initially. It started innocently enough: recipe swaps, lost pet alerts, recommendations for local contractors. But as the group grew, so did the negativity. Minor maintenance issues became blown out of proportion. Disagreements over board decisions descended into personal attacks, often anonymously, fueling a sense of mistrust.

The board, initially pleased with the "engagement," failed to anticipate the need for moderation. By the time they realized action was needed, the damage was done. Long-time residents, tired of the bickering and negativity, simply left the group, further isolating those fueling the discontent. Newcomers, seeing the hostile environment, were reluctant to join. What was intended as a community-building tool had the opposite effect. Attempts to establish rules and remove the worst offenders were met with cries of "censorship," dividing the community further. Whispering Pines, once known for its neighborly atmosphere, gained an online reputation as a place to avoid, potentially impacting property values and the ability to attract new residents.

What Could They Have Done Differently?

- **Preemptive Moderation:** Establish clear rules of conduct *from the outset* of creating the group: no personal attacks, respectful dialogue, etc. Name moderators and a process for reporting violations.

- **Board Oversight:** Have a designated board member or staff monitor the group regularly to catch issues early.
- **Zero-Tolerance Policy:** Enforce the rules consistently. When negativity takes hold, it's incredibly difficult to reverse.

Board Member Voice: "We were so excited to offer this new way for residents to connect. We honestly never thought it could backfire like this. We were naive."

Question for the Reader: If your community has, or is considering, a social media group, what safeguards are in place to prevent a similar scenario?

Key Takeaways

- Social media is a powerful tool, but it's not without risks.
- Rules and oversight are essential, even in seemingly friendly settings.
- Don't underestimate the potential damage of unchecked negativity.

Case Study: The Squeaky Wheel

Mr. Johnson was a fixture at board meetings, his voice echoing through the community room with a near-permanent air of grievance. His complaints ranged from the color of the petunias to the noise level of children playing in the pool. The board, initially sympathetic, grew weary. His rants dominated the allotted "resident comment" time. When they tried to cut him off, he cried censorship, fueling his sense of being wronged by the very system he was trying to influence.

A change came with the election of Ms. Patel, a new board member with a background in customer service. Instead of joining the chorus of exasperation, she reached out to Mr. Johnson. Over coffee, she listened. Much of his anger, it turned out, stemmed from feeling unheard. Yes, some of his complaints were about minor issues, but a few touched on genuine concerns – confusing signage about parking, inconsistent enforcement of noise regulations.

Ms. Patel didn't promise to fix everything, but she did two crucial things:

1. **The Power of Process:** She explained the board's procedures for formally submitting concerns, ensuring him that each item would be reviewed, even if the outcome wasn't to his liking.
2. **Bridging the Gap:** She became Mr. Johnson's informal liaison. If his written complaints were unclear, she'd help him rephrase them. If the board's response was jargon-filled, she'd translate.

The transformation wasn't overnight. Mr. Johnson still

occasionally slipped into his old patterns at meetings, but reminders about the process helped. The board, seeing him working within the system, became more receptive to the valid points he raised. While not a fairytale ending, the community benefited from a less disruptive dynamic.

What Could They Have Done Differently?

The board could have recognized early on that Mr. Johnson, while perhaps abrasive, was driven by a core desire to be heard and feel like his concerns mattered. A proactive approach, setting clear boundaries and offering guidance on how to communicate effectively within the board's procedures, might have diffused the situation much earlier.

Board Member Voice: "We were so focused on Mr. Johnson's delivery that we missed the message underneath. Ms. Patel helped us see he wasn't just the enemy, but a resident who deeply cared, even if he showed it in the worst possible way."

Question for the Reader: Are there any "squeaky wheels" in your community? Instead of dismissing them, could there be a way to channel their energy constructively?

Key Takeaways

- Even the most difficult residents sometimes have valid concerns masked by poor communication.
- Listening, even when someone is hard to listen to, can uncover the root of the problem.
- Setting clear expectations for communication and providing guidance benefits both the resident and the board.
- Finding a grain of truth in a mountain of complaints helps de-escalate situations and build trust.

Case Study: The Phantom Decision

Oak Ridge Condominiums had always prided itself on its well-maintained grounds. But the flower beds, once vibrant, looked tired. Residents longed for something more eye-catching, while the board hesitated due to the cost. Then came Mrs. Anderson's bombshell. A board member for over a decade, she insisted the previous board had actually approved a lavish landscaping makeover, complete with exotic blooms and a cascading water feature. Frustration boiled over. Why was the current board stalling on something already decided?

Meetings became a battleground. Residents, believing they'd been denied, demanded action. The board, unsure how to proceed, felt accused of obstruction. Every landscaping quote was met with suspicion – was the board inflating costs to squash the project? Then, Sarah, the board secretary known for her detailed minutes, had an idea. Despite Mrs. Anderson's certainty, Sarah requested minutes from the past two years. No mention of the grand landscaping plan existed. Confronted with this, Mrs. Anderson seemed genuinely confused, then sheepish. She admitted to misremembering a casual conversation as a formal decision.

It was a humbling moment, but also a breakthrough. The phantom decision vanished, but the desire for improved landscaping remained. Now, free from the baggage of the past, the board and residents could discuss options realistically. They settled on a scaled-down plan – more flowers, strategically placed for maximum impact, with a budget everyone could support.

What Could They Have Done Differently?

Oak Ridge could have prevented a lot of wasted time and frustration with better documentation practices. Meeting minutes should include not just decisions, but a summary of key discussions. Had the details of the earlier landscaping conversation been documented, the board could have quickly verified there was no formal approval process in place.

Board Member Voice: "At first, we were annoyed with Mrs. Anderson. We had new members on the board eager to make improvements, and it felt like she was dragging us backward. But honestly, I think we were also a bit defensive. No one wants to be told they're incompetent right from the start." – David, Board Treasurer

Question for the Reader: Does your board have a clear system for recording not just decisions, but the discussions and rationale leading up to those decisions?

Key Takeaways

- Accurate records protect against well-intentioned misinformation that can derail progress and erode trust.
- Detailed meeting minutes are essential, especially when dealing with potentially contentious topics.
- Even when someone is mistaken, approach the situation with empathy. It fosters a more collaborative environment.

Case Study: From Blame Game To Brainstorm

The Pine Valley Condominiums fee increase announcement landed like a bombshell. The board knew it was coming, bracing themselves for the backlash. Meetings descended into chaos. Mr. Thompson, a vocal resident, railed against the "incompetence" of previous boards for not having a larger reserve fund. Mrs. Patel, usually quiet, tearfully recounted how the increase would force her to choose between groceries and her condo fee. The new board members, though prepared for displeasure, felt ambushed by the level of vitriol. Their defensiveness poured fuel on the fire.

Sarah, recently elected, watched with growing dismay. She understood the residents' anger, but the blame game solved nothing. During a particularly heated exchange, she raised her hand. To her surprise, the room fell silent. "Look," she began, "I get that we're all upset. I wish this wasn't necessary. But pointing fingers at past boards changes nothing. We're the ones here *now*, and it's our job to deal with this. So, instead of attacking each other, does anyone have any ideas to actually help the situation?"

The shift was surprising. Mr. Thompson, still annoyed, grumbled about exploring refinancing options. Mrs. Patel, calmer, suggested a phased payment plan for those truly struggling. Others chimed in, the energy moving from accusation to brainstorming. It wasn't perfect – some resentments lingered. But by focusing on the "what now?", Sarah prevented deadlock. The board later implemented several of the resident-suggested ideas, softening the impact.

What Could They Have Done Differently?

- **Anticipate the Backlash:** The board knew the fee increase would be contentious. They could have prepared by proactively explaining the rationale, outlining the consequences of inaction, and even soliciting resident input *before* the final decision.
- **Empathy First:** Defensiveness is a natural human response, but boards must model the behavior they seek from residents. Acknowledging the hardship upfront, even while sticking to the decision, might have de-escalated the situation.

Board Member Voice: "At first, I admit, I bristled at the accusations. We hadn't even been on the board a year! Then I realized... the residents weren't truly invested in the past, they were scared about the future. That changed my perspective." – Sarah

Question for the Reader: When faced with strong emotions from residents, how can you separate their valid concerns from unproductive negativity?

Key Takeaways

- **Don't Get Defensive:** It fuels the fire, even when the criticism feels unfair.
- **Focus on the Present:** Dwelling on "what should have been" distracts from finding current solutions.
- **Residents Can be Part of the Solution:** Shifting from blame to brainstorming taps into their collective knowledge and may uncover workable ideas.

Case Study: The Overloaded Manager

Greenview Condominiums prided itself on its friendly atmosphere. Part of that was due to their manager, Mrs. Davis. She knew residents by name, responded to emails within a day, and genuinely cared. There was only one problem: the entire communication system revolved around her. The online portal was clunky and underused. Residents knew a direct email to Mrs. Davis got the fastest results, so they used it for everything – leaky faucets, barking dog complaints, even questions easily answered in the governing documents.

At first, Mrs. Davis kept up, working longer hours. But the community was growing. Soon, her inbox was a flood. Urgent requests got buried under minor ones. Residents, used to quick responses, grew frustrated at the delays. Some even accused her of ignoring them. The board saw the strain on their manager but assumed this level of service was simply the cost. Then, Mrs. Davis, exhausted, gave notice.

That was the board's wakeup call. Working with the management company, they didn't just hire a replacement – they revamped the system. They invested in user-friendly portal software, trained residents on its use, and the company assigned a dedicated support team to handle basic inquiries. This freed up Mrs. Davis to tackle complex issues and, importantly, proactively visit the property and interact with residents, building the relationships that made Greenview special. The change wasn't without bumps, but the result was a win-win: residents got timely service across the board, and their beloved manager was no longer on the verge of burnout.

What Could They Have Done Differently?

- **Proactive System Design:** Instead of waiting for a crisis, the board should have regularly assessed the community's communication flow. Early intervention would have prevented the overload.
- **Channel Education:** Emphasize to residents the appropriate use of the portal and email from the get-go, preventing the habit of going straight to the manager for all issues.
- **Recognizing the Manager's Limits:** Even dedicated managers have limits. The board should have noticed the unsustainable workload and collaborated with the management company to scale support *before* burnout set in.

Board Member Voice: "We genuinely appreciated Mrs. Davis's dedication. But in hindsight, we mistook her willingness to go above and beyond for a sign that everything was fine. We should've been more proactive in supporting her."

Question for the Reader: Does your community have clear guidelines for how residents should communicate different types of requests? If not, is your manager potentially becoming a bottleneck?

Key Takeaways

- The best managers can't sustain being the sole point of contact for a community of any significant size.
- Boards must partner with their management company to design scalable communication systems.
- Educating residents on proper channel use benefits everyone – residents get faster responses, and managers can focus on complex issues.

Test Your Knowledge! Answers

1. **Why is establishing a structured communication policy important for a condominium community?**

   - Sets clear expectations for residents and the board, reducing confusion and frustration.
   - Ensures consistency in how the community addresses issues.
   - Protects the board from potential misunderstandings and disputes.

2. **List three essential elements of active listening.**

   - Paying full attention to the speaker.
   - Demonstrating empathy and understanding, even if you disagree with their position.
   - Asking clarifying questions to ensure you understand their perspective.

3. **How can social gatherings and events foster a sense of community?**

   - Create opportunities for residents to meet and get to know each other.
   - Build a sense of belonging and shared experience.
   - Provide a relaxed setting to discuss community matters.

4. **What is one key benefit of resident committees?**

   - Distributes workload, preventing board member burnout.
   - Brings in diverse perspectives and skills.

- Creates a pipeline of potential future board members.

5. **What should a board member do if a resident becomes verbally abusive or disrespectful during a meeting?**

- Remain calm and avoid escalating the situation.
- Firmly but respectfully set boundaries, reminding the resident of appropriate conduct.
- If necessary, ask the resident to leave or adjourn the meeting.

6. **Why is documenting resident interactions important?**

- Creates an accurate record of events, especially in case of recurring issues.
- Prevents misunderstandings or misrepresentations of facts.
- Provides evidence if a dispute escalates.

7. **Describe one way to encourage resident feedback.**

- Conduct regular surveys – keep them short and focused for better participation.
- Have a dedicated feedback section in newsletters or on your website.
- Hold open forums at meetings, using facilitation techniques to ensure everyone has a voice.

8. **How can a board promote transparency in their communication?**

- Share meeting minutes and summaries of major decisions promptly.
- Provide clear explanations for decisions, especially if they're controversial.
- Ensure all residents have equal access to information.

9. **Why are private resident groups a double-edged sword for a community?**

- **Benefits:** Can foster connection and information sharing.
- **Risks:** Can become echo chambers of negativity if left unmonitored, driving residents away and undermining the board.

10. **What's the difference between "de-escalation" and "defensiveness" when handling difficult residents?**

- **De-escalation:** Focuses on calming the situation, finding common ground, and moving towards a solution.
- **Defensiveness:** Reacting emotionally, getting caught in arguments, and potentially making the problem worse.

CHAPTER 5: BOARD GOVERNANCE AND LEADERSHIP

Introduction

The Board of Directors serves as the guiding force of any condominium association. It holds the responsibility for making decisions that shape the community's well-being, both in the present and long-term. Board governance provides the framework for how the board operates, detailing systems, rules, and processes. It encompasses legal obligations like state statutes and the community's governing documents, along with the board's own best practices.

The Board's primary focus should be on leadership, not day-to-day management. Leadership means setting a vision for the community's future, inspiring and motivating owners toward common goals, and building consensus. The board must leverage its position to inspire residents and foster a collaborative spirit.

Day-to-day operations, rules enforcement, and the essential 'blocking and tackling' are best delegated to the management company and other third-party support partners. These entities manage the short-term tasks and processes, ensure adherence to existing systems, and offer strategic guidance. The management company executes the board's directives; they are the hands of the board, not its visionary body.

Strong governance coupled with focused leadership is crucial for thriving communities. Boards that understand this distinction drive property values, encourage resident satisfaction, maintain quality of life, minimize legal risks, and secure the community's long-term financial health.

Fast Fact: Many states have specific laws outlining the duties and responsibilities of condominium board members.

Roles And Responsibilities Of Board Members

Board members have several core functions. First, upholding the governing documents is essential. This means thorough familiarity with the declaration, master deed, bylaws, and any relevant rules and regulations. Your decisions and actions must align with these documents to protect the association from legal battles and declining morale.

Another core function is setting policy and strategic direction. Remember, the board's role is leadership, not management. Focus on the big picture, not daily operations. Develop long-term goals for the community's future, create policies that support the established vision, and provide guidance to your management company when needed.

The board also ensures financial oversight and accountability. As we discussed earlier, financial understanding is vital. Boards review and approve budgets (and may even create them), monitor income and expenses, and safeguard the community's funds through responsible decision-making.

Additionally, the board must represent the interests of *all* owners. Act in the best interests of the whole community, not specific individuals. While some residents might try to sway you for their own benefit, remain impartial. Balance diverse perspectives and aim for decisions that benefit the majority.

Now, let's discuss some vital board member responsibilities:

- **Regular Meeting Attendance:** Prioritize board meetings. These are where essential business occurs, and delegating

voting isn't always wise. Your presence ensures that all perspectives are considered and that you stay fully informed.
- **Preparation is Key:** Review agendas, reports, and relevant materials beforehand. Arrive ready to engage in constructive debate and voice thoughtful opinions.
- **Vote Responsibly:** Carefully evaluate information before making decisions. Uphold your fiduciary duty to the community with every vote.
- **Open Communication:** Maintain open lines of communication with residents. Be friendly and approachable, even for brief interactions. Share board decisions and processes transparently (without compromising privacy).
- **Ongoing Education:** Actively seek knowledge about community management best practices, legal requirements, and effective board governance. Attend seminars, read industry publications, and consult with your attorney when needed.

Finally, let's touch on the role of committees. Committees amplify the board's influence, improve the pipeline of future board members, get everyone on the same page, and let board members make a broader impact. However, committees aren't independent. Boards should work collaboratively with them, avoiding a single board member becoming the sole point of contact. This ensures all board members feel ownership and avoid disconnected members disregarding important committee work.

Checklist:

- **Review Governing Documents:** Become intimately familiar with the declaration, bylaws, and rules.
- **Board vs. Management:** Understand the division of duties between the board (setting policy) and the management company (day-to-day operations).

- **Know your Limits:** Seek professional guidance (legal, financial) when needed, don't make decisions outside the board's expertise.
- **Attendance Expectations:** Commit to regular meeting attendance and participation.

Action Step: Within your first 30 days as a new board member, schedule a meeting with your management company to review their responsibilities and discuss how you can best collaborate.

Effective Board Meetings

Effective board meetings require a roadmap in the form of an agenda. Agendas focus discussions, prevent wasted time, ensure coverage of important topics, and provide accountability. Place important voting issues early in the meeting for optimal focus. An effective agenda can help prevent rogue board members with ulterior motives from taking control and derailing progress.

Here are essential components of a typical meeting agenda:

- **Call to Order:** The president or designated meeting leader officially begins the meeting.
- **Approval of Previous Meeting's Minutes:** Review the prior meeting's minutes for accuracy, ensuring they reflect discussions, motions, and votes.
- **Old Business:** Updates or actions on ongoing matters.
- **New Business:** Discussion and decision-making on new topics.
- **Committee Reports (if applicable):** Updates on the work of board-created committees.
- **Management Report:** Details on finances, collections, delinquencies, and other essential information.
- **Open Forum (optional):** Opportunity for resident comments.
- **Adjournment:** Official end of the meeting.

Tips for Preparing Effective Agendas:

- **Solicit Input:** Seek agenda items from other board members well in advance.
- **Clarity of Purpose:** Clearly articulate the reason for each

agenda item.
- **Time Allocations:** Estimate time needed for each item to guide discussions and ensure a timely conclusion.
- **Advance Distribution:** Allow board members ample time to review the agenda, ideally several days prior to the meeting.

Effective Decision-Making

Boards employ different decision-making methods based on the situation and their community's needs. Understanding the pros and cons of each approach empowers more efficient and productive meetings.

Majority vs. Consensus

- **Majority Rule:** Decisions are made when more than half of the voting members agree. This is efficient for routine matters or when time is limited. However, minority viewpoints might feel disregarded. When to use it…best for straightforward decisions (approving routine expenditures, minor rule changes), or when seeking community input isn't crucial.
- **Consensus:** While time-consuming, consensus aims to find solutions everyone can live with. It emphasizes collaboration, compromise, and ensuring all voices are heard. Best suited for complex issues or when a unified decision is crucial to community harmony. When to use it…ideal for major changes impacting all residents (significant construction projects, large dues increases), or when past decisions have led to community conflict.

Robert's Rules of Order

- **Overview:** A formalized system of parliamentary procedure, designed to ensure orderly meetings with fairness and respect for all participants. It covers how to make motions, debate, and vote.
- **Benefits:** Can reduce confusion, prevent power

grabs, and help manage disagreements. Especially useful in communities with diverse or strongly opinionated members.
- **Considerations:** Full adoption can be overly formal for some associations. However, using aspects (like time limits on speakers, formal motion procedures) can streamline meetings without imposing the entire structure.

Fast Fact: Robert's Rules of Order is a formalized system, but boards can adapt elements to suit their community's needs.

Key Takeaway: It's not 'one size fits all'. Boards should choose the decision-making method which best suits the situation, promotes community well-being, and aligns with the association's governing documents.

Meeting Minutes

Along with a well-prepared agenda, accurate meeting minutes are another vital component of productive meetings.
- **Role of Minutes:** Minutes serve as the official record of board decisions, providing continuity and reference for future actions. Keep redacted minutes on file in digital format for reference by future boards, residents, and in potential legal matters.
- **Key Elements:** Include date, time, location, attendees (with absences noted), accurate summaries of discussions, motions (with who seconded them), voting outcomes, and action items with clear assignments of responsibility.
- **Best Practices:** Appoint a designated minute-taker (board member, management representative, or third party). Focus on clarity, objectivity, and avoid personal opinions. Review and approve minutes at the subsequent meeting.

Pro Tip: Board minutes aren't just a record of the past; they can be valuable references when similar issues arise in the future.

Checklist

- **Agenda Power:** Propose items, request materials in advance, know what should and shouldn't be on the agenda.
- **Preparation is Key:** Read the agenda packet thoroughly, make notes on questions or concerns.
- **Meeting Conduct:** Respectful discussion, focus on the issue at hand, avoid personal attacks.
- **Minutes Matter:** Review minutes for accuracy, ensure actions and decisions are documented.

Sample Timeline: Agenda Creation

- 10+ days before the meeting: Board members submit agenda items to management
- 7 days before: Management distributes draft agenda for board feedback
- 5 days before: Final agenda sent to residents

Board Member Training And Education

We've emphasized the importance of training throughout this book for good reason. Staying current on ever-evolving laws, regulations, and industry best practices is crucial for effective board members. Training prevents avoidable missteps, builds essential skills like financial management, conflict resolution, and strategic planning, and reinforces the board's duty to prioritize the overall community's well-being. It also reduces the likelihood of costly mistakes due to lack of knowledge, mitigating risks for the board and the community.

Here are some excellent sources of training:

- **Your Management Company:** Many provide board training programs, educational seminars, and resources, often at minimal or no cost.
- **Associations and Industry Groups:** Local, state, or national HOA associations often offer conferences, workshops, and certifications.
- **Specialized Events:** Industry workshops and conferences delve into topics like legal updates, financial management, and leadership skills.
- **Online Resources:** Webinars, articles, podcasts, and online courses provide convenient, on-demand learning.

Check with your management company and attorney to determine if your state or governing documents mandate specific board training requirements.

Structured Orientation is Essential For New Board Members

A well-designed orientation ensures a smooth transition for

newly elected board members. Here's why it's important:

- **Rapid Knowledge Acquisition:** Orientation introduces the fundamentals of board governance, the community's specific rules, finances, and procedures, getting new members up-to-speed quickly.
- **Clarity of Expectations:** A clear orientation outlines responsibilities and fiduciary duties, promoting accountability.
- **Continuity and Consistency:** Structured programs ensure all new board members receive the same essential information, maintaining consistency.
- **Networking Opportunities:** Orientations can include introductions to key players like management, committee members, or other support staff, fostering valuable connections.

Potential Elements to Include in a Comprehensive Orientation:

- **Review of Key Documents:** Cover the declaration, bylaws, rules, recent meeting minutes, budgets, and relevant policies.
- **Financial Overview:** Explanation of the budget process, how reserves are managed, the board's financial oversight role, and how to interpret financial statements within the monthly board packet.
- **Roles and Responsibilities:** Clarify board vs. management duties, committee structures, expected time commitments, and effective meeting preparation strategies.
- **Legal and Ethics Briefing:** Outline essential legal requirements, the board's fiduciary duty to the community, and the role of the community's attorney.
- **Community Overview:**
  - **Communication:** How the board communicates with residents (newsletters, websites, etc.) and how

residents can communicate with the board.
- ○ **Meetings:** Meeting protocols, voting procedures, and decision-making processes.
- ○ **Key Contracts and Policies:** List major vendors (landscaping, etc.), insurance coverage, and how to access relevant information.
- **Community Tour (if applicable):** A physical walk-through familiarizes new members with the properties and amenities.
- **Mentorship or Buddy System:** Pair new board members with experienced ones for ongoing support.

Considerations:

- **Timing:** Depending on the complexity of your community, the orientation might be spread over multiple sessions vs. cramming information into one long meeting.
- **Resources:** Consider providing a new board member "handbook" with summaries of crucial information for easy reference.
- **Who Conducts:** The outgoing board, management company, or a combination can lead the orientation. Ensure those leading it have the knowledge and resources needed.

Pro Tip: Don't neglect "soft skills" in your board member training. Communication, diplomacy, and teamwork are essential.

Checklist:

- **Identify Needs:** Are there specific skill gaps on the board (financial, legal, etc.)?
- **Resources:** Explore options provided by management companies, industry associations, or online.
- **Make it Ongoing:** Training isn't a one-time event; commit to continuous development.

- **New Member Orientation:** Have a comprehensive program in place.

Action Step: Set aside a portion of your annual budget specifically for board member development. Discuss potential training topics at your next meeting.

Fiduciary Duty And Acting In The Best Interests Of The Community

Board members have a fiduciary duty to their association, a legal obligation derived from state statutes and the community's governing documents. This duty has three key components:

- **Duty of Care:** Acting diligently and prudently when making decisions.
- **Duty of Loyalty:** Placing the community's interests above personal gain or the interests of specific individuals.
- **Duty of Good Faith:** Acting honestly and in a manner that reasonably furthers the community's goals.

Fast Fact: The term "fiduciary duty" comes from the Latin word for "trust". Board members hold a position of trust within the community.

Conflicts of Interest

A conflict of interest arises when a board member's personal or professional interests might unduly influence their decisions. This compromises objectivity. Common scenarios include:

- **Self-Dealing:** Conducting business with the association for personal gain. Examples include hiring one's own company without proper bidding or selling goods/services to the association at inflated prices.
- **Favoring Friends or Family:** Showing undue preference to relatives or close associates in matters like contracts or hiring.
- **Gifts and Incentives:** Accepting gifts or benefits from vendors seeking the association's business.

Importance of Disclosure and Recusal

If a board member recognizes a potential conflict, they must disclose it promptly to the rest of the board. Recusal means stepping away from discussions and voting on the matter in question. This ensures a fair and objective decision-making process.

Examples:

- A board member who owns a construction company cannot vote on awarding major renovation contracts without disclosing the conflict and recusing themself.
- Accepting free season tickets from a company proposing a new cable contract is likely a conflict.

Important Notes

- Even small gestures can create the appearance of a conflict. I recommend discouraging vendors from providing anything of value, even meals.
- Board members should make informed decisions, gathering relevant information and seeking professional advice (legal, financial) when needed.
- Prioritize the community's long-term well-being, balancing diverse resident needs while upholding the greater good.

Potential Liability

Violating fiduciary duty can lead to lawsuits, financial penalties, and damage to the board's reputation. Communities often have Directors & Officers (D&O) insurance for protection, but it's important to understand coverage limits.

Fast Fact: Directors & Officers (D&O) insurance can provide financial protection for board members if they are sued for actions related to their board service.

Proactive Approach

Board members should take a proactive approach, seeking guidance when in doubt rather than risking a breach. While honest mistakes or differences of opinion can occur, the guiding principle should always be acting in the community's best interests. A board member with past positive experiences with a vendor can advocate for them, as long as they act transparently and in the community's interest.

Non-Conflicts of Interest

It's important to remember that not every situation resembling a conflict of interest actually is one. Before making accusations against board members acting as fiduciaries, take the time to fully investigate any potential conflict. Thoroughness will help ensure a decision is based on facts, not assumptions.

Let's examine a few scenarios that might appear questionable at first glance, but upon closer consideration, are perfectly ethical:

1. Board Member with Relevant Expertise:
- A board member is a landscape architect by profession. The community needs to hire a new landscaping company. Their expertise can be invaluable in evaluating proposals and choosing a qualified company. To avoid any appearance of impropriety, the board member should:
    - Disclose their profession upfront.
    - Avoid advocating for any specific company.
    - Consider recusing themselves from the final vote, depending on the comfort level of the board and the member.

2. Family Member Works for a Qualified Vendor:
- A board member's child works for a company providing cleaning services to other communities. The board is considering new cleaning contracts. As long as

the child has no ownership stake or decision-making power in the company, and the company is objectively qualified and competitively priced, this wouldn't be a conflict of interest. However, disclosing the relationship is recommended for transparency.

3. Board Member Recommends Neighbor's Business:

- A board member's neighbor owns a reputable pool maintenance company. The community needs this service, and the board member suggests considering the neighbor's company. This is acceptable if the neighbor's business offers high-quality service at a competitive price. Ideally, the board member should encourage bids from other companies for comparison.

4. Helping a Struggling Business Owner:

- A board member might help a friend launch a business, recognizing their operational strengths but administrative weaknesses. Later, if that business offers quality work at competitive prices, it's perfectly ethical for the board member to recommend their services to the community. As long as the board member has no financial stake in the business, receives no personal benefit, and the recommendation is based solely on the business's merit, this is not a conflict of interest.

Checklist:

- **Understand the 3 Components:** Duty of Care, Duty of Loyalty, Duty of Good Faith
- **Know Your Red Flags:** Common conflict of interest scenarios (self-dealing, favoring friends, etc.)
- **Disclosure is Key:** If in doubt, disclose a potential conflict and seek guidance.
- **Focus on the Community:** Make decisions based on the long-term, collective good.

Action Step: At your next board meeting, dedicate time to an open discussion about potential conflicts of interest. Foster a culture of transparency.

Building A Strong And Sustainable Board

Building a strong and sustainable board requires a proactive approach to recruitment and succession planning. Here's how to create a pipeline of interested, qualified future board members:

Board Member Recruitment

- **Desirable Skills and Qualities:** Look for diversity in professional backgrounds (legal, finance), commitment to the community, strong communication and collaboration, and a willingness to learn.
- **Strategies for Finding Owners:**
  - Utilize committees as a stepping stone to board service.
  - Employ direct outreach (newsletters, events) to publicize openings.
  - Encourage nominations from board members and residents.
  - Conduct surveys to gauge interest.

Pro Tip: A committee system is a great way to get more residents involved in the community and build a pipeline of potential board members.

Succession Planning

- **Anticipate Vacancies:** Know term limits and board member plans to proactively fill openings.
- **Mentoring:** Create a shadowing program for potential board members and use committees as a way for residents to get involved in governance without the full pressure of board membership.

- **Smooth Transitions:** Have comprehensive documentation of board procedures, and establish a formal baton-pass process between outgoing and incoming members.

Addressing Potential Conflicts of Interest

- **Outline Clear Policies:** Discuss what constitutes a conflict within your community, establish disclosure requirements, and formalize recusal procedures when necessary.
- **Open Communication:** Hold regular discussions about conflicts of interest to maintain alignment and address potential misunderstandings.
- **Manage Difficult Situations:** Consider adopting a code of conduct for board members. In cases of persistent disagreement about conflicts, mediation or other resolution techniques can be helpful.

Remember: Effective governance is nuanced. While conflicts of interest can and do occur, not every situation with the appearance of a conflict is inherently problematic. Encourage a culture of transparency and open communication to ensure decisions are made in the community's best interests.

Checklist:

- **Desired Skills:** What does your board need? (legal, finance, communication, etc.)
- **Outreach Strategies:** Don't just wait for people to volunteer; use newsletters, events, and direct appeals to find candidates.
- **Mentorship Matters:** Have a program to guide interested residents into board service.
- **Succession Planning:** Anticipate vacancies well in advance, have a system to identify potential replacements.

Sample Timeline: Recruiting a New Member

- 3 Months Before Vacancy: Nominating committee identifies candidates
- 2 Months Before: Candidates attend a board meeting as 'observers'
- 1 Month Before: Board votes on new member

Conclusion

Throughout this chapter, we've emphasized the importance of strong board leadership in creating successful condominium communities. Effective governance safeguards property values, fosters resident happiness, enhances the overall quality of life, and helps prevent or reduce the impact of legal problems.

Board service should be viewed as a continuous learning experience. Proactively seek opportunities for further education and skill development in areas such as conflict management, legal compliance, budgeting, and strategic decision-making. Thankfully, there are abundant resources to support your growth, including your management company, industry groups, conferences, and online materials.

Investing in strengthening your leadership abilities is an investment in your community's present and long-term prosperity.

Pro Tip: Remember, the board's goal is the well-being of the *entire* community, not catering to specific individuals or interest groups.

Test Your Knowledge!

1. What are the three key components of a board member's fiduciary duty?
2. List two common scenarios that could create conflicts of interest for board members.
3. Besides attending board meetings, what's one way to prepare for effective board service?
4. What's the difference between majority rule and consensus decision-making?
5. Why is it important to maintain confidentiality about board discussions and decisions?
6. Name one advantage of having a structured orientation program for new board members.
7. Why might a board member choose to recuse themselves from a discussion or vote?
8. What is board member succession planning, and why is it important?
9. List two ways a board member can seek out continuing education opportunities.
10. Briefly explain how effective board governance benefits the overall community.

The answers are at the end of this chapter

Case Study: The Self-Serving Vendor (Conflict Of Interest)

The Pinewood Condominium Association faced a daunting task: their aging roofs were leaking, causing water damage and growing resident frustration. Getting estimates seemed straightforward until board member Sarah mentioned her cousin, Mike, who owned a successful roofing company.

Mike's reputation was stellar. Sarah was confident he'd do quality work, and initial bids suggested his pricing was fair. She believed hiring him was a win-win for Pinewood. However, other board members weren't so sure.

"Favoritism," one muttered. "This looks bad," said another. Trust was already a sensitive topic after the previous board mishandled reserve funds. Sarah understood the optics but felt stuck – ignoring a potentially great resource seemed wrong.

The board chair, recognizing the impasse, suggested a path forward. They couldn't risk accusations of self-dealing. Yet, Mike might be their best option. The solution: full transparency.

Sarah openly disclosed her connection to Mike during a resident meeting. She recused herself from further discussion on the roofing bids. Mike wasn't given preferential treatment – he was required, like all vendors, to provide references and detailed cost breakdowns. The other board members thoroughly vetted his company alongside other competitors.

In the end, Mike's proposal was chosen. Not only did his

bid prove the most competitive, but his references from other HOAs were glowing. With Sarah recusing herself from the final vote, the decision felt fair and objective.

The project was a triumph. Mike's team finished under budget and ahead of schedule. Residents were thrilled with the workmanship and reassured by the board's transparent process.

Pinewood's experience highlights a key point: potential conflicts don't always equal wrong-doing. By prioritizing disclosure, recusal, and treating all vendors equally, the board made an ethical decision that benefited the entire community.

What Could They Have Done Differently?

- Sarah could have anticipated potential concerns by proactively disclosing her relationship with Mike from the start, even if she didn't think it would influence the decision. This would further cement trust and demonstrate her commitment to transparency.

Board Member Voice: Sarah: "Look, Mike's work is top-notch. I know it might sound self-serving, but I genuinely believe he is our best option. However, I understand if that makes others uncomfortable. I'm willing to step aside if that's what makes this decision feel fair for everyone."

Question for the Reader: If you were a resident in Pinewood, how would Sarah's early disclosure and offer to recuse herself affect your perception of the situation?

Key Takeaways

- Proactive disclosure is always the best policy, even for seemingly minor potential conflicts.
- Recusal can be a powerful tool to address concerns about objectivity.
- Don't assume the best vendor is out there. Ensure even those with prior connections are thoroughly vetted

alongside competitors.
- Sometimes, the ethically sound choice aligns with the most practical one for the community.

Case Study: The Missing Minutes (Importance Of Documentation)

Sunset Hills Condos, a sprawling complex with aging infrastructure, faced an escalating crisis. Water intrusion during heavy rains was causing significant damage to multiple units. Residents were furious, flooding board meetings with complaints. Yet, the board seemed baffled by the problem, insisting that they were unaware of the extent of the issues.

Emily, a recently elected board member, felt something was amiss. The community's frustration hinted at a longstanding problem, not something that materialized overnight. She requested to review the past two years' meeting minutes, hoping for clues. To her shock, large gaps existed – some months were entirely missing, others had only a few cryptic bullet points.

Determined to get to the bottom of things, Emily partnered with the management company, combing through old emails, work order logs, and even resident newsletters. A disturbing pattern emerged. Emails detailed increasingly urgent resident complaints about leaks and water damage. Work orders revealed temporary fixes but no resolution. Newsletter articles even mentioned the growing drainage concerns, all seemingly ignored by the previous board.

Armed with this reconstructed timeline, Emily and the new board confronted their predecessors. The evidence was undeniable. Chronic inaction had worsened the situation. More importantly, this documentation proved crucial in negotiations with the insurance company. Initially, they balked at covering the extensive damage, but the records proved the problem was longstanding and due to negligence. The insurance claim was ultimately approved, saving the community hundreds of thousands in out-of-pocket repair costs.

The ordeal at Sunset Hills became a cautionary tale. It reinforced the absolute necessity of accurate and thorough meeting minutes. Minutes are not just a formality; they are the historical record of a community's decisions, discussions, and the evolution of issues. They safeguard both the present and future of the association.

What Could They Have Done Differently?

- **Enforce Minute-Taking Standards:** The previous board should have had a clear policy regarding minutes – detailing format, required content, and a review process for accuracy.
- **Prioritize Transparency:** Even if minutes were incomplete, the board had an obligation to communicate openly with residents about ongoing maintenance challenges.
- **Act with Urgency:** Dismissing resident concerns and deferring repairs was a recipe for disaster. A proactive approach could have mitigated the damage.

Board Member Voice: Emily: "I couldn't believe such important information was simply missing. It felt like the previous board was trying to hide something, and the whole community was paying the price."

Question for the Reader: Does your community have a system in place to ensure accurate meeting minutes? Are they easily accessible to residents? If not, what steps can you take to address this?

Key Takeaways

- Meeting minutes are a legal record and a vital tool for transparency and continuity.
- Boards cannot ignore ongoing maintenance issues. Proactive solutions, even if costly, are preferable to negligence leading to compounded expenses.
- Resident communication is paramount. Even when problems can't be fixed immediately, open dialogue builds trust during challenging times.

Case Study: Orientation Overload (Effective Onboarding)

Green Valley HOA prided itself on its robust new board member orientation. The intention was noble - provide every scrap of information upfront for transparency. Unfortunately, the reality was overwhelming. New member Tom received a binder thicker than a phonebook, sat through a daylong PowerPoint marathon, and was whisked on a dizzying tour of the vast property. His questions went unanswered in the rush, and he left feeling more lost than informed.

Tom stuck it out, but barely. He spent countless hours sifting through documents, felt uninformed during meetings, and hesitated to contribute. The experience discouraged him and other potential board members.

A year later, a leadership change sparked a re-evaluation. Feedback from new members revealed a common thread: the well-intentioned orientation was counterproductive. Green Valley took action:

- **Digital Handbook:** Key governing documents, policies, and contacts were compiled into a searchable digital resource. This reduced printing costs and allowed for easy updates.
- **Focused Briefing:** The in-person session was shortened and zeroed in on essentials: reviewing the current budget, understanding upcoming projects, and clarifying roles and responsibilities.
- **Mentorship Program:** Each newbie was paired with an experienced board member as a guide. This provided a go-to person for questions and helped foster a sense of belonging.

The results were striking. New board members felt prepared without being inundated. Participation in meetings increased, and the board benefited from fresh perspectives. Tom, now a second-year member, even became a mentor himself, offering advice and encouragement.

Green Valley learned a valuable lesson: Sometimes, less is more. A streamlined orientation focused on essentials empowers new board members, contributing to the community's overall success.

What Could They Have Done Differently?

Green Valley could have adopted an "essentials first" approach. Instead of overwhelming new members, prioritize the crucial information needed for immediate contributions. Follow-up with more in-depth materials as needed, allowing for gradual absorption.

Board Member Voice: "We wanted to be thorough and leave nothing out. In hindsight, we were basically handing new members a firehose of information and hoping they wouldn't drown." – Susan, Board President, Green Valley HOA

Question for the Reader: Is your community's onboarding

process designed to inform or overwhelm? Are new members set up to succeed, or is information overload setting them up for discouragement?

Key Takeaways

- A streamlined orientation focused on core knowledge empowers new board members for faster integration.
- Prioritize the "need-to-know" over the "nice-to-know." Additional information can be provided later.
- Mentorship creates support and helps new members find their footing quickly.
- Effective onboarding boosts confidence, encourages participation, and benefits the whole board.

Case Study: The Tiebreaker (Decision Making)

Lakeview Apartments' community pool, a popular gathering spot for hot summers, had seen better days. With peeling paint and outdated equipment, it was in desperate need of an upgrade. However, the board was deeply divided on how to address the issue.

Half the board championed a full-scale renovation: new decking, upgraded filtration system, even a zero-entry feature to attract young families. They argued the pool was an amenity that boosted property values and needed investment. The other half of the board vehemently disagreed. Citing cracked and uneven sidewalks throughout the complex, they saw the pool as a frivolous expense when basic safety hazards remained unaddressed.

Weeks of meetings turned into heated arguments. "How can you justify fancy pool upgrades when people could trip and get hurt?" shouted one faction. "A welcoming pool makes our community attractive! Neglecting it will drive people away," countered the other. The board chair, usually adept at mediating, felt the gridlock was becoming personal.

Finally, she proposed a change in tactics. "We're pitting resident needs against each other, and it's getting us nowhere. Let's break this down." The board painstakingly dissected the renovation proposal. The zero-entry was deemed non-essential and costly. The filtration upgrade, while desirable, could be delayed. Resurfacing the deck, repainting, and fixing obvious tripping hazards on the surrounding walkways were non-negotiable.

Suddenly, a path forward emerged. There was enough in the budget to cover those immediate needs and create a smaller reserve fund for the 'nice to have' pool additions down the road. It wasn't a perfect solution, but it addressed the core safety concerns while acknowledging the importance of the amenity.

The vote wasn't unanimous, but the motion passed. The board learned a critical lesson: Sometimes, finding common ground necessitates letting go of the ideal outcome and prioritizing based on what the community truly needs.

What Could They Have Done Differently?

- **Shift Focus Sooner:** The board got stuck on an 'all or nothing' approach. They could have reframed the discussion earlier, focusing on urgent needs vs. improvements, making it less about specific pool features and more about responsible budgeting.
- **Cost-Benefit Analysis:** Thoroughly analyzing the costs of each renovation component, alongside the potential risks of deferring sidewalk repairs, might have led to a more productive, less emotional debate.

Board Member Voice: "We were so focused on who was 'right', we lost sight of what was best for the whole community. Honestly, it felt more like a personal win-lose situation than trying to solve a problem for everyone."

Question for the Reader: When your board faces a similarly contentious decision with no easy solution, how might you shift the conversation towards compromise for the greater good?

Key Takeaways

- Don't let "perfect" be the enemy of "good enough." Sometimes compromise is necessary to move forward.
- Prioritize issues based on immediate need and potential

impact on the entire community, not just on strongly held personal preferences.
- Focusing on cost-benefit analysis can help depersonalize debates and lead to data-driven decisions.

Case Study: Bridging The Skills Gap (Training And Education)

Willow Creek Condominiums was a vibrant community with a board comprised of dedicated, long-time residents. While they had a deep love for their neighborhood, most lacked backgrounds in finance, legal matters, or business management. This created challenges when it came to making major decisions.

Reading the monthly financial reports was a chore. Numbers swam before their eyes, and terms like "capital reserves" and "accrual accounting" felt like a foreign language. Contracts for services, from landscaping to insurance, were filled with dense legalese that left the board uncertain and hesitant to sign. This led to delays, reliance on the management company for even routine matters, and a lingering sense of unease.

Recognizing the problem, a newly elected board member, Susan, suggested seeking targeted training. The board partnered with their management company, which had expertise in community association governance. They hosted a customized workshop designed specifically for Willow Creek's needs.

The first session demystified financial statements. The trainer broke down revenue, expenses, reserve funds, and how to spot both positive trends and warning signs. The second session focused on contracts. The trainer explained common clauses, red flags to look for, and strategies for negotiation.

The impact was immediate. Board members no longer felt intimidated by spreadsheets and legal jargon. They asked informed questions when reviewing the monthly financials and felt confident when negotiating contracts. This newfound knowledge wasn't just about efficiency; it also fostered trust. Residents sensed the board's increased competence, easing prior tensions.

Willow Creek made training an ongoing practice. They scheduled follow-up workshops and partnered with their management company to identify other knowledge gaps. Investing in their education transformed the board from well-intentioned volunteers to empowered community leaders.

What Could They Have Done Differently?

Years of operating on good intentions but limited knowledge likely took a toll. There might have been missed opportunities for cost savings, overlooked contractual issues, or a general sense of the board not being fully in control of the community's business affairs. Proactive training would have prevented those potential problems and instilled confidence earlier.

Board Member Voice: "Honestly, I felt embarrassed sometimes. We all want what's best for Willow Creek, but staring at those financial statements... I just got lost. The training finally made things click."

Question for the Reader: Does your board have specific areas of expertise? Are there aspects of community management where you feel additional knowledge would be significantly beneficial?

Key Takeaways

- Don't let "lack of experience" become an excuse for inaction. There are abundant resources and training specifically designed for community boards.
- Targeted training addresses the unique needs of your association.

- Investing in board education benefits not just the board, but the entire community through better decision-making and increased resident confidence.

Case Study: The Succession Success (Board Recruitment)

Oak Ridge HOA was stuck in a cycle of board burnout. Finding willing volunteers at the last minute became the norm. The few dedicated residents who did step up often felt overwhelmed and lacked the specific skills needed to address the community's challenges. Resident apathy was high, with many viewing board service as a thankless task.

Recognizing this pattern was unsustainable, the current board decided on a proactive approach. They established a Nominating Committee. Rather than waiting for people to raise their hands, this committee was tasked with actively identifying residents with valuable skills – those with backgrounds in finance, legal matters, or project management were highly sought after. Committee members reached out personally, highlighting how a resident's expertise could benefit the whole community.

To break down the barrier of board mystique, Oak Ridge created a "Board Member in Training" role. Interested residents could attend meetings, review the agenda packet, and witness board discussions without formal voting power. This shadowing program provided a low-pressure way to understand the inner workings of the board and gauge their genuine interest in future full membership.

These two strategies paid off. The Nominating Committee

built a roster of qualified residents open to serving when their term limits allowed. The "Board Member in Training" participants felt prepared and invested when they transitioned to full board positions. Oak Ridge experienced smoother handoffs, less board burnout, and notably, a shift in resident perception. Board service was no longer seen as a burden but an opportunity to contribute meaningfully to the community.

What Could They Have Done Differently?

In the past, Oak Ridge relied heavily on general pleas for volunteers during annual meetings or the occasional newsletter notice. This passive approach failed to target the skills they needed and didn't address residents' hesitation in stepping into an undefined, potentially overwhelming role.

Board Member Voice: "We were tired of the same cycle – dedicated people burning out, and then scrambling to find anyone willing to fill the seats. We knew we needed to change our approach," [Board President, Oak Ridge HOA]

Question for the Reader: Is your community's board primarily composed of 'usual suspects' who serve out of obligation, or do you have a system for identifying fresh talent and building leadership capacity?

Key Takeaways

- **Proactive Recruitment:** Don't just wait for volunteers; strategically seek out individuals with skills the board needs.
- **Demystify the Role:** Offer ways for potential board members to experience what it's like before fully committing (shadowing, committee work).
- **Change the Culture:** Emphasize that board service is an opportunity to contribute to the community, not a thankless burden.

Test Your Knowledge! Answers

1. **Key Components of Fiduciary Duty:**
   - Duty of Care: Acting diligently and prudently
   - Duty of Loyalty: Prioritizing the community's interests
   - Duty of Good Faith: Acting honestly and furthering the community's goals
2. **Common Conflict of Interest Scenarios**
   - Self-dealing (conducting personal business with the association)
   - Favoring friends or family members
   - Accepting gifts or incentives from vendors
3. **Preparing for Board Service**
   - Review the governing documents (declaration, bylaws, rules)
   - Read recent meeting minutes
   - Familiarize yourself with the budget
   - Speak with other board members or the management company
4. **Majority vs. Consensus**
   - Majority Rule: Decisions are made when more than half agree. Efficient but can disregard minority views.
   - Consensus: Emphasizes finding a solution everyone can accept. Time-consuming, but promotes collaboration.
5. **Importance of Confidentiality**
   - Prevents the spread of misinformation
   - Builds trust within the board
   - Protects the community during sensitive matters

(legal, personnel issues)
6. **Advantage of Structured Orientation**
   - Provides new members with essential knowledge quickly, enabling effective contributions. (Other possible answers include consistency, maintaining board continuity)
7. **Reasons for Recusal**
   - A board member has a direct personal or financial interest in the matter being decided.
   - A relationship with a party involved could compromise their objectivity.
8. **Succession Planning**
   - The process of proactively anticipating board vacancies and identifying/preparing potential replacements.
   - It ensures smooth transitions and prevents leadership gaps.
9. **Continuing Education Opportunities**
   - Conferences and workshops offered by industry associations
   - Training programs from management companies
   - Online courses, articles, and webinars
10. **Benefits of Effective Governance**
    - Protects property values
    - Increases resident satisfaction
    - Enhances quality of life
    - Helps avoid or minimize legal disputes
    - Contributes to the community's long-term financial health

CHAPTER 6: ASSESSING YOUR COMMUNITY'S HEALTH

Introduction

A condominium community is like a living organism, and just as a doctor regularly assesses a patient's health, a condo board must proactively evaluate the well-being of their community. We've emphasized the importance of proactive versus reactive approaches in maintenance, and this principle remains true for the overall health of the community. The difference between reacting to problems as they arise versus proactively monitoring for potential issues is significant. Proactive management ensures long-term stability and prevents major crises that reactive management might miss.

This chapter will get into three key areas of focus:

- **Financial Health:** As established earlier, a strong financial foundation is essential for any successful community.
- **Physical Condition:** Maintaining community assets and infrastructure protects property values.
- **Resident Satisfaction:** A happy and engaged community creates a thriving environment.

We'll discuss specific red flags within each of these areas. Even board members without prior experience can learn to recognize these warning signs and use the tools provided in this chapter to make informed decisions.

The board's role in assessment is crucial for three key reasons:

- **Financial Responsibility:** Assessments ensure adequate reserve funding, responsible budgeting, and the ability to handle unexpected costs.
- **Smart Maintenance Planning:** Proper assessments help prioritize repairs and replacements, preventing costly emergencies.
- **Resident Happiness and Retention:** Community health is directly linked to resident satisfaction. Assessments contribute to a welcoming environment that builds a sense of belonging and reduces conflict.

Fast Fact: Many management companies offer reserve study services to help communities accurately assess their infrastructure funding needs.

Recognizing A Community In Crisis

Condominium communities can decline for a multitude of reasons. These problems often become apparent in the community's financial health, physical upkeep, and overall resident happiness. It's essential for the board of directors to understand these warning signs so they can act quickly to protect the community's future.

Fast Fact: Ignoring red flags rarely makes them go away – they usually worsen and become more expensive to fix over time.

Signs of Financial Trouble

- **Recurring Special Assessments:** Frequent additional assessments or special assessments highlight potential budget mismanagement or surprise expenses. This signals a need to closely examine the community's financial planning.
- **Rising Delinquent Accounts:** Accounts in arrears hurt the community's ability to pay its bills and maintain operations.
- **Difficulty Securing Loans or Insurance:** Problems obtaining financing or affordable insurance damage the community's reputation with outside financial institutions.
- **Inadequate Budgets:** If operating budgets consistently fall short, it creates a cycle of deferred maintenance that leads to further decline.

Evidence of Physical Neglect

- **Deferred Maintenance:** Obvious deterioration, like

peeling paint, damaged walkways, and leaking roofs, shows a lack of care that harms property values and quality of life.
- **Ignored Safety Hazards:** Equipment failures (like fire alarms), persistent plumbing problems, or unresolved ice buildup create a dangerous environment and increase the community's liability exposure.
- **Unkempt Appearance:** Neglected landscaping, aging entry signage, and inoperable exterior lights send a message of decline, which can dampen residents' pride in their community.

Fast Fact: A well-maintained community can see, on average, a 5-10% increase in property values compared to those in decline.

Pro Tip: Walk your property regularly with a critical eye. Look beyond the obvious and make a list of things that need attention to start prioritizing repairs.

Resident Frustration and Apathy

- **High Turnover:** If residents leave at an unusually high rate, it suggests the community isn't as desirable as others, impacting property values.
- **Unresolved Complaints and Conflicts:** Ongoing disputes breed negativity and make residents feel like they don't have a voice.
- **Low Meeting Attendance:** Poor turnout at annual meetings is a sign that communication has broken down and residents have lost trust in the board or that the residents don't have a strong connection to the community.
- **Decreased Participation:** When residents don't volunteer, it creates a ripple effect. The community might have to hire and pay for services that could otherwise be handled by volunteers, leading to increased costs for everyone. Amenities, events, or even the upkeep of

common areas may suffer without sufficient volunteer support, potentially leading to their decline or removal altogether.

Fast Fact: Regular resident surveys are a simple, low-cost tool to gauge community satisfaction and identify issues early.

Pro Tip: Address even minor resident complaints promptly. This builds trust and prevents issues from escalating.

How Professional Management Helps

Professional management companies are trained to spot early indicators of trouble. Their skills benefit the community by:

- **Identifying Subtle Signs:** Managers notice shifts in financial patterns, vendor problems, or escalating resident tensions, things the board might miss.
- **Offering Unbiased Solutions:** Outsiders have the objectivity to focus on practical solutions, without the emotional investment of residents.
- **Understanding the Industry:** Managers are aware of changing regulations, best practices, and potential dangers that could harm the community.

Pro Tip: When evaluating management companies, ask for references and specific examples of how they've helped other communities address challenges.

The Board's Duty

The board of directors has the ultimate responsibility to be alert to these red flags. By acting swiftly and decisively, they can protect the community's long-term health and stability.

Checklist: Red Flags

- **Financial Distress**
  - Frequent special assessments
  - Delinquent accounts
  - Difficulty obtaining financing or favorable insurance
  - Underfunded budgets

- **Physical Decline**
  - Deferred maintenance (peeling paint, leaky roofs, etc.)
  - Unresolved safety hazards
  - Unkempt appearance
- **Resident Dissatisfaction**
  - High turnover
  - Frequent complaints and unresolved disputes
  - Low meeting attendance
  - Lack of resident involvement

Timeline: Addressing Red Flags

- **Immediate:**
  - Consult with management company or relevant professionals (attorney, engineer, etc.) for urgent issues.
  - Communicate any safety hazards or major disruptions to residents.
- **Short-Term (1-3 months):**
  - Review budget and identify areas for potential cost savings or increased revenue.
  - Prioritize repairs, balancing safety concerns with financial capacity.
  - Assess resident concerns and develop a plan to address major issues.
- **Long-Term (6+ months):**
  - Revise budgeting practices to avoid future crises.
  - Create a long-term maintenance plan and update the reserve study, if needed.
  - Explore ways to improve resident communication and involvement.

Hallmarks Of A Stable Community

Successful condominium communities share specific traits that ensure their continued well-being, appeal, and rising property values. Let's examine what these traits are.

Strong Financial Footing

- **Healthy Reserves:** Adequate reserve funds, tailored to the community's specific needs, allow for handling unexpected expenses or major projects without resorting to special assessments.
- **Responsible Budgeting:** Thoughtful budgeting accurately reflects the community's financial requirements, avoiding shortfalls and surprises. Long-term planning ensures stability.
- **Low Delinquencies:** Timely fee collection is essential for maintaining cash flow and operations. It also demonstrates that residents value and support the community.

Well-Maintained Assets

- **Proactive Approach:** Preventing problems through regular maintenance saves money, reduces resident frustration, and protects valuable assets.
- **Preventive Schedules:** Proactive maintenance extends the lifespan of infrastructure and avoids costly emergencies. For example, replacing problematic underground drainage piping prevents disruptive sewer backups, saving the community from expensive repairs and the hassle of using insurance for preventable issues.
- **Curb Appeal:** Well-kept common areas, landscaping, and

building exteriors enhance resident pride and positively impact property values.

Positive Resident Engagement

- **Open Communication:** Using a variety of channels for constructive communication between the board and residents builds trust and collaboration.
- **Resident-Driven Committees:** These committees empower residents to take ownership of improvements and projects, supporting the board and creating a shared vision for the community.
- **Strong Event Attendance:** Social events build community spirit, promote neighborliness, and attract potential new residents who want to belong to a vibrant community.

Pro Tip: Encourage a variety of residents to join committees. This brings diverse perspectives and helps create a sense of shared ownership in the community.

Stability in Action

While challenges are inevitable, communities possessing these hallmarks have proactively positioned themselves for success. This forward-thinking approach ensures their continued strength and attractiveness, maintaining their strength and appeal for the long term.

Checklist: Assessing Your Community

- **Financial Footing:**
    - Are reserves sufficient to meet projected needs?
    - Does budgeting accurately reflect the community's costs?
    - Are fee collections timely, and delinquencies low?
- **Asset Maintenance:**
    - Is there a proactive maintenance plan in place?
    - Are inspections performed regularly?

- How does the community's curb appeal compare to similar properties?
- **Resident Engagement**
  - What communication channels are available (meetings, website, newsletter)?
  - Are resident committees active?
  - Are social events well-attended?

Action Steps

- **Identify Weak Areas:** Use the checklist to pinpoint which hallmarks aren't fully present in your community.
- **Prioritize Actions:** Focus on strengthening financial stability first, followed by asset maintenance and resident engagement improvements.

A Well-Functioning Community: Going Above And Beyond

A successful community isn't merely about fulfilling basic obligations. To truly flourish, a condominium association must aim higher, offering a lifestyle that elevates resident satisfaction, protects property values, and builds a strong reputation. Let's get into the key elements that define this "above and beyond" mindset:

Attractive Amenities

Well-chosen amenities become an extension of residents' living spaces. Pools, fitness centers, clubhouses, golf courses, and walking trails all offer the potential to add tremendous value to the community experience. Boards play a crucial role in selecting amenities that are both desired by residents and financially sustainable over the long run, ensuring these assets continue to bring joy for years to come.

Proactive Sustainability

Embracing sustainability isn't just about being environmentally conscious; it's also fiscally responsible. Initiatives like upgrading to energy-efficient appliances, implementing water conservation measures, and offering comprehensive recycling programs can significantly reduce operating costs. Moreover, these efforts appeal to a growing number of eco-conscious residents, boosting the community's marketability.

Embracing Technology

In today's world, technology plays a vital role in streamlining communication and improving the delivery of services within a community. Online portals that allow residents to pay fees, submit maintenance requests, and access important information enhance the resident experience. Additionally, enhanced security systems provide peace of mind. When selecting any technology, boards must prioritize user-friendliness to ensure widespread adoption and maximize the benefits.

Fast Fact: Online portals and communication tools can streamline resident communication and help boards stay organized.

Building a Sense of Community

A true sense of community goes beyond well-maintained grounds and buildings. It's about creating an environment where everyone feels welcome and included. Initiatives like welcome committees, small gifts for new residents, and clear communication channels set a positive tone from the moment someone moves in. Offering diverse events – from large celebrations to smaller interest-based gatherings – encourages participation from residents with different personalities and schedules. Finally, recognizing both community-wide achievements and individual contributions cultivates a sense of pride and shared purpose, reminding residents that they are an essential part of something special.

The Competitive Advantage

Boards should always be mindful of the market. Communities that offer these desirable elements stand out, attracting new residents, maintaining strong property values, and encouraging current residents to stay for the long term. Going above and beyond isn't just a feel-good strategy – it's a sound investment in the community's future.

Sample Project Timeline: Implementing an Amenity

1. **Needs Assessment (1 month):** Survey residents to determine their interests and gauge support for various amenities.
2. **Cost and Feasibility (1-2 months):** Obtain price quotes, research potential regulations, and assess the impact on maintenance costs.
3. **Financing (if applicable):** Explore funding options.
4. **Decision and Communication:** If the project proceeds, present the detailed plan to residents and address questions transparently.
5. **Implementation:** Obtain permits (as needed), create a construction timeline, and keep residents informed of progress.

Action Steps:

- **Start Small:** Begin with more easily achievable enhancements (e.g., upgraded community signage rather than a new pool).
- **Resident Input:** Involve residents in selecting and planning amenities and initiatives.

Call To Action

As we've discussed throughout this chapter, identifying potential issues early is crucial for preventing major crises, saving money, and protecting property values. Your board has a responsibility to be vigilant in recognizing these red flags – or to seek expert help when needed. Ignoring problems when they first appear can have severe negative consequences for the community.

For complex issues, I strongly urge boards to leverage the expertise of professionals like management companies, consultants, attorneys, and industry associations. These resources offer specialized knowledge and experience that can save you time and prevent costly mistakes.

Addressing Red Flags: Time for Action

We've learned how to spot the warning signs – now it's time to implement solutions. Remember, acting swiftly is essential to stop small problems from turning into crises.

Tackling Financial Distress

- **Analyze Your Budget:** Scrutinize your community's income and expenses. Identify areas to cut costs or, if absolutely necessary, adjust fees to meet financial obligations.
- **Special Assessments:** These may be the only solution if major infrastructure needs are unfunded. Transparency is key – explain to residents the reasons, how the money will be spent, and how it will impact them.
- **Explore Cost Savings:** Consider these strategies:

- Negotiate better rates with existing vendors or find new ones.
- Bulk purchase supplies while carefully managing inventory to avoid waste.
- Invest in energy efficiency for long-term savings.
- Spread out non-urgent projects to improve cash flow.

Pro Tip: When reviewing budgets, don't just compare them to the previous year. Analyze trends over multiple years to identify potential problem areas.

Addressing Physical Decline

- **Prioritize Repairs** Prioritize urgent repairs, especially safety hazards. Balance immediate needs while planning for long-term financial health.
- **Proactive Maintenance:** A well-structured maintenance plan prevents minor issues from becoming costly disasters. Include regular inspections to stay ahead of potential problems.
- **Consult the Experts:** For major projects (like replacing a roof), seek advice from engineers or specialized contractors. This ensures the best outcome for your investment.

Managing Resident Dissatisfaction

- **Communication is Key:** Keep residents informed through newsletters, the community website, and meetings. Make it easy for them to provide feedback and voice concerns.
- **Act on Feedback:** Show residents their input matters. Create a system to track complaints and address them in a timely manner.
- **Resident Power:** Form resident committees for specific areas (like landscaping or social events). This builds a sense of ownership and lessens the burden on the board.

The Path to Recovery

Turning a troubled community around is possible but may involve temporary discomfort, both financially and emotionally. The deeper the problems, the harder the recovery will be. There's no avoiding this, but the only way to improve is to confront the challenges. Management companies can offer guidance, but the board ultimately bears the responsibility to lead.

Commit to fixing the issues facing your community. Be open with residents about the challenges and your plan to address them. A healthy, well-run community benefits everyone – board members and residents alike – with increased property values, stronger community bonds, and a more enjoyable place to call home.

Checklist: Is Your Board Ready to Act?

- Do we have a clear understanding of our community's current challenges?
- Are we open to seeking professional guidance when necessary?
- Are we committed to transparent communication with residents?

Action Steps:

- **Set Goals:** Create a list of specific improvements the board aims to achieve, along with a realistic timeline.
- **Share the Vision:** Communicate these goals to the community, inviting feedback and building support for the path forward.

Test Your Knowledge!

1. Name three major areas to evaluate when assessing your community's health.
2. What are some key indicators of financial distress within a community?
3. Describe the difference between deferred maintenance and aesthetic neglect.
4. Why is it important to address resident dissatisfaction, even if the complaints seem minor?
5. What is the role of a professional management company in identifying potential risks?
6. Why is a well-maintained community important for property values?
7. What does it mean to manage your community proactively versus reactively?
8. List two benefits of having resident committees.
9. Explain the concept of a community's "curb appeal" and why it matters.
10. What is the purpose of a reserve study?

The answers are at the end of this chapter

Case Study: Financial Foresight – A Cautionary Tale

Sunset Hills was once the pride of its neighborhood. Well-kept homes, manicured lawns, and a sparkling community pool drew in young families and retirees alike. But beneath the surface, a financial storm was brewing. The reserve fund, meant for major repairs, had been consistently underfunded. Board members, focused on keeping dues low, had turned a blind eye to warnings from concerned residents and recommendations within past reserve studies.

Then, a severe weather event swept through, causing widespread roof damage. The cost of repairs was staggering – far beyond what the limited reserves could cover. Faced with a massive special assessment, the community fractured. Longtime residents on fixed incomes felt betrayed, their retirement savings threatened. Younger families, already stretched thin, questioned whether they could stay.

Panic set in. Some desperate homeowners listed their properties at reduced prices, further destabilizing the market. Delinquencies in monthly fees skyrocketed, creating a vicious cycle. The once-vibrant community spiraled into a state of financial crisis. Maintenance was deferred on other areas, accelerating the decline.

Sunset Hills became a cautionary tale. Residents had prioritized artificially low dues in the short term, only to pay a far greater price later. The fallout lasted for years – eroded property values, lingering resentment, and the loss of the community spirit that had once defined them. It served as a stark reminder that responsible budgeting and long-term financial planning aren't just smart practices – they're essential for a community's survival.

What Could They Have Done Differently?

- **Heed Reserve Study Recommendations:** These studies are invaluable for identifying funding needs. Ignoring them is like dismissing a doctor's warnings.
- **Prioritize Responsible Budgeting:** Low fees might look appealing today, but they mortgage the community's future. Reserves are crucial.

- **Communicate Transparently:** Residents deserved to understand the financial risks and have a voice in long-term planning.

Board Member Voice: "We wanted to make everyone happy...thought we could keep fees low and still fix problems as they came up. Boy, were we wrong!"

Question for the Reader: Is your community tempted to put off essential repairs or underfund reserves in the name of keeping dues low? What are the potential long-term consequences of this approach?

Key Takeaways

- Short-term savings can lead to long-term disaster.
- Reserve studies are vital tools, not optional documents.
- Transparency builds trust, even when discussing difficult financial realities.

Case Study: The Power Of Proactive Maintenance

Oak Creek had always prided itself on being a well-run community. But beneath the surface, a hidden threat was lurking. Over decades, the original plumbing system was slowly deteriorating. Tiny leaks within the walls remained undetected, the moisture silently fueling mold growth and causing unseen damage to the building's structure.

One winter, the problem erupted. A pipe burst in a resident's unit, flooding their home and the one below. Investigations unveiled a much larger problem. Mold remediation was required in several units along with extensive plumbing repairs. The crisis led to a substantial special assessment, months of construction noise, and frayed nerves for the affected residents.

It was a costly and disruptive wake-up call for Oak Creek. They vowed that this would never happen again. Working with a consulting engineer, the board developed a comprehensive maintenance plan. This included:

- Regular plumbing inspections with specialized equipment to detect hidden leaks early.
- Proactive replacement of aging infrastructure elements based on their projected lifespan.
- Budgeting for both routine maintenance as well as unexpected repairs, avoiding crisis-funding.

In the years since, Oak Creek has benefited tremendously. Several minor leaks have been caught and fixed while still manageable, saving money and preventing resident displacement. The community has avoided surprise assessments, and the enhanced maintenance has contributed to overall stability and resident satisfaction. While the initial crisis was painful, Oak Creek now serves as a model for how a proactive mindset protects a community's long-term health and value.

What Could They Have Done Differently?

Oak Creek could have prevented this costly crisis by:

- **Prioritizing Regular Inspections:** Investing in professional inspections using thermal imaging or other leak detection technology would have caught the deteriorating pipes before a major failure occurred.
- **Understanding Infrastructure Lifespan:** Knowing the expected lifespan of their plumbing system would have allowed them to proactively plan and budget for a replacement, instead of being blindsided.

Board Member Voice: "At the time, we thought we were being responsible. If something broke, we fixed it. We never imagined problems could be brewing where we couldn't see them."

Question for the Reader: Is your community relying on a "break-and-fix" mentality, or do you have a plan in place to proactively address hidden infrastructure issues?

Key Takeaways

- Even well-maintained communities can have unseen problems.
- The costs of deferred maintenance almost always exceed the costs of proactive solutions.
- Inspections and a long-term maintenance plan are essential investments in the community's future.

Case Study: Decline Due To Neglect – The Downward Spiral Of Whispering Pines

Whispering Pines had once been a sought-after address. Its well-maintained townhomes, tree-lined streets, and sparkling community pool had attracted young families and retirees alike. But a slow but steady decline began to creep in. Budget constraints led to deferred maintenance – the repainting of faded trim kept getting pushed back a year, then another. Landscaping became less meticulous as contracts lapsed, and the once-manicured lawns grew patchy.

The community pool, a centerpiece of summer fun, developed cracks. Instead of a quick repair, the board debated for months: patch it temporarily or invest in a full resurfacing? The pool closed for the season...then for another. Residents, frustrated by the inaction, became less invested. Small infractions added up: uncollected pet waste, overflowing trash bins, toys left scattered. The decline felt both intangible, yet impossible to ignore.

Potential buyers were immediately turned off by the shabby appearance. Whispering Pines was no longer a place people aspired to live. Those who could afford to move began to list their properties. As property values dipped, the community's financial woes worsened. Arguments erupted at board meetings: Should they raise fees to address the decay, or would that drive even more residents away?

Whispering Pines became a stark example of how neglect can snowball. The visual decline eroded resident pride, leading to further apathy and a vicious cycle that became difficult to break. It served as a harsh reminder that addressing even seemingly minor aesthetic issues is essential to protect a community's reputation, resident morale, and long-term financial health.

What Could They Have Done Differently?

- **Prioritized Small Repairs:** Addressing minor issues early prevents them from escalating into larger, budget-busting problems.
- **Phased-in Approach:** Develop a multi-year maintenance plan, tackling smaller projects alongside major replacements to manage costs and avoid neglecting upkeep entirely.
- **Proactive Budget:** Factor in regular upkeep expenses and create a contingency fund for minor, unexpected repairs.
- **Resident Communication:** Be transparent about maintenance challenges and the financial impact of deferring repairs. This increases buy-in when fee increases become necessary.

Board Member Voice: "At the time, we were focused on keeping fees low. We thought residents would be happier not paying more. We didn't fully grasp the connection between how the community looked and its overall health."

Question for the Reader: Are there areas in your community where maintenance might be slipping? Don't wait for them to become major problems – address them now!

Key Takeaways

- Neglect, even with good intentions, has a negative ripple effect on everything from property values to resident happiness.
- Proactive maintenance is always more cost-effective than large-scale fixes resulting from inaction.
- Transparent communication helps residents understand the "why" behind necessary repairs and potential costs.

Case Study: From Conflict To Collaboration At Maplewood

Maplewood had a problem: residents seemed constantly at odds. From noise complaints to disputes over the use of common areas, a steady stream of negativity flowed toward the board. Board meetings became tense affairs, dominated by arguments instead of problem-solving. Residents felt unheard, leading to a sense of mistrust and a general feeling of discontent within the community.

Recognizing the pattern, the board made a bold decision. Instead of trying to silence the complaints, they'd overhaul their communication. First came a monthly newsletter summarizing board actions, upcoming events, and sharing resident success stories. Next, they upgraded their online portal, making it easier for residents to pay fees, submit maintenance requests, and access community documents. But the most impactful change was creating a formalized suggestion process, encouraging residents to share ideas and concerns constructively.

The board took another key step: forming resident-led committees. These weren't just for planning parties – residents were now involved in landscaping upgrades, revising community rules, and even budget discussions. This shift from just complaining to active participation was transformative. People felt like they had a stake in the community's success. With direct channels for involvement, the barrage of petty complaints lessened.

Maplewood's board meetings changed. Instead of arguments,

there were discussions focusing on the issues residents had helped define. The sense of community grew. Neighbors who were once adversaries worked together on projects. Maplewood's journey teaches a vital lesson: sometimes the best way to combat conflict is to give people a meaningful way to channel their energy and work with, not against, one another for a shared vision of a better community.

What Could They Have Done Differently?

- Acted sooner to address the communication gap and resident frustrations.
- Implemented a more proactive approach to gathering resident feedback, potentially through surveys or focus groups.
- Created resident committees earlier to provide a positive outlet for involvement.

Board Member Voice: "We were tired of the arguing. Honestly, we were starting to resent the residents instead of seeing them as part of the solution. We had to break that cycle."

Question for the Reader: Are there issues in your community where residents feel their voices aren't being heard? How could you change your communication channels and processes to address that?

Key Takeaways

- Unresolved conflict is toxic to a healthy community. Don't ignore resident concerns, even if they seem minor.
- Clear communication channels and transparency build trust.
- Resident committees and opportunities for involvement give people ownership over their community, shifting them from critics to collaborators.

Case Study: Help From The Professionals

Greenfield was a bustling community with aging infrastructure and a dedicated but inexperienced board. While they had the best intentions, their lack of specialized financial knowledge led to mounting problems. Operating costs steadily increased with no clear reason why. Reserves were dwindling, and residents began to worry about the long-term health of their community.

The board realized they needed outside help. They researched several management companies and selected one with a proven track record in financial turnaround and board education. Here's what the partnership achieved:

- **Deep Dive into the Finances:** The management company conducted a forensic audit, uncovering hidden expenses like unfavorable vendor contracts and billing errors. They identified areas where costs could be streamlined without sacrificing services.
- **Renegotiating for Savings:** Armed with industry knowledge and detailed analysis, the management company renegotiated contracts with Greenfield's existing vendors. Many agreed to lower rates or provided additional services for the same price to retain the community's business.
- **Best Practices Training:** The company didn't just fix the problems; they empowered Greenfield's board. Regular training sessions focused on budget creation, financial reporting, and strategies for long-term planning.
- **Transparency and Communication:** The management company helped the board develop a clear plan to

communicate the community's financial situation and necessary adjustments to residents. Transparency built trust and understanding.

What Could They Have Done Differently?

- **Sought Help Earlier:** Greenfield's board waited until problems became urgent. Seeking professional guidance sooner could have prevented mounting costs and resident anxiety.
- **Regular Budget Reviews:** Independent reviews by a management company or financial consultant could have caught issues before they reached a critical point.

Board Member Voice: "We were committed to doing what was best for Greenfield, but we were in over our heads. Financial stuff isn't easy, and we were starting to lose sleep over it. Bringing in the experts was the best decision we made." – Janet Miller, Board President

Question for the Reader: Is your board equipped with the knowledge to make complex financial decisions? Are you confident you could spot hidden expenses or negotiate optimal contracts?

Key Takeaways

- Don't let pride prevent you from seeking expert help when needed.
- Management companies offer specialized knowledge that can save your community money and stress.
- Proactive financial management is essential for a community's long-term health.
- Transparency builds trust with residents, especially when facing challenges.

Case Study: Curb Appeal's Impact

Rose Garden had always been a decent community, but it lacked that "wow" factor. Landscaping was uninspired, buildings were showing their age, and there was an overall sense of things being just a little bit tired. The board recognized that while there were no major problems, boosting the community's visual appeal could pay significant dividends.

Their transformation began with landscaping. Overgrown, outdated bushes were replaced with vibrant flower beds, flowering trees, and neatly trimmed hedges. Rose Garden's entrance was overhauled; they added a new, prominent sign with elegant lettering and integrated lighting for nighttime. The board then turned to common areas. Clubhouse exteriors and pool areas received fresh paint in a modern color scheme.

It didn't stop there. Recognizing the power of resident involvement, Rose Garden transformed a patch of unused land into a community garden. Residents could sign up for plots, creating opportunities to connect with neighbors and adding to the visual appeal. These seemingly small changes ignited something unexpected. Pride began to bloom. Residents started sprucing up their own patios and balconies. Properties that lingered on the market suddenly sold. Rose Garden drew interest from new buyers attracted by its fresh, inviting atmosphere.

The most important change, however, wasn't about financials. It was the revived sense of community. The garden became a social hub, the pool area buzzed with activity, and more residents attended meetings. Rose Garden proved that strategic investments in curb appeal aren't just about property values, they are about creating a place people are proud to call home.

What Could They Have Done Differently?

- **A proactive approach:** Rose Garden could have tackled the lack of curb appeal earlier, preventing the gradual decline it created. Regular assessments of the property's appearance would have highlighted potential areas for improvement.
- **Including Resident Input:** The board could have surveyed residents to get their ideas and gauge support before implementing significant changes. This can generate buy-in, potentially even volunteering to assist with the projects.

Board Member Voice: "Honestly, we always thought the community was good enough. It didn't occur to us that investing some money into the way things looked could make such a huge difference."

Question for the Reader: Does your community prioritize curb appeal and make regular investments in its upkeep? How could even small enhancements boost both its visual appeal and your residents' sense of pride?

Key Takeaways

- **Curb appeal matters:** First impressions have lasting power and directly impact perceived value.
- **A catalyst for change:** Improvements in curb appeal can encourage resident involvement and revitalize the entire community.
- **Pride in ownership:** A well-maintained property fosters a sense of pride and belonging amongst residents.

Test Your Knowledge! Answers

1. **Three major areas of assessment:**
   - **Financial Health:** Adequate reserves, responsible budgeting, timely fee collection.
   - **Physical Condition:** Maintenance of buildings, common areas, and major infrastructure.
   - **Resident Satisfaction:** Communication, responsiveness to concerns, sense of community.
2. **Indicators of financial distress:**
   - Frequent special assessments
   - Rising delinquencies in fees and payments
   - Difficulty obtaining loans or favorable insurance
   - Budgets that struggle to cover basic operating costs
3. **Deferred maintenance vs. aesthetic neglect:**
   - **Deferred Maintenance:** Essential repairs to infrastructure (roofs, plumbing, etc.) are postponed, potentially leading to safety hazards and larger expenses later.
   - **Aesthetic Neglect:** Unkept landscaping, outdated fixtures, lack of attention to visual appeal, which impacts resident pride and property values.
4. **Addressing resident dissatisfaction:**
   - Untended complaints can escalate, create negativity, and damage the community's reputation.
   - Addressing issues builds trust, supports open communication, and helps prevent larger conflicts.
5. **Role of professional management:**
   - Trained to spot subtle warning signs (financial inconsistencies, vendor issues, minor resident disputes)

- Offer objective assessment without emotional investment in the community
- Have up-to-date industry knowledge on potential risks and best practices

6. **Well-maintained community and property values:**
   - Attracts potential buyers and maintains strong demand
   - Protects the investment of existing owners
   - A visually appealing community suggests care and responsibility, which translates into higher values

7. **Proactive vs. reactive management:**
   - **Proactive:** Prevents problems through regular upkeep, budgeting, and long-term planning.
   - **Reactive:** Crisis-driven responses, leading to rushed decisions, higher costs, and resident frustration.

8. **Benefits of resident committees:**
   - Empowers residents and lessens the workload on the board
   - Brings diverse expertise and perspectives to community improvements

9. **Curb appeal:**
   - The first impression of a community, created by landscaping, building exteriors, and overall upkeep.
   - Good curb appeal attracts buyers, boosts resident pride, and positively impacts property values.

10. **Purpose of a reserve study:**
    - A professional assessment of the community's major infrastructure components (roofs, roads, etc.)
    - Projects their lifespan and determines the necessary funding levels to maintain them over time.
    - Helps prevent financial surprises from major repairs and replacements.

CHAPTER 7: STRATEGIES FOR IMPROVEMENT

Introduction

Living in a condominium community offers many benefits, but it also comes with a unique set of management complexities. Even with the most dedicated board members and experienced managers, challenges can arise in areas like finances, building maintenance, or resident relations. However, it's important to remember that these challenges present opportunities for improvement and growth within communities of any size or functionality.

Challenges are a natural part of community management. Some common hurdles include:

- **Financial Constraints:** In a world of unlimited resources, we'd make different choices, but that's not our reality. Financial limits create the need for careful budgeting and prioritization.
- **Maintenance Issues:** Unexpected maintenance problems can strain budgets and disrupt residents' lives. Proactive planning helps mitigate these issues.
- **Resident Disputes:** Differing expectations, misunderstandings about rules, and personality clashes are all potential sources of conflict within a community.
- **Evolving Regulations:** Legislatures continuously update laws affecting condominium communities, requiring boards to adapt and ensure compliance.

Even well-managed communities face challenges. However, confronting these hurdles leads to innovation, improved operations, enhanced resident lifestyles, and the elimination of outdated practices. While we briefly discussed distressed communities in a previous chapter, we'll revisit the topic here to highlight the contrasting strategies, tools, and priorities for stable and well-functioning communities. Remember, any condominium association can boost its effectiveness, regardless of its current state.

- **Distressed Communities:** These communities face significant financial, operational, and resident relation issues.
- **Stable Communities:** These communities have a mix of strengths and weaknesses, with generally sound finances, operations, and infrastructure.
- **Well-Functioning Communities:** These communities are running smoothly, with strong reserves, satisfied residents, and well-maintained amenities. Yet, there's always room to improve.

Remember, there's no one-size-fits-all solution for condominium management. Think of this book as a toolkit – providing different tools for different situations. Understanding your community's specific strengths, weaknesses, and goals, as outlined in previous chapters, is key to selecting the right tools for improvement.

Prioritizing Actions For Distressed Communities

Recognizing and Fixing a Distressed Community

We've talked about this before, but here's a recap of how to spot a financially distressed community: budget problems, unpaid dues piling up, trouble paying bills. These are warning signs, and boards need to figure out the root cause – maybe it's overspending, dues set too low, or people just not paying.

Another red flag is neglected maintenance. Things falling apart can become dangerous or make problems worse. This causes property values to drop, makes residents frustrated, and might even create legal trouble for the community.

Fast Fact: Ignoring a small maintenance problem can often lead to much more expensive repairs down the road.

Poor communication and resident conflict are also common in struggling communities. Lack of clear updates, unresolved arguments, and empty meetings are signs that trust is broken and it's tough to solve problems.

Finally, if rules aren't followed or enforced fairly, that just adds to the instability and sense of unfairness.

Strategies for a Comeback

First, a distressed community has to get a grip on its finances. This means a deep dive into the books, then a realistic budget – which might mean cuts and finding new income.

Special assessments might be necessary, but get legal advice first and make them fair. Be clear with residents about why this is needed, even if you don't require their vote (sometimes you do, so check the rules!).

Prioritize the most urgent repairs for safety and to stop things from getting even worse. Balance quick fixes with a plan for long-term upkeep.

Pro Tip: When evaluating bids for maintenance or repairs, don't just look at the bottom line – consider the contractor's experience and reputation.

Update policies and be ready to consistently enforce them – especially with finances and maintenance. Explain procedures for violations, and be ready for people playing the "but what about them?" game.

Communication is key! Open meetings, newsletters, anything to keep residents informed.

Remember: Distressed communities often need professional help – managers, accountants, lawyers. Also, stress in the community is high – acknowledge that and get residents involved in finding solutions.

Pro Tip: A well-maintained community is more attractive to buyers and can command higher property values.

Identifying the Core Issues

- **Checklist**
    - Delinquent dues report (amounts, how long overdue)
    - List of vendors with unpaid invoices
    - Maintenance issues list (prioritize urgent/safety hazards)
    - Resident complaints log
    - Review of governing documents
- **Timeline:** 1-2 weeks to gather data

- **Action Step:** Analyze the data to pinpoint the largest areas of financial distress, critical maintenance needs, and major sources of resident dissatisfaction.

Stabilization Strategies
- **Checklist:**
  - Current budget vs. actual income/expenses
  - Financial audit (if not already done)
  - Reserve fund balance
  - Legal counsel contact information
  - Delinquent accounts list
- **Timeline**
  - Budget Revision: 1-2 Weeks
  - Special Assessments (if necessary): Consult lawyer, then 1-2 months to implement
  - Collection Efforts: Ongoing, immediate start
- **Action Steps:**
  - Designate a "finance team" from the board.
  - Communicate the financial situation transparently to residents, emphasizing the need for urgent action.

Enhancing A Stable Community: Focus And Strategies

Even financially stable communities need to focus on the long haul. Here's what to prioritize:

1. **Beef Up Your Reserves:** A healthy reserve fund is like a safety net for your infrastructure, property values, and the community's overall appeal. Regularly check how much you've got compared to what you'll need. Keep your reserve study up-to-date and use it as your budgeting guide.

Fast Fact: The average lifespan of a roof in many climates is 20-30 years. Knowing this helps plan for major expenses.

2. **Get Expert Eyes on Your Buildings:** For the most accurate picture of your building's condition, hire qualified engineers or contractors. Board members, handymen, and even generalist management companies might not have the in-depth knowledge you need. Use these professional reports to create a smart maintenance plan, fixing things before they become major emergencies. A little routine maintenance, like cleaning gutters or servicing your HVAC system, can save you big money down the line.

Fast Fact: Regularly cleaning gutters can prevent costly water damage issues to your building's foundation and interior.

3. **Keep Residents Involved and Happy:** Get feedback from residents using surveys, focus groups, or suggestion boxes. Form resident committees to tap into their skills and interests—think landscaping, events, or even helping review the budget. This gives residents a voice and lightens the board's workload.

Additionally, host community events like potlucks, holiday gatherings, or clubs to help people connect and feel like they belong.

4. **Update Policies and Contracts:** Take a close look at your governing documents. Do they need updates on tech usage, pets, or rentals? Consult your lawyer before big changes. Share updates with residents, listen to feedback, but ultimately, make decisions based on what's best for the whole community. Regularly check your service contracts (landscaping, snow removal, etc.). Get the best deal you can, and make sure the services actually meet your community's needs.

Pro Tip: Before making major policy changes, consider holding a resident forum for open discussion and feedback.

Important: When suggesting improvements that cost money, explain the long-term benefits to residents. These investments will make their homes more valuable and their community life that much better!

Fast Fact: Resident surveys can uncover hidden dissatisfaction and provide valuable insights before issues escalate.

Pro Tip: Creating a resident welcome packet with essential community information creates a sense of belonging for new residents.

Proactive Maintenance and Planning

- **Checklist:**
    - Reserve study (update if needed)
    - Professional building assessment report
    - Routine maintenance schedule
- **Timeline**
    - Reserve Study Update: As needed (every few years)

- Building Assessment: 1-2 months to arrange and receive the report
- Maintenance Schedule: Ongoing

- **Action Steps**
  - Create a maintenance calendar with long-term replacements and routine tasks.
  - Budget for preventive maintenance.

Resident Engagement and Satisfaction

- **Checklist:**
  - Design a resident survey
  - Communication methods (newsletter, website, etc.)
  - Resident interest survey (hobbies, skills)

- **Timeline**
  - Survey Creation: 1 week
  - Survey Distribution & Collection: 2-3 weeks
  - Committee Formation: Based on survey results, ongoing

- **Action Steps**
  - Publicize survey widely
  - Share summarized results transparently
  - Form committees quickly to capitalize on enthusiasm

Reviewing and Updating Policies and Procedures

- **Checklist:**
  - Governing documents (CC&Rs, bylaws, etc.)
  - Recent resident disputes
  - State/local regulations
  - Attorney contact info

- **Timeline:**
  - Initial review: 2-3 weeks
  - Attorney consultation (if needed): timeline varies
  - Proposed revisions and resident communication:

1-2 months
- **Action Steps:**
    - Focus on the most outdated or problematic policies first
    - Involve residents in the review process (with board oversight)

Taking A Well-Functioning Community To The Next Level

When a community is already running smoothly, boards have the chance to focus on enhancements that elevate it even further. Consider these areas:

A. Innovative Improvements

- **Go Green:** Projects like solar panels, LED lighting, and better insulation save money, show environmental commitment, and attract eco-minded residents.
- **Smart Upgrades:** Balance the cost of security tech (access control, cameras) and convenience features (package systems, community apps) against the benefits residents will actually use.
- **Boost Value and Satisfaction:** Tailor amenities to what your residents want. This could be a modern gym, community garden, pet-friendly spaces, or even EV charging stations.

B. Building a Stronger Board

- **Invest in Training:** Keep your board sharp with training on finances, legal changes, conflict management, and big-picture planning. Use resources from industry organizations, webinars, or your management company's recommendations.
- **Plan for the Future:** Mentor interested residents to create a pool of potential future board leaders. This keeps things running seamlessly and preserves valuable community knowledge.
- **Stay Agile**: Regularly check if your board's size,

committees, and decision-making processes are still the best fit for your community's needs.

Fast Fact: Many states have laws outlining board member training requirements – check yours!

Pro Tip: "Soft skills" like communication and conflict resolution are just as important for board members as financial or technical understanding.

C. Long-Term Financial Health

- **Look Ahead:** Use your reserve study to predict major expenses well in advance (think roofs, HVAC, pavement, etc.).
- **Be Proactive:** Gradual dues increases can be easier to manage than sudden special assessments. Explain your reasoning to residents clearly.

Also Remember:

- **Don't Bite Off More Than You Can Chew:** Prioritize projects carefully, balancing enthusiasm with realistic budgets and resident support.
- **Needs vs. Wants:** Some exciting upgrades may not be truly essential. Focus on those that provide lasting value and address real resident needs.

Sample Project Timeline: Implementing Smart Technology

- **Phase 1: Needs Assessment:** (2-4 weeks)
  - Resident survey on desired features
  - Research security/convenience options
  - Obtain bids from vendors
- **Phase 2: Decision & Budget:** (1-2 months)
  - Board presentation of options
  - Resident vote (if required by bylaws)
- **Phase 3: Implementation:** (Timeline varies based on the scope)

- **Action Steps:**
    - Form a "tech team" for research
    - Communicate clearly with residents throughout the process

Conclusion: The Journey Of Continuous Improvement

As you can see, the best strategies for your community depend on its current state. Boards aren't always trained to think this way – they might be told there's a single "best practice" for everyone. While some fundamentals apply to all communities, different types require different areas of focus.

Regardless of your community's current level, improvement is always possible. Even the most successful communities will face challenges – it's the nature of things. Improvement is a journey, not a destination.

Boards have a responsibility to think strategically. This means anticipating future needs, trends, and finding the resources to address them. Proactive planning is far better than waiting for problems to arise and then reacting.

Seek out ongoing education and resources for both new and experienced board members. Regularly evaluate your community's finances, infrastructure, and resident satisfaction. Be prepared to make course corrections as needed – that's normal and a sign of strength, not weakness.

Remember, the tools and knowledge in this book are meant to be used continuously, not just read once and then forgotten. With dedication and a constant focus on improvement, any board can guide its community to greater success.

Test Your Knowledge!

1. What are three common symptoms of financial distress in a condominium community?
2. Why is creating a prioritized maintenance plan essential, especially in distressed communities?
3. List at least two ways to collect resident feedback in a stable community.
4. What's the difference between proactive and preventive maintenance?
5. Why is it important to communicate updates about policy changes transparently to residents?
6. What is succession planning, and why is it crucial for well-functioning communities?
7. Give two examples of how technology can enhance security or convenience in a community.
8. Describe how neglecting to update governing documents can negatively impact a community.
9. Why are reserve studies essential, particularly for long-term financial planning?
10. Explain why improvement should be viewed as an ongoing process, not a destination.

The answers are at the end of this chapter

Case Study: From Crisis To Stability (Distressed Community)

Oceanview Condominiums was on the brink of collapse. Decades of deferred maintenance had left buildings with leaking roofs, cracked foundations, and an overall air of decay. Morale was just as bad — residents were furious, blaming each other and the overwhelmed volunteer board. Finances were a black hole of unpaid dues, overdue vendor bills, and a sense of impending doom.

Then came Sarah, a new board member with an accounting background. She refused to let Oceanview fail. First, she demanded a thorough financial audit. The results were eye-opening: years of overspending, lax collection practices, and a total lack of budgeting discipline. Next, Sarah spearheaded a collections crackdown. Some residents needed payment plans, others faced legal action, but the message was clear: non-payment wouldn't be tolerated.

The board knew they were in over their heads. They partnered with a property management firm specializing in distressed community turnarounds. Together, they created a bare-bones budget. Fancy landscaping was out, fixing hazardous balconies was in. It wasn't popular, but it was necessary. Sarah held town-hall-style meetings, not sugarcoating things. "If we don't fix this, we'll lose our homes—literally and financially," she warned. Residents, used to neglect, were skeptical at first. But then came the engineer's report, prioritizing repairs: safety hazards first, then what would prevent further deterioration and hopefully even raise property values.

With professional guidance, they secured a modest loan to tackle the most critical issues. Progress was slow at first. Some residents complained about any expense. But as the worst problems were fixed, and the financials stabilized, a shift happened. People started volunteering to help with smaller projects—painting, weeding. It took years, but Oceanview was clawing its way back. They weren't just financially sound anymore, they were a community pulling together, a place people were starting to feel proud to call home.

What Could They Have Done Differently?

- **Acted sooner:** Years of neglect created a crisis. Regular maintenance assessments and proactive budgeting could have prevented the extent of the damage and financial disarray.
- **Communication from the start:** Transparency about the problems and the need for tough measures might have gained more resident support earlier.

Board Member Voice: Sarah: "When I saw the state of things, it was scary, but also a wake-up call. We couldn't wish problems away. Someone had to step up, even if it meant being unpopular for a while."

Question for the Reader: Is your community avoiding difficult conversations or delaying essential repairs, creating bigger problems for the future?

Key Takeaways

- **Don't ignore red flags:** Financial distress and building decay fester over time. Early intervention is crucial.
- **Transparency builds trust:** Residents are more likely to accept tough decisions when they fully understand the crisis.
- **Seek professional help:** Distressed communities often need outside expertise (accountants, managers,

attorneys) to get back on track.

Case Study: Small Change, Big Impact (Stable Community)

Greenwood Estates was a pleasant place to live. Finances were stable, the grounds well-kept, but something was missing. There was little sense of community; people kept to themselves. The board, while competent, had fallen into a routine. A few new board members decided it was time to shake things up.

They started with a resident survey, asking not just about satisfaction with services, but what people wished was different. The top answer? A desire to connect with neighbors. Armed with this, the board got to work. They created a simple monthly newsletter, highlighting community news, resident profiles, and upcoming events. Next was a summer potluck at the clubhouse – casual and inviting. To encourage a greener and prettier Greenwood, they formed a "Gardening Buddies" group, sharing tips and pooling resources.

At first, participation wasn't overwhelming, but those who took part were enthusiastic. These events became seeds for connections. Seeing the momentum, the board empowered a newly formed social committee, led by residents with a knack for planning. A winter holiday decorating contest sparked friendly competition. The summer block party, with games and food trucks, became a can't-miss tradition.

Word spread. Greenwood wasn't just a collection of houses anymore, it was a neighborhood with a vibe. Young families were drawn in, seeing playmates for their kids and a place to put down roots. Property values began a steady climb, due not to fancy amenities, but that precious sense of belonging. The changes were gradual, driven by the residents themselves. The board provided a spark, but the ongoing success was owed to the newfound community spirit they had nurtured.

What Could They Have Done Differently?

- **Going Bigger Sooner:** The board could've been bolder, risking a flop with a bigger initial event. However, the small, low-budget successes built trust and attracted early champions.
- **More Focus Groups:** Beyond the survey, focus groups could've gone deeper into the specific kinds of activities residents wanted, perhaps uncovering untapped interests.

Board Member Voice: "Honestly, at first, I wasn't sold on this 'social stuff'. Seemed like extra work for little gain. But watching those faces at the potluck, people laughing who barely knew each other before... that's when I got it." - Mark, Greenwood Estates Board Treasurer

Question for the Reader: Could relatively simple, low-cost initiatives make a significant difference in your community's sense of connection? What might be some first steps to explore?

Key Takeaways

- **Resident Input is Key:** Surveys or focus groups reveal what your community *actually* wants, not what the board assumes they want.
- **Small Starts, Big Potential:** Don't be afraid of modest beginnings. Enthusiasm is contagious!
- **Empower Committees:** Social events thrive when driven by passionate residents, not just overloaded board members.
- **Don't Underestimate "Soft" Benefits:** A sense of belonging enhances quality of life and has tangible value

(attracting buyers, boosting property values).

Case Study: Tech Upgrade - Winning Over The Skeptics (Well-Functioning Community)

Sunset Hills prided itself on its manicured lawns and quiet charm. Yet, the board knew they couldn't ignore the world around them. Petty theft was on the rise, package deliveries were haphazard, and the single gate with a passcode felt outdated. They envisioned a tech upgrade: key-fob building access, strategically placed cameras, and a package room with digital notifications to residents. The potential benefits were clear: enhanced safety, reduced package theft, and the kind of modern convenience younger buyers increasingly expected.

However, Sunset Hills had a significant population of older residents, some less tech-savvy and wary of the expense. The board knew they had to build consensus. Their strategy was multi-pronged:

- **Informational Workshops:** They held town hall-style meetings with tech vendors present. Instead of just talking benefits, they had residents try out fob systems, see how user-friendly package notification apps were, and watch demos of how camera systems deterred crime.
- **Show, Don't Just Tell:** They partnered with a similar, slightly larger community that had already made the tech transition. A group of Sunset Hills residents took a "field trip" to see the system in action and talk to residents who were initially hesitant but were now converts.
- **Cost Transparency & Phasing:** The board openly presented projected costs and sought multiple bids to get the best deal. They also broke the project into phases (security gates first, package room later) to ease any

sticker shock and allow for adjustments based on initial results.

It took time, and there were still some holdouts. But, by patiently addressing concerns, demonstrating value, and showing the tech wasn't as scary as some thought, the majority of residents got on board. The upgrade went smoothly. Now, Sunset Hills boasts about its safe, convenient community, attracting new residents while keeping long-time owners feeling secure and valued.

What Could They Have Done Differently?

- **More proactive outreach to tech-resistant residents:** Offer one-on-one, personalized tutorials to ease fears and build tech comfort before major decisions.
- **Pilot program:** Start with a small-scale test (cameras in one building, or fob entry at a secondary gate), proving the concept and allowing residents to experience the benefits.

Board Member Voice: "At first, I was hesitant too. We're proud of our traditional feel, and change can be unsettling. But seeing those crime stats, and how unhappy residents were with package issues…it wasn't just about 'gadgets,' it was about protecting our community and the life we cherish here." – Margaret, Board President

Question for the Reader: Is your community hesitant about a change that could bring long-term benefits? How could you use a similar strategy of information, demonstration, and phased implementation to win them over?

Key Takeaways

- Change, even positive change, can stir up anxieties in some residents. Empathy with their concerns is just as important as highlighting the benefits.
- Don't dismiss those who are tech-wary. Offer support,

training, and opportunities to "try before they buy" to build confidence.
- "Show, don't tell" is powerful. Seeing other communities, vendor demos, or real-world examples often seals the deal.
- Transparency about costs and willingness to consider phasing projects helps manage financial concerns.

Case Study: When Bylaws Get Dusty (All Communities)

Whispering Pines Condominiums, built in 1982, had a peaceful name but a combative reality. Their governing documents hadn't been seriously revised since their creation. What was once a quiet, mostly retiree community had changing demographics. Suddenly, arguments flared over issues those old bylaws never mentioned:

- **The Airbnb Boom:** Units turned into short-term rentals, bringing strangers and noise. Some owners liked the extra income, others felt it ruined the residential feel.
- **Tech Wars:** Giant satellite dishes sprouted on balconies. Rules mentioned "aesthetic appearance," but were those eyesores legal?
- **Charging Disputes:** With electric vehicles on the rise, who paid for charging station installation? Could someone with a garage outlet charge their neighbors a fee?

The overwhelmed board was caught between residents yelling, "it doesn't say I can't!" and others demanding action. They realized an overhaul was essential, not optional. First step: Hiring an attorney specializing in condominium law. This wasn't cheap, but better than endless lawsuits down the line.

The board held multiple town hall meetings, expecting pushback. Surprisingly, most residents were just frustrated by the ambiguity. Workshops helped identify the biggest pain points and brainstorm fair solutions. It took a year of wrangling, but the revised bylaws addressed:

- **Short-term Rentals:** A balance was struck – some permitted, but with time limits and owner responsibility for guest behavior.
- **Visual Standards:** Balcony use was clarified, allowing for smaller, discreet satellite dishes where cable access was poor.
- **Charging Stations:** The community would install a few, with usage fees to recoup costs over time.

The final vote to adopt the new bylaws passed overwhelmingly. Whispering Pines still had occasional disputes, but now, there were clear rules and procedures. The board gained respect, and residents stopped feeling like their community was stuck in the past.

What Could They Have Done Differently?

- **Proactive Updates:** Ideally, bylaws should be reviewed every few years, proactively addressing changes in resident needs and technology. Whispering Pines let them get seriously outdated, creating a crisis.

Board Member Voice: "We thought, 'if it ain't broke, don't fix it.' Well, things break when you ignore them! Should've tackled this sooner."

Question for the Reader: When was the last time *your* community thoroughly revised its governing documents? Are there potential time bombs lurking?

Key Takeaways:

- **Outdated bylaws fuel conflict and make communities vulnerable.** Rules need to evolve with the times.
- **Resident input is vital when making significant changes.** Workshops and communication build understanding and support.
- **Investing in expert legal advice is wise.** It helps craft enforceable rules and prevents costly mistakes.

Case Study: The Power Of Planning (Long-Term Finance)

Lakeview Towers had always prided itself on its well-maintained grounds and amenities. Residents assumed their monthly dues covered everything, including setting aside money for future repairs. For years, the board had relied on a reserve study done when the buildings were relatively new. But time marches on, and Lakeview wasn't getting any younger.

Then came the double whammy. A series of storms caused major roof leaks throughout the complex. Just as repairs were wrapping up, the aging central HVAC system gave out, leaving residents sweltering in an unexpected heatwave. The board tapped into their reserve fund... and found it woefully inadequate.

A hastily arranged special assessment caused an uproar. Residents who thought they'd planned responsibly felt betrayed. The new board, elected amidst the chaos, knew they had to regain trust and prevent this from ever happening again. They made long-term financial planning a top priority.

Their first step was commissioning a comprehensive reserve study from a reputable engineering firm. This detailed report didn't just list future expenses – it laid out what was needed *when*, helping them visualize the aging of their buildings. Next, they worked with a financial advisor to create a multi-year reserve contribution plan. This involved modest but regular dues increases, phasing in the needed funds.

Communication was key. The board held town halls, explaining why reserves had been low and how their new plan ensured future stability. They used visual presentations to break down complex numbers. While some grumbled about higher dues, most understood. Lakeview now has a predictable, well-funded plan for its future. Residents sleep easy, knowing their biggest asset – their home – is protected.

What Could They Have Done Differently?

- **Proactive reserve study updates:** Relying on an outdated study is a major risk. Regular professional assessments (ideally every few years) would have alerted them to growing shortfalls.
- **Gradual adjustments:** A big surprise is always worse. Smaller, gradual dues increases over time would have been easier for residents to accept.

Board Member Voice: "Honestly, we fell into the 'out of sight, out of mind' trap. The buildings looked fine, so we took the reserves for granted. Now we know better!"

Question for the Reader: When was your community's last reserve study? Is it time for a refresh to ensure your reserves are actually aligned with future needs?

Key Takeaways

- Reserve studies are not a one-and-done deal. They are a vital, ongoing planning tool.
- Don't let complacency lead to financial crisis. Proactive budgeting protects your community and your residents' investments.
- Transparency with residents regarding long-term financial planning builds trust and avoids nasty surprises.

Case Study: Building A Future Board (Succession Planning)

Rosewood Village was thriving, but its board of directors had a looming concern: they were all long-serving retirees. While their experience was invaluable, they knew the community's future depended on attracting fresh leadership.

Linda, the board president, had seen other communities stagnate or fall into conflict when long-term boards clung to control. She proposed a proactive approach. First, they launched a "Shadow a Board Member" program. Interested residents could attend meetings as observers, ask questions, and gain insight into the decision-making process. This demystified board service and revealed the commitment required.

However, Rosewood's bylaws had a residency requirement – board candidates had to be owners for several years. This unintentionally shut out newer residents who might have valuable skills. Working with their attorney, the board carefully revised the bylaws, balancing the desire for experience with the need for fresh perspectives.

The changes weren't an instant revolution, but word-of-mouth spread. Sarah, a marketing professional new to Rosewood, attended a few meetings. Impressed by the board's dedication, she cautiously offered her social media expertise to revamp their outdated community newsletter. The board welcomed her input. A few years later, Sarah was elected board treasurer, modernizing their budget tracking.

Other new leaders emerged – an accountant, a project

manager, even a tech-savvy college student with a passion for sustainability. The "old guard" didn't vanish. They transitioned into advisory roles, mentoring their successors.

Rosewood's board became a diverse and dynamic team. The smooth transitions enhanced stability, and the blend of experience and innovation led to exciting new initiatives. The community gained a reputation for both its welcoming atmosphere and its forward-thinking approach – a prime example of how succession planning ensures long-term success.

What Could They Have Done Differently?

- **Started Even Earlier:** Succession planning is best when it's an ongoing process, not something done out of a looming sense of urgency.
- **More Formalized Mentorship:** While the "shadow" program was good, pairing new potential leaders with specific board members for structured mentorship could boost their preparation.

Board Member Voice: "We take our responsibility to the community incredibly seriously. Yes, we've been here a long time, but Rosewood isn't about us – it's about making sure it thrives long after we're gone." - Linda, Board President

Question for the Reader: Does your board have a formal or informal succession plan in place? If not, what could the first small step be to begin the process?

Key Takeaways

- Succession planning isn't about getting rid of experienced board members, but about ensuring a pipeline of future leaders.
- Balancing experience with new energy and skills is crucial for long-term success.
- Mentorship and transparency attract potential leaders

and make transitions smoother.
- Small steps, like bylaw revisions or shadow programs, can have a significant impact over time.

Test Your Knowledge! Answers

1. **Symptoms of financial distress:** Budget deficits, significant unpaid dues (arrears), difficulty paying vendors.

2. **Prioritized maintenance plan:** Distressed communities often have many urgent repairs. A plan helps focus limited funds on the most critical issues, preventing safety hazards and further costly damage.

3. **Resident feedback methods:** Surveys (tailored questions), focus groups, suggestion boxes (physical and digital).

4. **Proactive vs. preventive:**

   - Proactive: Addressing issues *before* they become emergencies (hiring professionals for building assessments).
   - Preventive: Routine maintenance to avoid problems (gutter cleaning, filter changes).

5. **Transparent communication about policy changes:** Builds trust, reduces the chance of residents feeling blindsided, and helps avoid misunderstandings.

6. **Succession planning:** Mentoring interested residents and creating leadership pipelines ensures smooth board transitions and preserves institutional knowledge.

7. **Technology for security/convenience:**

    o   Secured access control systems, smart cameras
    o   Package delivery lockers, community communication apps
8. **Neglecting governing documents:** Outdated rules can be unfair, unenforceable, and may not address current needs (like technology use or changing resident demographics).

9. **Importance of reserve studies:** These professional assessments project future major repair/replacement costs, allowing for proactive budgeting and avoiding the need for sudden, large special assessments.

10. **Improvement as a journey:** Communities evolve, regulations change, and resident needs shift. Boards that embrace continuous learning and adaptation position their communities for long-term success.

CHAPTER 8: WORKING WITH PROFESSIONALS

Introduction

Managing a condominium effectively is no simple task. Your board's commitment is vital, but you also need specialized knowledge to handle legal matters, ensure financial health, and tackle everyday community challenges. While you hold ultimate decision-making authority, professionals like attorneys, accountants, and management companies offer the expertise to guide those choices.

This chapter focuses on getting the most out of these partnerships. Strong collaboration is crucial. Consider this example: A community was planning separate wood replacement and painting projects. Their management company suggested using one contractor for both jobs. The board agreed, leading to smoother logistics, less hassle, and a superior result.

Successful condominium management is a team effort. Never feel like your board carries the burden alone. Your professional partners are there to support you. The key is understanding what they bring to the table and how to work hand-in-hand for the community's benefit. Ask yourselves: Are we maximizing our professional relationships? Is there room to improve our teamwork?

"No surprises" is a good rule. Contracts with professionals should clearly outline potential additional fees or charges beyond their base rate.

The Role Of A Management Company

What is a Management Company?

Think of a management company as a specialized team you hire to handle the day-to-day tasks of running your condominium smoothly. Importantly, the board stays in the driver's seat, setting the direction, while they handle the details. They're a powerful tool to help your community succeed.

Typical Responsibilities

- **Daily Operations:** Answering resident requests, finding reliable contractors, and keeping common areas in good shape.
- **Financial Management:** Collecting fees, paying bills, creating clear reports, and helping with the budget.
- **Administrative Tasks:** Organizing meetings, keeping records, and communicating with residents.
- **Rule Enforcement:** Addressing issues according to your policies, working with the board on any potential fines or actions.

Why Hire a Management Company

- **Expert Help:** They know the ins and outs of condominium law, management practices, and how to avoid common problems.
- **Saves You Time:** Volunteer board members can focus on the community's future, not everyday tasks.
- **Reduced Risk:** Their experience and insurance can help protect the board and the association from legal trouble.

Picking the Right Partner

- **Essentials:** Check their reputation, references, size (do they fit your community well?), services offered, and if their fees are clear.
- **Deeper Questions:**
  - Do they make you feel valued, or like just another client?
  - Do they truly understand condominiums, not just general property management?
  - How do they manage resident requests to avoid communication breakdowns?
  - Can you easily speak with decision-makers when you need to?
  - Do they solve problems before they happen, not just react?

Go Beyond the Sales Talk

- **Visit Other Communities:** See how places they manage actually look and feel.
- **Test Their Response:** How fast do they answer questions, and who handles issues outside regular hours?
- **Understand Their Reports:** Are they clear and easy to use, or confusing?

Bottom Line: Choose a company committed to a partnership that makes your community stronger in the long run.

Check a professional's online presence. Reviews, their website, and any articles they've written can offer insights into their communication style and approach.

"Good fit" isn't just about expertise. If a professional's personality clashes with your board, it will hinder effective collaboration.

Example: A condo inherited a foreclosed unit that sat empty, causing problems. Their management company stepped up, got the unit fixed, found a realtor, and it sold quickly –

something the board couldn't have handled alone.

Even Self-Managed Condos Benefit: Sometimes, fully self-managed condominiums still use management companies for specific things, like complex financial reports, to make life easier.

Checklist:

- **Assess Community Needs:**
    - List current pain points in management (maintenance, communication, financials, etc.)
    - Prioritize areas where a management company could provide the most value.
- **Understanding Management Models:**
    - Research full-service management vs. specific task delegation (e.g., only accounting).
    - Identify the model that best aligns with your community's needs and budget.
- **Define Your Ideal Company:**
    - Size: Boutique vs. large firm?
    - Niche: Do they specialize in your type of community?
    - Values: What company culture resonates with your board?

Timeline:

- **Week 1-2:** Needs assessment within the board
- **Week 3-4:** Research management company models
- **Week 5-6:** Draft a list of "must-haves" in a management company

Action Steps

- Consult with similar communities to learn from their experiences with management companies.
- Attend industry conferences or webinars to gain insights into the latest management trends.

Selecting And Managing Attorneys, Accountants, And Other Specialists

Beyond the Boardroom: When to Call in the Experts

Your board handles a vast range of responsibilities, but sometimes, specialized knowledge is essential. Here's a breakdown of the areas where outside professionals often provide invaluable support to condominium communities:

- **Legal Matters: Finding the Right Attorney:** When facing governing document revisions, complex contracts, collections, or disputes, an attorney specializing in condominium law is crucial. They guide you through the legal complexities of these situations.
- **Accounting & Financial Reporting:** Audits, financial statement preparation, tax compliance, and budget forecasting can be overwhelming. A qualified accountant, particularly one experienced with condominiums, brings clarity and ensures your association's financial health.
- **Insurance Advisors:** Choosing the right insurance coverage and navigating claims can be a headache. An insurance advisor helps you assess your needs, find the best policies, and assists with the claims process if trouble arises.
- **Engineering & Structural Assessments:** Major repairs like roofing or balcony projects require specialized expertise. Engineers or structural specialists ensure projects are done correctly, provide preventative maintenance evaluations, and help preserve your community's assets.
- **Other Potential Specialists:** Depending on

your community's unique situation, you might also benefit from environmental consultants, reserve study professionals (to aid with long-term financial planning), or construction defect experts.

Condominium law is complex! Even experienced attorneys may need to consult niche specialists within the field for issues like construction defects or unique governing documents.

Finding the Right Fit: Guidance for Boards

- **Tap Your Network:** Seek referrals from other condominiums, your management company, and industry organizations like the CAI (Community Associations Institute).
- **The Interview:** Emphasize the importance of experience working specifically with condominiums. Inquire about their communication style and problem-solving approach.
- **Verify Credentials:** Check their licensing (attorneys with the bar association, CPAs), professional standing, and any relevant industry certifications.
- **Fee Transparency:** Understand their fee structure (hourly, flat rates, retainers) along with billing increments and potential additional costs.

Building Successful Partnerships

- **Designated Contact:** Appoint a specific board member or manager as the main point of contact for each professional.
- **Be Prepared:** Provide clear project instructions and all necessary background information upfront.
- **Balanced Oversight:** Establish a regular update schedule, respecting the professional's time while ensuring the project stays on track.

- **Trust and Transparency:** Recognize their expertise, be open to their recommendations, and maintain open communication from your side as well.

Additional Tips

- **Formalize it:** Ensure contracts clearly outline the scope of work, responsibilities, and fee arrangements.
- **Regular Reviews:** Periodically assess your satisfaction with each professional's services.
- **Easy to Understand:** Insist on clear, jargon-free reports and communications that your board can easily understand and act upon.

Ask about contingency plans. What happens if your regular contact at the firm is ill or unavailable?

Checklist

- **Identify Essential Services:**
    - Legal (HOA law expertise)
    - Accounting (HOA-specific)
    - Insurance broker (if not included with a management company)
    - Potential future specialists (e.g., engineers, reserve study experts)
- **Get Referrals:**
    - Ask your management company (if you have one).
    - Network with other communities.
    - Consult industry association lists of professionals.
- **Interviewing Tips:**
    - Ask for case studies relevant to your community type.
    - Inquire about communication style/frequency.
    - Get detailed fee breakdowns.

Timeline:

- **Week 1-2:** Prioritize your immediate and potential future

needs.
- **Week 3-6:** Gather referrals and narrow down the candidate list.
- **Week 7-10:** Conduct interviews.

Action Steps

- Check references thoroughly! Talk to current or past clients of the specialists you consider.
- Develop clear contracts outlining scope of work, responsibilities, and communication protocols.

Defining Expectations And Ensuring Effective Collaboration

Setting Clear Expectations for Success

Strong partnerships with professionals aren't just about their expertise, but also about clear communication and mutual respect. This leads to better decisions, saves your board time, and reduces risks for your association.

The Importance of Open Communication

Share expectations early and often with any professional you engage. Don't wait, harbor frustrations, and then explode later. This is ineffective and damages the relationship. Professionals can't adjust their approach if they don't know what you need, so be proactive in sharing timely feedback.

Project Outlines: Even Simple Tasks Need Them

Detailed project outlines are crucial. Include the specific issue, the desired outcome, and relevant background. In other words, tell them exactly what you need. Consider the saying "garbage in, garbage out" – clear instructions are vital for the professional to deliver what you expect.

Break It Down, Set Deadlines

For larger projects, break them into manageable steps with estimated deadlines. Coordinate with the professional to set mutually agreeable timelines. This helps the board track progress and allows the professional to manage their workload accordingly. Remember, you can't hold them accountable for deadlines they weren't aware of!

Establish Communication Channels

How will you communicate with each other? Emails, phone calls, scheduled meetings? Determine the best methods for routine updates versus urgent matters. Also, discuss realistic expectations for response times to inquiries, acknowledging that professionals may have other clients too. Flexibility is key, as unexpected situations may require adjusting your usual communication methods.

Regular Feedback and Reviews

Offer timely feedback throughout the project – both positive and constructive. Don't just save it all for the end. Formal reviews are also important to assess overall satisfaction, identify areas for improvement, and renew/adjust contracts if needed.

Feedback is a two-way street. Be open to hearing constructive criticism from professionals about the board's processes as well.

Finding the Right Attorney (and Other Professionals)

Seek out attorneys who offer clear, concise guidance. Lengthy, confusing written responses without specific recommendations are unacceptable. Address these issues directly with your legal counsel.

Building Trust and Respect

- **Recognize expertise:** Value the professional's knowledge and treat them as a true partner.
- **Transparency:** Open communication and information sharing build trust.
- **Address Issues Promptly:** Raise concerns professionally to avoid problems festering.

Clear timelines benefit everyone. Professionals can manage their workload more effectively when boards are upfront about deadlines.

Don't ghost your professionals! A quick email acknowledging a report or update shows you value their time.

Additional Considerations

Ask yourself these key questions about any professional: Will they work collaboratively with your board? Do they focus on sharing expertise, or on taking control?

Examples

- **Insurance Dispute:** A resident attempted to make a claim on their association's policy for a flooded basement that was finished after the initial sale. The insurance advisor guided the board, explaining resident responsibility, and the board successfully pushed back on the resident's claim.

- **Garage Licensing:** A community lost track of who held licenses for separate garages. Their attorney proposed a solution, which the board accepted due to the attorney's clear and respectful guidance.

Checklist

- **Board Responsibilities:**
    - What does the board retain control of, even with a management company?
    - How often will the board and management company meet?
- **Communication Protocols:**
    - Preferred channels (email, management portal, phone)
    - Response time expectations
    - Resident communication procedures
- **Performance Metrics:**
    - Financial health indicators

    - Resident satisfaction surveys
    - Project completion timelines

Timeline (assuming a management company is already in place)

- **Month 1:** Initial collaborative meeting to set baseline expectations.
- **Month 2-3:** Establish regular communication channels and reporting formats.
- **Ongoing:** Quarterly or semi-annual reviews for adjustments/feedback.

Action Steps:

- Avoid micromanagement. Trust your chosen professionals while setting clear oversight.
- Provide timely feedback, both positive and constructive, for continuous improvement.

Conclusion: The Power Of Professional Partnerships

Working with professionals has major benefits. They bring specialized knowledge, improving your decision-making. They also reduce your community's risk by ensuring you follow best practices and legal guidelines. Plus, it saves your board valuable time, allowing you to focus on the community's future, not reinventing the wheel on everyday tasks.

However, boards need to take an active role. It's a partnership, not handing over control. You should always question, seek clarification, and leverage your professionals' expertise. Remember, the board is ultimately in charge. Successful partnerships are built on clear expectations, timely feedback, open communication, and mutual respect.

By actively partnering with excellent professionals, you empower yourselves to take your community to new heights. This collaborative approach ensures the best possible outcomes and helps your community achieve its long-term goals.

Document everything! Meeting minutes, important emails, and project updates protect both the board and the professional in case of miscommunication.

Test Your Knowledge!

1. When hiring an attorney, what's the most important question to ask besides their hourly rate?
2. Why is a detailed project outline essential even for tasks that seem simple?
3. What's one way to build trust with a professional?
4. If you have an urgent issue to raise with a professional, what's the best communication method?
5. Why are formal reviews with professionals important, even when things are going well?
6. What does it mean for professionals to be "collaborative" with the board?
7. Give an example of timely feedback a board might offer to a professional.
8. What's the risk of a board choosing a professional solely based on the lowest fee proposal?
9. Why is it important to agree on response times with a professional?
10. How can a board tell if a professional respects their expertise and decision-making authority?

The answers are at the end of this chapter

Case Study: The Bylaw Blunder

Greenwood Condominiums was a charming community with a close-knit feel. Most board members had served for years, priding themselves on maintaining harmony within the association. Their bylaws, however, were a relic of the past – a dense document full of antiquated legal jargon no one truly understood. The board figured, "if it ain't broke, don't fix it," until it was...

The trouble started with Mrs. Jenkins' beloved magnolia tree. Its branches extended over Mr. Smith's fence, causing leaves to clutter his meticulously manicured lawn. Mr. Smith, a stickler for rules, searched for guidance in the bylaws, but found nothing specific about trees or property lines. The ensuing argument escalated, with both neighbors demanding the board take their side.

Feeling out of their depth, the board realized a vague set of bylaws was a recipe for disaster. They contacted a local attorney, but his long-winded explanations and focus on billable hours only added to their confusion. Desperate, they reached out to a fellow board member at a neighboring condo for advice. This connection proved invaluable. They were referred to an attorney specializing in condominium law, known for his ability to translate legalese into practical terms.

This attorney took a different approach. He patiently reviewed their bylaws, pinpointing ambiguities and outdated sections. He even held a short workshop for the board, focusing on the areas most likely to cause conflict. The board members felt like a lightbulb went on! Armed with this knowledge, they actively participated in revising the bylaws, ensuring they reflected the community's current needs.

Greenwood Condominiums now has a clear, modernized set of bylaws. The magnolia incident was resolved amicably (a compromise on trimming was reached), and future disputes are far less likely thanks to the proactive work of the board and their collaborative attorney.

What Could They Have Done Differently?

- **Proactive Review and Updates:** Bylaws shouldn't be treated as static documents. Regular reviews with legal counsel specializing in community associations would have caught potential issues before they escalated.
- **Prioritized Clarity:** Seeking out legal advice focused on translating complex legalities into practical terms for the board would have prevented confusion and feelings of being overwhelmed.

Board Member Voice: "Honestly, those bylaws were like a foreign language. We just hoped for the best, but that magnolia situation really opened our eyes."

Question for the Reader: When was the last time your association's governing documents had a thorough review? Are they clear enough for everyone to understand and apply consistently?

Key Takeaways

- **Bylaws are not "set it and forget it":** Community needs and laws evolve. Proactive review keeps your governing documents relevant and effective.
- **Clarity is key:** Investing in legal counsel that prioritizes plain-language explanations empowers boards to make informed decisions.
- **Prevention is better than cure:** Addressing outdated or ambiguous bylaws proactively helps avoid costly disputes

and strained relationships within the community.

Case Study: The Missing Money Mystery

The board of Sunnyside Condos prided themselves on responsible financial management. So, when their quarterly report showed reserve funds alarmingly below what they anticipated, shockwaves went through the boardroom. Fear gripped them – had there been theft? Perhaps a resident, or even a disgruntled former board member, was siphoning off their hard-earned savings?

Their veteran property manager, sensing the rising panic, calmly suggested a less nefarious explanation might be at play. She recommended a forensic audit by a CPA firm specializing in condominium finances. The board, while skeptical, saw the wisdom in this approach before launching accusations.

The CPA arrived, armed with spreadsheets and a meticulous eye. Days turned into weeks as they scrutinized bank statements, invoices, and the community's accounting software. Finally, they delivered their findings. There had been no embezzlement. The culprit was far more insidious: a simple data entry error made years ago. A misplaced decimal had thrown off calculations related to reserve contributions. Over time, this seemingly minor mistake had compounded into a major discrepancy.

The board was equal parts relieved and embarrassed. No one had stolen their funds, but their own oversight had let this problem fester. The CPA didn't just leave them with bad news; they provided a detailed plan for correcting the records, adjusting future reserve calculations, and implementing a system of double-checks. They also ran a training session on understanding financial reports, ensuring future boards at Sunnyside could spot issues early.

While not the scandal they'd feared, this incident served as a powerful lesson for Sunnyside Condos. It reinforced the importance of specialized expertise, proactive audits, and why even well-meaning boards must be vigilant when it comes to their community's finances.

What Could They Have Done Differently?

- **Instituted regular audits:** Even without suspicion of wrongdoing, periodic forensic audits by a qualified CPA could have caught the data error much earlier, minimizing its impact.
- **Implemented stronger financial controls:** Double-checks and review processes before major reports are finalized might have detected the misplaced decimal.
- **Prioritized board financial training:** Greater understanding of financial statements and reserve calculations could have empowered the board to identify anomalies sooner.

Board Member Mindset: "We thought we were doing everything right. I was so angry, ready to call the police! If someone hadn't suggested we get an expert opinion... well, it could have ruined someone's life over a stupid typo!"

Question to Ponder: Does your own board have the systems and knowledge in place to prevent a similar situation, or is a small error waiting to snowball into a major problem?

Key Takeaways

- **Don't let pride blind you to vulnerabilities:** Even well-run communities can benefit from independent, expert scrutiny.
- **Regular reviews are crucial:** Mistakes happen; proactive audits help you find them before they become crises.

- **Invest in knowledge:** A financially literate board is a community's best defense against unforeseen problems.

Case Study: Communication Breakdown

Riverbend Condos faced a nightmare scenario when severe storms caused a significant roof leak in several buildings. Water poured into units, damaging residents' belongings and creating a slip hazard in the common areas. The board scrambled to contact their insurance carrier, who promised a prompt adjuster visit.

The adjuster arrived, took some photos, and informed the board that the damage appeared to fall within their policy coverage. Relieved, the board then sought bids from several roofing contractors. But the process stalled. Communication between the board, their chosen contractor, and the insurance adjuster became a tangled mess. They bickered over the scope of work – was it just patching, or a full replacement? Approval for the repairs dragged on for weeks, during which time the leaks worsened.

Tensions rose. Residents were furious with the delays, the board felt powerless, and the contractor was exasperated by the lack of clarity. Just as it seemed things couldn't get worse, a board member remembered a presentation they'd attended on the benefits of insurance advisors. Desperate, they reached out to a specialist recommended by a neighboring condominium association.

The insurance advisor arrived and swiftly took control. They reviewed the policy, the adjuster's notes, and the contractor's bid. With their knowledge of the industry, they identified where miscommunications had occurred. They facilitated a meeting with all involved parties, clarified the scope of the claim, and smoothed out the approval process. Finally, with everyone on the same page, repairs began. The work was completed efficiently, and further damage was prevented. Riverbend Condos learned a hard lesson about the importance of clear communication channels, especially when dealing with insurance claims.

What Could They Have Done Differently?

- **Bring in an insurance expert early:** Waiting until the situation was dire meant hasty decisions and added stress. Having an advisor on board from the start could have prevented many misunderstandings.
- **Establish a single point of contact:** Designating one board member to handle all communication with the adjuster and contractor would have streamlined the process.
- **Document everything:** Keeping detailed records of conversations and agreements would have provided clarity and accountability for all parties.

Board Member Voice: "We felt like we were in over our heads. We know condos, not insurance policies. If only we'd realized sooner how much we didn't know."

Question for the Reader: When facing complex situations outside your area of expertise, do you have a process for identifying and bringing in the necessary support?

Key Takeaways

- Complex claims often require specialized knowledge. Don't hesitate to seek expert guidance early in the process.
- Centralized communication channels prevent confusion and ensure important information isn't lost.
- Careful documentation is essential for protecting your interests and preventing future disputes.

Case Study: The Power Of Proactive Planning

The board of Oakwood Condos knew their aging balconies were a ticking time bomb. The wrought iron railings showed rust, and some of the wood supports felt concerningly soft. However, money was tight, and they feared a major assessment if repairs became an emergency. They decided that putting their heads in the sand wasn't leadership and instead sought professional guidance.

A fellow board member from a neighboring community recommended a structural engineer who specialized in condominiums. The engineer conducted a thorough inspection, providing a detailed report that surprised the Oakwood board. Yes, repairs were needed, but the situation wasn't as dire as they had feared. With this knowledge, they had leverage.

Armed with the engineer's report, the board confidently approached contractors. It was the off-season for balcony work, meaning they secured competitive bids. Oakwood also phased the repairs over two years, easing the financial impact further. Residents were inconvenienced, but having the work proactively scheduled on their terms minimized complaints compared to dealing with an emergency closure.

Months later, Oakwood Condos boasted balconies that not only looked beautiful but were structurally sound. Because they sought expert advice and acted early, they achieved this with less financial burden and stress than they had anticipated. The lesson stuck with them: proactive maintenance, done in partnership with the right professionals, often saves money and headaches in the long run.

What Could They Have Done Differently?

The board could have sought professional advice even sooner. While their fear of uncovering a major issue was understandable, delaying action can result in a scenario where fewer options are available with potentially higher costs in the long run.

Board of Directors Member Voice: "Honestly, we were dreading the whole balcony situation. We figured it was going to be a financial nightmare that the residents would revolt over."

Question for the Reader: Are there areas within your own community where you suspect a problem might be developing? Is it better to face the issue now, or risk having it unexpectedly worsen?

Key Takeaways

- Ignoring a potential problem doesn't make it go away; often, it just makes it worse.
- Proactiveness allows for greater control – you can schedule repairs on your timeline and budget strategically.
- Seeking expert opinions early gives you valuable information to make informed decisions.
- Well-timed proactive maintenance projects can actually improve resident satisfaction compared to emergency repairs.

Case Study: Seeking A Second Opinion – When

"Good Enough" Isn't Good Enough

Lakeside Condos, a mid-sized community, had been locked in a costly construction defect lawsuit for years. The original developer had cut corners, leading to water intrusion issues that damaged several units. Their initial attorney, while experienced, seemed weary of the protracted battle. When a settlement offer finally came, the attorney strongly encouraged the board to accept it.

The dollar figure looked sizable, but something didn't sit right with the board. The terms included broad language that could release the developer from future liability, even for undiscovered defects. Sensing their responsibility to the entire community, the board hesitated. They decided it was worth investing in a second opinion. Through a referral, they found another attorney specializing in condominium construction litigation.

This new attorney had a fresh perspective. She meticulously reviewed the settlement offer, highlighting clauses that might restrict Lakeside's ability to pursue future claims if more damage was found later. She also identified potential weaknesses in the developer's case, suggesting that Lakeside might have more leverage than their initial attorney had led them to believe.

Armed with this knowledge, the board felt confident in reopening negotiations. The new attorney skillfully argued their points, emphasizing the potential for additional, as-yet-unseen damage the settlement could leave the condo association liable for. Ultimately, Lakeside secured a significantly larger settlement amount and included a clause allowing them to pursue additional claims should further defects be discovered in the future.

Key Takeaway: Sometimes even experienced professionals can

be influenced by factors like case fatigue. Boards have a duty to act in their community's best interest. A second opinion can uncover overlooked options and ensure the board makes the most informed decision possible.

What Could They Have Done Differently?

The Lakeside Condos board could have sought a second opinion earlier in the process. While their initial attorney may have been competent, the prolonged nature of the lawsuit suggests a different approach might have been beneficial sooner.

Board Member Voice: "Honestly, we were tired. This whole legal thing had been a nightmare for years. When that first offer came, we just wanted it over with. But deep down, we knew that accepting could mean more problems for our homeowners down the line."

Question for the Reader: Have you ever been in a situation where settling for 'good enough' felt like the easy way out, but risked causing bigger issues later?

Key Takeaways

- **Don't mistake fatigue for resolution.** Sometimes a long struggle can desensitize you to the full implications of decisions.
- **A fresh perspective is invaluable.** A new expert may provide insights that have been missed.
- **Your duty is to the long-term.** Boards must balance the desire for a quick end with their responsibility to protect the community's future well-being.

Case Study: The Power Of Finding The Right Cultural Fit

Hilltop Condos, a thriving homeowner's association, had always prided itself on its self-management model. The volunteer board members handled all aspects of running the complex, from landscaping to budget management. However, as the community grew, the workload became overwhelming. Recognizing the need for specialized support, particularly in the realm of accounting, the board embarked on the search for a CPA firm.

The search presented a unique challenge. Hilltop Condos wasn't just looking for technical expertise; they needed a partner who truly understood their unique dynamics. Interviews with several firms yielded candidates with impressive qualifications, yet something was missing. Finally, a firm emerged that shone in both capability and compatibility. This firm's approach aligned seamlessly with the board's preferences. They demonstrated:

- **Clear and Concise Communication:** They offered transparent reporting and explanations, empowering the board to make informed decisions.
- **Respect for Volunteerism:** Appreciating the board's dedication, they streamlined processes, minimizing unnecessary time commitments.
- **Shared Values:** Their commitment to fiscal responsibility and community well-being mirrored the Hilltop Condos' own mission.

The decision to partner with this firm proved transformative.

It wasn't simply a delegation of tasks; it was the formation of a collaborative relationship. The board still maintained ultimate control, but now felt genuinely supported by their accounting experts. Key benefits of this successful cultural fit include:

- **Reduced Stress and Increased Efficiency:** Confident in the handling of the financial aspects, the board could focus on other core responsibilities.
- **Enhanced Decision-Making:** Access to accurate, timely financial data led to more informed choices for the community's future.
- **Boosted Morale:** The feeling of being understood and valued fostered a sense of teamwork and a renewed enthusiasm for their volunteer roles.

What Could They Have Done Differently

Hilltop Condos could have made a more hasty decision and chosen a CPA firm based solely on technical expertise or cost. This might have resulted in a functional accounting solution, but would likely have missed the deeper benefits of finding a true cultural fit.

Board of Directors Member Voice: "At first, we were tempted to just go with the firm that had the biggest name recognition. But as we interviewed people, something clicked with this other team. It wasn't just about their accounting skills – it was about how they talked about our community."

Question for the Reader: When seeking external partners or service providers, how much weight do you place on factors beyond the core deliverables? Do you consider communication style, shared values, and overall "fit" to be as important as the technical aspects of their service?

Key Takeaways:

- **Cultural fit is crucial:** A good working relationship goes beyond skills alone. Aligning communication styles,

respecting each other's constraints, and sharing core values fosters long-term success.
- **Compatibility leads to partnership:** Finding a service provider who 'gets' you transforms the relationship from merely transactional to truly collaborative.
- **Don't undervalue the intangibles:** Factors like ease of communication, sense of support, and shared commitment can have a profound impact on overall satisfaction and the potential for growth.

Test Your Knowledge! Answers

1. **Ask about their experience in condominium law.** Hourly rates are important, but an experienced attorney will efficiently guide you, potentially saving money in the long run.

2. **Details prevent miscommunication and ensure the right outcome.** Even a simple task can derail if expectations aren't aligned between the board and the professional.

3. **Transparency builds trust.** Be open about information and challenges. This allows the professional to provide the best possible advice and support.

4. **For urgent matters, a phone call is usually best.** This ensures your issue is addressed quickly, with the opportunity for immediate follow-up questions.

5. **Formal reviews prevent surprises and allow for

course correction. Things may seem fine, but issues could be brewing. Reviews also build relationships and renew agreements.

6. **A collaborative professional listens to the board's goals and concerns.** They share knowledge to empower good decisions, rather than simply dictating solutions.

7. **There are many possible answers.** One of those is "Thank you for the draft bylaw revision. Please add a section on [specific issue] to proactively address similar situations in the future."

8. **The lowest fee may mean less experience or cut corners.** This can lead to costly mistakes, legal trouble, or work that needs to be redone later.

9. **Setting response time expectations prevents frustration and ensures timely handling of issues.** It respects both the board's need for information and the professional's workload.

10. **A respectful professional values the board's input and decision-making.** They'll explain their recommendations, answer questions patiently, and work with the board's direction.

CHAPTER 9: LEGAL AND REGULATORY COMPLIANCE

Introduction

Condominium associations must operate within a complicated network of laws that exist at all levels of government. It's essential to understand these regulations, as following them is key to the community's financial stability and overall positive atmosphere. Not complying can lead to expensive legal battles, fines, and a damaged reputation.

The financial consequences of non-compliance can be severe. This includes potential legal costs, fines for breaking fair housing or ADA regulations, and the strain of losses not covered by insufficient insurance. Damage to the association's reputation is just as serious; it can break trust with residents, make it harder to attract buyers, and create a negative perception of the community.

This chapter offers board members a valuable foundation by outlining the legal environment for condominiums. It's important to stress, however, that this information shouldn't replace the advice of a qualified condominium attorney. To protect your community and manage risk properly, seeking legal advice on specific matters is crucial.

Fast Fact: Ignoring legal compliance can cost you. Penalties, lawsuits, and damage to your community's reputation are all consequences of non-compliance.

Key Federal Laws

In Chapter 1, we briefly introduced the Fair Housing Act (FHA) and the Americans with Disabilities Act (ADA). Let's go deeper into these important laws.

The Fair Housing Act (FHA)

The FHA protects individuals from discrimination in housing based on several protected classes: race, color, religion, sex, national origin, familial status, and disability. This means a condominium association cannot implement rules like rental restrictions or screening processes that unfairly target people within these protected classes.

Additionally, the FHA addresses reasonable accommodations and modifications. Residents with disabilities have the right to request changes to policies or physical alterations to their units. There's a specific process residents must follow, and the community has a responsibility to understand and comply with the FHA. That said, there are limitations on when a community can deny such requests.

To ensure FHA compliance, communities should follow best practices, including:

- **Developing a Clear Fair Housing Policy:** This outlines how the community will respond to resident requests, including who is responsible, required documentation from residents, and response times.
- **Training the Board and Staff:** Everyone involved in decision-making should be well-versed in FHA provisions.
- **Documentation:** Meticulously document all interactions related to accommodation requests for easy reference if needed.

The Americans with Disabilities Act (ADA)

Title III of the ADA is particularly relevant to condominiums, as it focuses on accessibility standards in public spaces. Common areas within a condominium community must be accessible to individuals with disabilities. The ADA provides guidelines for paths of travel, parking, entrances, and more.

Responsibility for ADA compliance is often shared:

- **Condominium Association:** Responsible for common areas like the clubhouse, pool, fitness center, property grounds, sidewalks, and building entrances.
- **Individual Owners:** May be responsible for compliance within their own units.
- **Coordination is Key:** The community and residents need to work together to ensure overall ADA compliance.

Residents can request modifications under the ADA. For instance, readily achievable changes might be simple adjustments, while larger structural modifications can be more complex. It's essential to understand the difference and have a plan in place (such as a reserve fund) to address ADA-related requests.

Key Takeaway: While both laws address discrimination, the FHA focuses on protected classes, and the ADA centers on accessibility for individuals with disabilities.

Fast Fact: ADA compliance applies to common areas. Accessibility isn't just about unit interiors.

Fair Housing Act (FHA)

- **Checklist**

    - Does your Board have a clear anti-discrimination policy based on FHA protected classes?
    - Are your resident screening processes FHA

compliant (avoiding questions/criteria that could have discriminatory impact)?
- Do you have a procedure for handling reasonable accommodation requests from residents with disabilities?
- Is your staff (and ideally your Board) trained on FHA basics?

- **Timeline**

  - **Within 30 days:** Review policies and screening processes, consult your attorney if needed.
  - **Within 60 days:** Schedule FHA training for management and Board members.
  - **Ongoing:** Revisit FHA compliance annually as part of legal checkups.

- **Action Steps**

  - Create/update your Fair Housing policy and post it prominently in the management office and on your community website (if applicable).
  - Work with your attorney to develop standard forms for accommodation requests and a clear decision-making process.

Americans with Disabilities Act (ADA)

- **Checklist**

  - Are common areas accessible (paths of travel, parking, entrances, etc.)?
    - If not, have you considered what "readily achievable" changes are feasible?
  - Do you have a process for residents to request modifications to their units based on disability needs?
  - Is your community budgeting for potential future ADA-related changes to common areas?

- **Timeline**

    - **Immediate:** Conduct a basic visual assessment of common areas, note potential barriers.
    - **Within 6 months:** If major accessibility issues exist, consult an ADA specialist AND your attorney.
    - **Ongoing:** Include ADA in your reserve studies and long-term budgeting.
- **Action Steps**

    - Start an "ADA Accessibility Fund" even if contributions are initially small.
    - Educate residents about the difference between the association's responsibility (common areas) and individual owners' responsibilities within units.

State And Local Regulations: A Navigational Guide For Boards

State Laws: Unique to Your Location

Condominium governance is heavily influenced by state-specific laws. The Board has a duty to fully understand and abide by the regulations that apply to your community. Typical areas covered by state laws include:

- **Governance:** How the Board is structured, how elections are conducted, and meeting procedures.
- **Financial Management:** Rules surrounding budgets, reserve funds (how they're used and maintained), and different types of assessments.
- **Maintenance:** Clearly defining which areas are common property and which are the responsibility of individual owners.

Local Ordinances: Community-Specific Rules

In addition to state laws, condo associations must follow local ordinances. These typically cover:

- **Zoning:** Restrictions on building size, how far structures must be from property lines, and the maximum number of units allowed.
- **Noise:** Designated quiet hours and rules about construction noise.
- **Parking:** Regulations regarding street parking, guest parking, and the number of spaces per unit.
- **Other:** Potentially include pet restrictions, rules about renting units, and more.

Compliance and Enforcement: The Association's Role

Associations have a two-fold responsibility:

- **Abide by** all relevant local ordinances.
- **Enforce** these rules within the community, using the authority granted by your governing documents (such as fines).

Pro Tip: "Reasonable" is key. Courts often judge condominium rules by whether they are reasonable restrictions. Avoid overly strict or arbitrary rules.

When Rules Collide

There may be times when local ordinances and your association's bylaws disagree. Knowing which rules take priority and how to address these situations is crucial.

Where to Find Help

- **State Laws:** Your community attorney is the best source for interpreting state laws and how they impact your association.
- **Local Ordinances:** Get the most accurate information directly from your municipality's government offices. Your management company may also offer guidance.
- **Staying Updated:** The Board must keep up with changing regulations. Work closely with your attorney, attend conferences, and stay informed – this task involves every Board member!

Checklist:

- **Identify Relevant Laws:**
    - Start with your state's Secretary of State website or the department regulating condominiums.
    - Search your city/municipal government website for local ordinances.
- **Focus on Key Areas:**
    - Governance (elections, meetings, etc.)
    - Financial Management (budgets, reserves, etc.)
    - Maintenance Responsibilities

- Zoning Restrictions
- Noise Ordinances
- Parking Regulations
- **Understand Compliance Hierarchy:**
    - Federal laws generally supersede state laws
    - State laws generally supersede local ordinances
    - Your governing documents must comply with all applicable laws

Action Steps:

- **Consult your attorney:** They are the best source for interpreting laws and their application to your association.
- **Contact relevant government agencies:** If you have questions about specific regulations or how to obtain copies.

Sample Timeline:

- **Week 1-2:** Identify relevant state and local government websites.
- **Weeks 3-4:** Review state laws, focusing on key areas for condominium governance.
- **Weeks 5-6:** Review local ordinances, highlighting potential overlap with state laws.
- **Ongoing:** Schedule a consultation with your attorney to clarify any questions and address areas where your governing documents might need updates.

Understanding Insurance Fundamentals

Pro Tip: Review insurance annually, not just at renewal time. Your community's needs and risks change – your coverage should too.

Understanding Your Insurance Coverage

It's crucial to work with a qualified insurance broker, but let's dive a bit deeper to understand how different insurance policies protect your community.

1. Property Insurance

- **What's Covered:** Think buildings, common areas, association-owned stuff, and legal liability if someone gets hurt on the property.
- **Who Pays for What:** Your main policy covers the original structure. Unit owners usually insure their own upgrades or customization within their units. Check your master deed and talk to your insurance broker to be sure.

2. Directors & Officers (D&O) Insurance

- **Peace of Mind:** Protects Board members from having to pay out-of-pocket if someone sues the Board over a decision. Covers lawyers, court costs, and potential settlements.

3. Fidelity Insurance

- **Protection from Within:** Safeguards your community's money against fraud or theft by Board members, management, or anyone handling association funds.

4. Additional Coverages

- **It Depends on Your Risks:** Work with your broker to figure out what else you need. Think about:

- o Flood Insurance (especially if you're prone to flooding)
- o Earthquake Coverage (if relevant to your location)
- o Other Special Protections (windstorm, equipment failure, cyber attacks, etc.)

5. Know Your Policy Terms

- **Deductibles:** This is what you pay BEFORE insurance kicks in.
- **Coverage Limits:** The maximum amount the insurance company will pay out.
- **Exclusions:** Read the fine print! These are things your policy DOESN'T cover.

6. The Claims Process

- **The Board's Job:**
    - o Report problems to your broker ASAP.
    - o Take photos, videos, and keep careful records of the damage.
    - o Work with the insurance company to help them investigate.
- **Important Note about Disasters**
    - o Your community might have a preferred vendor on standby, or your fire department might send someone to secure the site.
    - o You can choose your own company for repairs, but you likely have to pay the initial stabilization costs.
    - o These initial costs are usually covered by insurance (minus your deductible).

7. When Insurance Might Not Help

Insurance is usually for sudden disasters (floods, etc.). It likely won't cover things that go wrong slowly over time (like a slowly failing foundation).

8. Working with Insurance Pros

- **Find a Specialist:** Look for a broker who knows the ins and outs of condominium insurance.
- **They're Your Guide:** A good broker will:
  - Check out your property and suggest the right coverage.
  - Examine your governing documents for potential liability issues.
- **Stay Up-to-Date:** Your insurance needs change! To make sure you're protected:
  - Listen to lenders if they raise concerns about your coverage when buyers apply for mortgages.
  - Shop around for better prices every few years.

Checklist:

- **Types of Coverage:**
  - Property Insurance
  - Directors & Officers (D&O) Insurance
  - Fidelity Insurance
  - Additional Coverages (flood, earthquake, etc.)
- **Understanding Your Policy:**
  - Deductibles
  - Coverage Limits
  - Exclusions
- **The Claim Process**
  - Documenting Damage
  - Timeframes for Filing
  - Cooperation with Insurer

Action Steps:

- **Work with an Experienced Broker:** Seek a specialist in condominium insurance.
- **Annual Review:** Assess your coverage needs as your community's assets and risks evolve.
- **Know Your Claim Protocol:** Ensure all Board members understand the steps to take in case of an incident.

Sample Timeline

- **Month 1:** Contact 2-3 insurance brokers specializing in condominiums and get quotes.
- **Month 2:** Review quotes, compare coverage, and select the best fit for your community.
- **Month 3:** Meet with your chosen broker to go over your policy in detail.
- **Annually Thereafter:** Schedule policy review with the broker, noting any changes in your community.

Staying Informed And Proactive

Fast Fact: "We've always done it this way" isn't a defense. Laws and best practices change. Boards need to stay informed.

Staying Informed: Your Guide to Tracking Legal Changes

As a condominium Board member, it's vital to stay up-to-date on the ever-evolving legal landscape. Here are several ways to track changes and ensure your community remains compliant:

Government Websites

- **State Agencies:** Your state's Secretary of State office or the specific department overseeing condominiums often provides valuable resources and updates on relevant regulations.
- **Federal Agencies:** The Department of Housing and Urban Development (HUD) is your go-to resource for updates and guidance on the Fair Housing Act.

Industry Publications

- **Condominium Management Publications:** Subscribe to magazines, newsletters, websites, and blogs that specialize in condominium law. These publications offer insights and analysis on current legal issues specifically affecting your community.

Your Condominium Attorney: The Ultimate Resource

Your attorney is your most valuable asset when navigating legal complexities. They provide:

- **Clear Explanations:** They break down complex legal changes into understandable terms.
- **Proactive Updates:** Attorneys keep you informed about new laws or court decisions that directly impact your

community.

Fast Fact: Your management company isn't a substitute for legal advice. They can be helpful partners, but legal matters should be discussed with your attorney.

Best Practices for Proactive Compliance

- **Know Your Documents:** Regularly review your community's bylaws and CC&Rs (at least annually, if not more frequently). Be aware of potential conflicts with state or local laws.
- **Consult Your Attorney Regularly:** Proactive consultations are key. Discuss emerging legal trends and potential areas of concern for your association – don't wait for problems to arise.
- **Board Education is Essential:** Encourage all Board members to attend industry conferences and workshops. Utilize online training resources created specifically for condominium boards.
- **Informed Residents are Engaged Residents:** When the community understands legal requirements, they're more likely to follow the rules and proactively report potential issues.

Additional Tips:

- **Be Proactive, Not Reactive:** Anticipating legal changes helps you avoid costly issues down the road.
- **Embrace Technology:** Explore online legal research platforms or subscription services designed to track legislative updates.
- **Build a Network:** Connect with other condominium boards in your area to share information, resources, and best practices.

By utilizing these resources and strategies, your Board can stay informed, proactive, and ensure your community operates within the boundaries of the law.

Pro Tip: Don't DIY legal matters. Seemingly minor issues can have major consequences. Consult your attorney early and often.

Checklist:

- **Resources:**
    - Government Websites
    - Industry Publications
    - Your Attorney
- **Best Practices**
    - Review Governing Documents Regularly
    - Periodic Legal Check-ups
    - Board Education
    - Transparency with Residents

Action Steps

- **Assign Responsibilities:** Different Board members could monitor different types of updates (legal, industry trends, etc.).
- **Create a Resource Hub:** Have a shared folder or section of your website for relevant updates.
- **Budget for Proactive Measures:** Include funding for conferences, consultations, and educational materials in your annual budget.

Sample Timeline

- **Immediate:** Designate Board member(s) to find relevant websites and publications.
- **Within 1 Month:** Have an initial "check-up" with your attorney to establish a proactive consultation schedule.
- **Ongoing:** Set a cadence for reviewing governing documents (annually, bi-annually, etc.). Encourage participation in conferences or workshops throughout the year.

Staying Ahead Of The Curve: Addressing New Legal And Social Trends

Evolving Areas of Concern for Condominium Boards

As a Board member, it's essential to be aware of emerging issues that can create challenges within your community. Here are a few key areas to focus on:

1. Pet Policies: Finding the Right Balance

Pets can be a source of joy for residents, but they can also lead to disputes within a condominium community. Finding a balance between pet lovers and those concerned about noise, potential damage, and liability is essential. Even seemingly minor issues, like cats sitting in windows or wandering briefly outdoors, can spark conflict among neighbors.

Legal Restrictions to Keep in Mind

Navigating pet policies requires understanding the legal landscape:

- **The Fair Housing Act (FHA):** This law protects individuals with disabilities who rely on service animals or emotional support animals (ESAs). With a doctor's note, residents generally can't be denied an ESA. However, there are limits to how many animals can receive ESA designation and what types of animals qualify.
- **State and Local Laws:** These may further restrict your community's ability to enforce bans on specific breeds or impose weight limits on pets.

Checklist:

- **Legal Restrictions:**
    - Fair Housing Act protections for service/emotional support animals.

- State or local laws on breed restrictions or weight limits.
- **Crafting Effective Policies**
  - Define allowable pets (species, breed clarifications if any, maximum number).
  - Rules on pet behavior (noise, leashing, waste removal).
  - Enforcement mechanisms – warnings, fines, etc.
- **Resident Input:** Consider surveying residents for feedback before major policy changes.

Action Steps

- **Attorney Consultation:** Discuss legal requirements and ensure your policy language is compliant.
- **Resident Communication:** If changes are being considered, be transparent about the process and rationale.
- **Enforcement Plan:** Ensure the Board and management understand how to handle complaints fairly and consistently.

Crafting Effective Pet Policies

For a successful pet policy, consider these elements:

- **Clear Definitions:** Explicitly state which types of pets are permitted within your community.
- **Reasonable Rules:** Set expectations for pet behavior, including noise levels, leash requirements, and waste cleanup procedures.
- **Enforcement:** Establish a system of warnings and escalating fines for those who violate the pet policy.

Fast Fact: "Emotional Support Animals" (ESAs) have specific legal protections. Boards must follow Fair Housing Act guidelines on ESAs.

2. Short-Term Rentals: A Potential Source of Conflict

The rise of short-term rentals platforms like Airbnb can create challenges for condominium communities. Before crafting a policy, it's crucial to understand potential conflicts. Zoning restrictions may come into play, as local ordinances could prohibit or heavily limit short-term rentals. Additionally, your community's governing documents (CC&Rs) may have specific rules about rentals. Balancing the resident's right to use their property with the community's need to manage noise, security, and potential wear and tear on common areas is vital.

Here are some policy options to consider:

- **Outright Ban:** If legally permissible, a community might choose to fully prohibit short-term rentals.
- **Limitations:** Restrictions on the frequency or length of rentals can offer a compromise.
- **Registration Requirements:** Asking those renting out units to register their renters can help the community track who is coming and going, improving security awareness.

Checklist:

- **Zoning Restrictions:**
    - Check local ordinances – are short-term rentals even allowed in your area?
    - Are there limitations on duration or frequency?
- **Governing Documents Check:**
    - Do your CC&Rs address rentals in any way?
    - Ensure any new rules don't conflict with existing provisions.
- **Balancing Interests:** Consider:
    - Residents' desire to use their property vs.
    - Community concerns about noise, security, etc.
- **Policy Options:**
    - Outright ban (if legally permissible)
    - Limitations (length of stay, frequency)

- Registration requirements for renters

Action Steps:

- **Research is Key:** Investigate local zoning and any existing restrictions in your documents.
- **Attorney Consultation:** Discuss legal options and how to effectively draft new or revised rules.
- **Resident Input:** Gather resident feedback before implementing major changes – this can help avoid conflict later.

3. Additional Evolving Issues

Beyond pets and short-term rentals, condominium Boards face a range of emerging challenges. Here's a look at a few key areas:

- **Electric Vehicle (EV) Charging Stations**

  As more residents switch to EVs, your community will likely need to provide charging stations. This requires thoughtful planning:

  - **Infrastructure:** Where will stations be located? How many are needed? What type of chargers are most suitable?
  - **Cost Allocation:** How will the costs of installation and electricity usage be fairly distributed among residents?
  - **Legal Considerations:** Some states have laws dictating requirements for EV charging in condominiums. Check your state's regulations.

- **Cannabis Regulations**

  The legalization of marijuana (whether recreational or medical) varies drastically across states. Boards must navigate this complex issue, balancing individual rights with the community's well-being:

- o **Balancing Concerns:** Residents might have legitimate reasons for using cannabis, but others may have concerns about secondhand smoke or strong odors.
- o **Setting Clear Boundaries:** If your community allows cannabis use, clearly define designated areas (if any). This helps manage potential conflicts.

- **Data Privacy and Security**

Condominiums store a wealth of resident information. As your community goes digital, protecting this data is paramount:

- o **Safeguarding Information:** Limit access to sensitive data, use secure storage methods, and educate staff and residents on best practices.
- o **Cybersecurity Measures:** Invest in firewalls, antivirus software, and regular system updates to minimize the risk of breaches.
- o **Legal Compliance:** Understand and adhere to all relevant data privacy laws at the state and federal level.

Checklist:

- **Protection of Resident Information:**
    - o How do you store resident data? (physical files, electronic systems)
    - o Who has access?
    - o Security measures in place (passwords, encryption, firewalls, etc.)
- **Cybersecurity:**
    - o Do you have a plan for preventing data breaches?
    - o Are there incident response procedures in place?
- **Legal Compliance:**
    - o Are you familiar with relevant data privacy laws in

your state?
- Do you have a privacy policy that's been communicated to residents?

Action Steps:

- **Conduct a Data Audit:** Understand where resident information is stored and how it's protected.
- **Technology Assessment:** If you use online systems, work with an IT professional to evaluate their security.
- **Attorney Consultation:** Ensure you understand any legal requirements for data handling and disclosure.

Important Reminder: Your community's rules can never supersede local, state, or federal laws. Always consult your attorney for guidance when navigating these complex issues!

Conclusion: Compliance As A Continuous Journey

Pro Tip: Document EVERYTHING. Meeting minutes, incident reports, communications with residents – meticulous records are crucial if a legal issue arises.

Legal Compliance: An Ongoing Commitment

Legal and regulatory compliance is a core responsibility for any condominium board. It's crucial to remember that this isn't a one-time task. Laws change, communities evolve, and new legal challenges can emerge. Staying compliant requires continuous effort and a proactive approach.

Here's how Boards can stay ahead of the curve:

- **Schedule Regular Legal Checkups:** Meet with your community attorney proactively, not just when there's a crisis. This helps identify potential risks and address changes in the law.
- **Stay Informed:** Attend industry conferences, workshops, and utilize online resources specifically about condominium law.
- **Seek Expert Guidance:** While conferences and resources are valuable, they cannot replace the tailored advice of a qualified condominium attorney. Your attorney is your partner in protecting your community.

Why Compliance Matters

Yes, avoiding costly penalties is the immediate benefit of compliance, but its importance goes far beyond that. Here's why your Board should prioritize staying legally compliant:

- **Protect Your Community's Finances:** Sound legal practices directly safeguard your association's financial

stability. This avoids unnecessary fines and potential lawsuits.
- **Supports a Harmonious Community:** When residents feel their rights are respected and rules are applied fairly, it builds trust and creates a more positive, conflict-free environment for everyone.
- **Attract Potential Buyers:** Communities known for good governance and compliance are more attractive to potential buyers. This supports property values and makes your community a desirable place to live.

Pro Tip: A good relationship with your attorney is worth its weight in gold. Find an attorney who specializes in condominiums and is responsive to your needs.

Parting Advice

Boards have a fiduciary duty to their community. While you're not expected to be legal experts, you have a responsibility to seek expert guidance. Build a strong relationship with a qualified condominium attorney. They are your essential resource for navigating the complexities of community law and making the best decisions for the long-term well-being of your association.

Test Your Knowledge!

1. What are the two main types of insurance coverage that every condominium association should have?
2. Name two specific areas often covered by state condominium laws.
3. What is the difference between a condominium association's master policy and an individual unit owner's insurance policy?
4. Why is it important to review your governing documents regularly, even if no major changes are being considered?
5. What is the purpose of a reserve study, and how often should one be conducted?
6. List two common restrictions that might be found in a condominium's CC&Rs.
7. What does the term "fiduciary duty" mean in the context of a condominium board?
8. Briefly explain the Fair Housing Act and how it applies to condominiums.
9. What should a Board do in the immediate aftermath of a catastrophic event like a fire or a flood?
10. Why is it important to attend industry conferences and workshops as a Board member?

The answers are at the end of this chapter

Case Study: The Pet Policy Problem

Sunnyview Condominiums had always prided itself on its clear and consistent rules. One of the longest-standing provisions in their CC&Rs was a weight limit for dogs: no resident could own a dog over 30 pounds. It seemed straightforward enough, designed to prevent larger, potentially more disruptive breeds from residing in the community.

Then came Mrs. Johnson, a widowed senior who moved into Sunnyview with Buddy, her affectionate, six-year-old golden retriever. Buddy was well beyond the weight limit, but anyone who met him knew he was the gentlest of souls. He never barked excessively, was impeccably house-trained, and quickly became a beloved figure in the community, known for his friendly tail wags and eagerness to greet residents in the hallways.

However, the Board felt obligated to uphold the rules. They sent Mrs. Johnson a notice, politely but firmly informing her the dog had to go. The community was shocked. Petitions circulated, and several residents confronted the Board, outraged that kind Mrs. Johnson and her sweet dog might be forced to leave. The Board was caught in a difficult situation – the rule was intended to protect the community, but this situation seemed to demand an exception.

Unsure how to proceed, they consulted their attorney. What they learned was eye-opening. First, their state had recently passed legislation restricting overly narrow pet weight limits in condos. Second, the attorney explained the Fair Housing Act and how it might apply. Buddy, with a doctor's note confirming Mrs. Johnson's need for an Emotional Support Animal (ESA), might be protected even if he didn't meet the usual pet policy.

Realizing they were navigating a legally complex issue, the Board decided to revise their pet policy. They removed the weight restriction and replaced it with language focused on behavior: no aggressive breeds, excessive barking, or off-leash pets in common areas. They also established a clear process for residents to request ESA accommodations, including the necessary documentation.

Mrs. Johnson was thrilled and relieved. The broader community was also satisfied, seeing the Board adapt fairly while still prioritizing a peaceful environment. Sunnyview's case became a reminder that while rules are important, compassion and knowledge of the law are essential for creating a harmonious living community.

What Could They Have Done Differently?

- **Proactive Policy Review:** The Board could have avoided this situation by proactively reviewing their pet policy against state law and Fair Housing Act guidelines on a regular basis.
- **Early Consultation with Attorney:** Consulting their attorney before sending a notice to Mrs. Johnson would have alerted them to the legal complexities and potential for an ESA accommodation.

Board Member Voice: "We thought we were just following the rules. It never occurred to us that a sweet dog like Buddy could be why someone sues our association – but our eyes were opened."

Question for the Reader: Could your community's pet policy create a similar situation? When was the last time you reviewed your rules in light of the Fair Housing Act and any relevant state laws?

Key Takeaways

- Rules are necessary, but they must comply with current

laws and regulations. Don't assume old policies are still valid.
- The Fair Housing Act extends beyond rental restrictions; it applies to any community rules that might be discriminatory.
- Consult your attorney early in situations with potential legal implications. Being proactive can save significant stress and expense.

Case Study: Insurance Nightmare – When Coverage Isn't Enough

The skies above Riverbend Condominiums turned an ominous shade of green. The ensuing hailstorm pummeled the community, the ice chunks sounding like gunfire against the roofs and siding. In the aftermath, the Board surveyed the damage with a sinking feeling. This was bad.

They filed a claim with their insurance carrier, confident they had adequate coverage. Weeks later, the adjuster's report arrived. The claim was mostly denied. "Wear and tear," the report stated, not storm damage. The small amount offered barely scratched the surface of the needed repairs. Panic swept through Riverbend.

How could this happen? The Board scrambled, digging into their policy. They made two shocking discoveries. First, the property hadn't had a professional replacement cost valuation in over a decade. Their coverage was woefully inadequate to rebuild in the current market. Second, they hadn't scrutinized their policy's exclusions – and "gradual deterioration" was listed in bold. They'd mistakenly assumed "old age" wouldn't prevent payouts for storm damage.

The Board was forced to levy a massive special assessment on the residents. Residents' dreams of upgrades, vacations, and even retirement savings vanished overnight. The once-friendly community became a place of anger and accusations. Some residents blamed the Board for negligence, while the Board felt betrayed by their insurer.

Through painful trial and error, the Board vowed to do better. They found a qualified broker specializing in condominiums. They invested in an up-to-date property valuation. They painstakingly compared policies with their broker, not just focusing on price but on the fine print of what was, and wasn't, covered. They also developed an emergency fund, separate from their operating budget.

It took years for Riverbend to fully repair the physical damage, and even longer to heal the distrust that had grown among neighbors.

What Could They Have Done Differently?

- **Regularly Assess Coverage:** Have a replacement cost valuation done on the property every few years to ensure the insurance keeps pace with market values.
- **Work with A Specialist:** Use a broker who understands the nuances of condominium insurance, not a generalist.
- **Understand Exclusions:** Carefully review what ISN'T covered. Don't assume everything is included.
- **Build an Emergency Fund:** Special assessments can be devastating. Having an emergency fund helps soften the blow of unexpected events.

Board Member Voice: "We thought we were doing the right thing. We had insurance... what else were we supposed to do? Now I realize, you can't just 'set it and forget it' when it comes to protecting your community."

Question for the Reader: When was the last time your association had a professional property valuation? Do you fully understand your policy's exclusions?

Key Takeaways

- Insurance isn't a one-time expense; it needs regular review and adjustment.
- Working with a qualified condominium insurance broker is crucial.
- Don't let low premiums blind you to inadequate coverage. Read the fine print!
- Having an emergency fund provides a safety net for the

unexpected.

Case Study: The Bylaws Backfire

Greenwood Condominiums had always prided itself on its uniform appearance. But as the community aged, residents' desires for customization grew. When Mr. Smith submitted his plan for a small backyard patio off his ground-floor unit, he expected routine approval. After all, a quick glance around Greenwood revealed similar structures already in place.

The Board's denial came as a shock. They cited a provision in the CC&Rs requiring Board approval for all exterior modifications, a provision designed to maintain the community's aesthetic. Mr. Smith was furious. He gathered photos of patios, decks, and awnings in various states of disrepair, highlighting the lack of consistency in enforcement. A heated community meeting followed, splitting residents into camps: those wanting more flexibility and those fiercely protective of the original architectural vision.

The Board realized they were in a bind. Their outdated bylaws were both vague and inconsistently enforced, creating fertile ground for conflict. Determined to find a solution, they consulted with their attorney. The path forward was clear but far from easy: a comprehensive revision of their governing documents.

This wasn't a quick fix. It involved surveys to gauge resident preferences, careful drafting to balance individual desires with overall cohesion, and a lengthy approval process as defined by their bylaws. The Board worked with their attorney to create detailed guidelines specifying permissible materials, dimensions, and setbacks for exterior modifications. They proactively communicated updates to the community, fostering transparency.

While some residents grumbled about the time involved, the

majority appreciated the Board's willingness to address a long-standing problem. The revised documents not only clarified the rules but also provided a clear process for future requests, minimizing the potential for future disputes like Mr. Smith's.

In the end, Greenwood Condominiums learned a tough lesson: bylaws aren't meant to be set in stone forever. Revisiting these documents regularly was essential to prevent them from becoming a source of conflict rather than a tool for community harmony.

What Could They Have Done Differently?

- **Proactive Review:** Regularly reviewing their governing documents, even when no major issues were apparent, would have revealed the outdated provision regarding exterior modifications.
- **Community Input:** Before major changes were planned, surveying residents to gauge their evolving needs and preferences might have revealed a desire for more flexibility.
- **Anticipating the Future:** Acknowledging that tastes and acceptable standards change over time could have prompted the Board to draft some pre-approved modifications instead of requiring full Board approval for every little change.

Board Member Voice: "At the time, we truly believed we were doing the right thing – upholding the rules everyone agreed to when they moved in. Looking back, we should have been more adaptable, realizing that even a great community needs to evolve."

Question for the Reader: Are there areas in your community's governing documents that seem overly rigid, potentially outdated, or ripe for inconsistent enforcement?

Key Takeaways

- Bylaws and CC&Rs are not static – they need regular review to stay aligned with community needs and current laws.
- Proactive communication and gathering resident input can prevent seemingly routine decisions from escalating into major conflicts.
- Striving for a balance between upholding a community's vision and allowing reasonable flexibility makes for a more harmonious environment in the long run.

Case Study: The Reserve Fund Crisis

Oak Creek Condominiums had always been a place where residents appreciated the affordability. The Board prided itself on keeping assessments low, year after year. However, beneath the surface, problems were brewing. The elevator made creaking noises concerning to residents, patches on the roof hinted at leaks, and cracks in the pool tiles were getting wider.

Then, it all hit at once. The elevator broke down completely, requiring not just repairs, but a major overhaul. A torrential rainstorm proved the roof was no longer reliable. The pool was deemed unsafe by an inspector. Quotes for the repairs were staggering, and the reserve fund was a mere shadow of what was needed.

Residents were furious. They faced a massive special assessment – on top of their regular fees – to fix problems they felt the Board should have seen coming. Trust vanished, accusations flew, and some residents threatened to sell their units.

The newly elected Board faced a daunting task. They dug into the records and made a shocking discovery. Reserve studies had been conducted every few years, as recommended. Each had warned that major expenses were on the horizon. But the previous Board had consistently ignored these warnings, opting for the short-term popularity of keeping assessments artificially low.

The new Board knew they couldn't fix this overnight. They hired a reputable management company specializing in financial turnarounds. Transparency was key. They held town hall meetings, explaining the situation and the long road ahead. They increased assessments significantly but did so gradually, giving residents time to adjust their budgets.

The path to financial stability was slow and painful. Some residents did sell, but those who stayed saw gradual progress. The elevator was modernized, the roof was fully replaced, and the pool sparkled once again. It took nearly five years, but Oak Creek Condominiums regained its financial footing.

Most importantly, the Board had rebuilt a foundation of trust. Residents understood that assessments weren't arbitrary; they were safeguarding the community they all called home. Today, Oak Creek serves as a cautionary tale AND a success story, reminding everyone that responsible budgeting isn't just about numbers; it's about protecting the long-term well-being of the entire condominium community.

What Could They Have Done Differently?

- **Taken Reserve Studies Seriously:** The previous Board had the information but chose to ignore it. Reserve studies aren't just a formality; they are essential financial planning tools.
- **Prioritized Long-Term Health:** Popularity in the short term came at the expense of the community's future stability. Boards must balance current needs with preparing for predictable future expenses.
- **Communicated Transparently:** Even if assessments had to increase, residents might have been more understanding if the "why" was explained proactively, not just when the crisis hit.

Board Member Voice: "We thought we were doing the right thing, keeping costs down for our residents. We didn't realize we were just kicking the can down the road and setting our community up for disaster."

Question for the Reader: Does your Board have a long-term financial mindset? Are you reviewing reserve studies carefully and creating realistic, responsible budgets?

Key Takeaways

- Reserve studies are not optional; they are roadmaps to financial health.
- Short-term popularity can lead to long-term disaster.
- Transparency builds trust, even in difficult situations.
- Financial crises can be overcome, but it takes time, honesty, and a commitment from both the Board and residents.

Case Study: The Short-Term Rental Showdown

Bayside Condos, a beachfront community known for its relaxed vibe, suddenly became a battleground. The rise of Airbnb and similar platforms led to a surge in some units being used as short-term rentals. What started as a trickle of unfamiliar faces turned into a steady stream.

Complaints poured into the Board's inbox. Late-night parties spilled into the pool area. Parking spaces meant for residents were always full. Long-term residents felt a sense of unease, unsure of who was coming and going next door. On the other side, unit owners who used short-term rentals as an income source were furious at the thought of restrictions. The community was divided on what was once a non-issue.

The Board realized their governing documents were silent on short-term rentals. They began researching. Their city had been grappling with the same problem, and the council was debating potential ordinances that could severely limit or even ban short-term rentals outright.

Knowing they needed to act decisively, the Board followed several key steps:

- **Gather Information:** They surveyed residents to gauge the extent of the problem and get a sense of overall sentiment.
- **Consult the Attorney:** They discussed the legalities – what restrictions could they impose within their CC&Rs, and what might be preempted by potential city regulations?
- **Hold Community Meetings:** These were initially heated, with both sides passionately arguing their points. The Board focused on listening and facilitating discussion, not rushing to judgment.

It became clear that an outright ban wouldn't fly, as some owners relied on rental income. Yet, doing nothing wasn't an option either. The Board crafted a compromise:

- **Amend the CC&Rs:** They added rules limiting how often units could be rented short-term and the minimum stay length. This addressed noise and turnover concerns.
- **Registration System:** Owners renting short-term had to register with the association and provide contact information for guests. This reassured residents that the community knew who was on-site.
- **Clear Enforcement:** The CC&Rs now included fines for violations, providing teeth to the new rules.

The Board communicated the changes transparently, explaining the rationale. While not everyone was thrilled, most residents felt their concerns had been heard and a fair compromise was reached. And importantly, Bayside Condos acted proactively, avoiding potentially harsher restrictions if they had waited for the city ordinance to pass.

What Could They Have Done Differently?

- **Anticipate the Trend:** Short-term rentals weren't new. The Board could have been more proactive in discussing this issue with their attorney and potentially amended their CC&Rs *before* the situation became a major source of friction.

- **Early Communication:** A bit of preemptive communication to residents about the rise of short-term rentals, and the Board's intention to monitor the situation, might have eased some tensions when it was time to make changes.

Board Member Voice: "At first, we honestly thought this was a fad that would blow over. We didn't realize how quickly it would change the whole feel of our community." - Linda, Board President

Question for the Reader: Are there emerging trends within your community (electric vehicle charging, evolving resident demographics, etc.) that might require proactive policy discussions, even if they aren't a major problem yet?

Key Takeaways

- **Don't ignore evolving issues:** What starts small can quickly escalate and lead to division.
- **Proactive policymaking is better than reacting to a crisis:** Doing the work upfront gives you more room to find compromises and avoid overly restrictive knee-jerk reactions.
- **Communication is key:** Keeping residents informed helps them understand the 'why' behind the Board's actions and increases buy-in to new rules.

Case Study: The Power Of Proactive Compliance

The Board of Hilltop Condominiums wasn't content with just getting by. They believed in continuous improvement and staying ahead of the legal curve. This meant making proactive compliance a core value. Here's how they did it:

- **Knowledge is Power:** Board members regularly attended industry conferences and workshops. They didn't just send one representative – they made it a priority that the entire Board gain valuable insights into emerging trends and legal updates.
- **Partnership, Not Just Legal Services:** The Board viewed their condominium attorney as a strategic partner. They scheduled proactive consultations twice per year to discuss potential areas of vulnerability and changes on the horizon, not just calling when a crisis erupted.
- **Documents Under the Microscope:** The Board made an annual "date" with their governing documents. They reviewed the bylaws and CC&Rs line by line, cross-referencing them with current state and local laws to ensure nothing was in conflict.

This approach paid off when a new state law passed, significantly altering the requirements for condominium association financial reporting. Instead of scrambling, the Hilltop Board had already been discussing similar changes with their attorney. They understood the law's intent and were able to implement the new reporting standards smoothly, even providing resources to help residents understand the changes.

Benefits Beyond Compliance:

Proactive compliance wasn't just about avoiding trouble for Hilltop. It created a ripple effect of positive outcomes:

- **Resident Trust:** Residents saw that the Board was dedicated and responsible. This led to smoother adoption of rule changes, willingness to serve on committees, and less conflict within the community.
- **Reputation Matters:** Hilltop became known within the region as a well-managed community. This made it a highly desirable place to live, boosting property values and attracting new buyers.
- **Avoiding the Unexpected:** With proactive legal "checkups" and diligent review of their documents, the Hilltop Board was able to anticipate potential issues and address them before they became costly problems. This contributed to the financial health and long-term stability of the association.

What Could They Have Done Differently?

While the Hilltop Board took many positive steps, there's always room for improvement:

- **Resident Education:** They could have been even more transparent with residents about their proactive approach, explaining the "why" behind their dedication to staying informed.
- **Resource Sharing:** Sharing industry updates or articles with the community could further solidify Hilltop's commitment to informed governance.

Board Member Mindset: "At first, some of us thought regularly attending conferences would be a waste of time. But we quickly realized that the knowledge we gain and the connections we make are invaluable. It's what allows us to act, not just react, on behalf of our community."

Question for the Reader: Does your Board view legal compliance and continuing education as a "nice to have" or as an essential investment in your community's success?

Key Takeaways

- Proactive compliance builds trust and enhances the value of your community.
- Treat your attorney as a partner in protecting the association, not just a crisis hotline.
- Make staying informed a Board-wide priority, not the sole responsibility of one individual.

Test Your Knowledge! Answers

1. **What are the two main types of insurance coverage that every condominium association should have?**

    - **Property Insurance:** Covers physical structures (buildings, common areas) and liability for injuries on the property.
    - **Directors & Officers (D&O) Insurance:** Protects Board members from personal financial liability for decisions made on behalf of the association.

2. **Name two specific areas often covered by state condominium laws.**

    - **Governance:** How Boards are elected, meeting requirements, etc.
    - **Financial Management:** Budgets, reserve funds, assessments.
    - **Maintenance Responsibilities:** Defining common areas vs. the unit owner's responsibility. (Answers will vary slightly by state)

3. **What is the difference between a condominium association's master policy and an individual unit owner's insurance policy?**

- **Master Policy:** Covers the original structure, common areas, and association-owned property.
- **Unit Owner's Policy:** Covers upgrades within the unit, personal belongings, and additional liability protection for the unit owner.

4. **Why is it important to review your governing documents regularly, even if no major changes are being considered?**

- To ensure they align with current laws. State or local laws may change and potentially supersede your existing community rules.
- To identify outdated or unenforceable provisions that might cause future problems.

5. **What is the purpose of a reserve study, and how often should one be conducted?**

- **Purpose:** A reserve study analyzes the long-term repair and replacement needs of major common components (roofs, siding, etc.). It helps the association create a funding plan to avoid large special assessments.
- **Frequency:** A full reserve study is recommended every 3-5 years, with annual updates.

6. **List two common restrictions that might be found in a condominium's CC&Rs.**

- **Pet Restrictions:** Limitations on breeds, size, or the number of pets allowed.
- **Rental Restrictions:** Outright bans, minimum lease lengths, or requirements for tenant screening.

7. **What does the term "fiduciary duty" mean in the context of a condominium board?**

- Fiduciary duty means Board members have

a legal and ethical obligation to act in the best interests of the community as a whole. They must make decisions based on sound judgment and avoid conflicts of interest.

8. **Briefly explain the Fair Housing Act and how it applies to condominiums.**

    o   The Fair Housing Act (FHA) prohibits discrimination in housing based on protected classes (race, religion, disability, etc.).
    o   Condominium associations must comply with the FHA in areas like resident screening, making reasonable accommodations for disabilities, and handling complaints of discrimination.

9. **What should a Board do in the immediate aftermath of a catastrophic event like a fire or a flood?**

    o   **Safety First:** Ensure the safety of residents and contact emergency services if needed.
    o   **Notify Your Insurer:** Contact your insurance broker as soon as possible.
    o   **Document Everything:** Take photos and videos of the damage. Keep meticulous records of all communications and expenses.

10. **Why is it important to attend industry conferences and workshops as a Board member?**

    o   **Stay Updated:** Laws and best practices evolve. Conferences provide the latest information.
    o   **Learn from Experts:** Access to legal professionals and experienced community managers.
    o   **Networking:** Share knowledge and problem-solve with other Boards facing similar challenges.

CHAPTER 10: AMENITIES AND LIFESTYLE MANAGEMENT

Introduction

Amenities are the shared facilities and services that go beyond the basic living space in a condominium community. Examples include fitness centers, pools, community rooms, clubhouses, outdoor spaces, concierge services, spas, and the like. These amenities play a crucial role in condominium living, shaping the lifestyle experience by providing convenience, opportunities for leisure, and spaces for residents and their guests to interact. They distinguish a condominium from a simple apartment complex, creating a sense of added value.

Well-managed amenities offer several benefits. They increase resident satisfaction and create a sense of community by providing spaces for residents to socialize, pursue hobbies, and feel proud of where they live. Attractive and functional amenities also enhance property value, making a condominium complex more desirable and increasing individual unit values. Additionally, a strong suite of amenities can be a significant selling point, especially in a competitive real estate market.

Fast Fact: Well-maintained amenities can increase property values by up to 25%.

Understanding Your Current Amenities

Amenities play a crucial role in shaping the resident experience at your condominium community. They provide spaces for relaxation, leisure, and connection. However, are your current amenities truly meeting the needs and desires of your residents? To find this out, the first step is to go straight to the source – your residents themselves. Gathering their feedback lays the foundation for informed decision-making. This allows you to make strategic choices about how to manage existing amenities, identify areas for improvement, and even uncover potential for exciting new additions.

Understanding Your Current Amenities

1. Inventory and Assessment

- **Take Stock:** Create a comprehensive list of all amenities, including physical spaces, services, and any regular programs.
- **Evaluation Factors:**
  - **Condition:** Consider cleanliness, functionality, repair needs, and overall appeal.
  - **Usage:** Track how often each amenity is used and any noticeable patterns (peak times, user types).
  - **Maintenance:** Record schedules, past repairs, and associated costs.

2. Resident Feedback

- **The Value of Input:** Resident opinions help you understand what's working, what's not, and where there might be unmet needs.

- **Methods:**
    - **Surveys:** Use a mix of rating questions and space for detailed comments.
    - **Focus Groups:** Gather small groups for deeper discussions.
    - **Suggestion Box:** Offer a way for less vocal residents to share ideas.
- **What to Ask:**
    - Satisfaction levels with each amenity.
    - Why some amenities are underutilized.
    - Ideas for improvement.
    - Interest in potential new offerings.

Pro Tip: Usage Data Tells a Story - Go Beyond Foot Traffic: Don't just track if an amenity is used, track how it's used. Are residents using the gym mostly at 6 AM, suggesting later hours might be wasted? Is the pool packed on weekends but empty during weekdays? This reveals usage patterns and potential for adjustments.

Pro Tip: The "Silent Majority" Matters - Don't Overlook Those Who Don't Speak Up: Surveys and focus groups are valuable, but some residents might hesitate to offer feedback. A suggestion box (physical or digital) provides an anonymous avenue for input, potentially revealing valuable insights from those who are less likely to speak up.

Checklist:

- **Inventory:**
    - List every amenity space, service, and program
    - Note physical condition, cleaning needs, equipment functionality
- **Usage Tracking**
    - Systems in place? (sign-in sheets, smart tech, etc.)

- ○ Peak/low times, user demographic notes
- **Maintenance:**
  - ○ Detailed records of schedules, costs, recurring issues

Timeline:

- **Week 1:** Compile initial inventory. Identify gaps in usage/maintenance data.
- **Week 2-3:** Implement tracking systems. Observe amenities at different times.
- **Week 4:** Compile data, hold preliminary board discussion on findings.

Action Steps:

- Identify amenities needing immediate attention
- Decide on long-term tracking (digital tools, staff responsibilities)
- Prepare resident survey for feedback (see next section)

Amenity Evaluation For Beginners

Amenities are a major investment in your condominium community. Whether you're a seasoned board member or completely new to the role, taking the time to evaluate your amenities is crucial. Even if you've never done this before, don't worry! Simple evaluations go a long way. Here's why they matter:

- **Prevent Problems:** Catching small issues early stops them from turning into costly headaches later.
- **Enhance Resident Experience:** Well-maintained and thoughtfully planned amenities are a major contributor to resident satisfaction.
- **Make Smart Budget Decisions:** Understanding the condition of your amenities helps you prioritize spending for maximum impact.

Simple Evaluation Tools

- **Checklists:** Create a standard checklist for each type of amenity (pool, fitness center, etc.). Include key things to check, like equipment condition, signage, lighting, and overall appearance.
- **Walk-through Observations:** Do regular walk-throughs with your checklist. Note any issues, but also pay attention to how residents are using the space – this can reveal a lot!
- **Usage Logs:** Where possible, track how often amenities are used (sign-in sheets, key fobs, etc.). This helps identify any amenities that might be going unused.

Focus on the Basics

- **Cleanliness:** Is the amenity clean and inviting? First impressions count!
- **Functionality:** Does everything work as it should? Are the spaces well designed for their purpose?
- **Safety:** Look for potential hazards and make sure proper safety signage and emergency equipment (if needed) are in place.
- **Accessibility:** Can residents of all abilities comfortably access and use the amenity?

Understanding Budgetary Impact

- **Maintenance and Upkeep** Consider routine cleaning, equipment servicing, and supplies. When evaluating an amenity's condition, also try to estimate the cost of long-term repairs or replacements.

Remember, even basic evaluations make a huge difference!

Fast Fact: Resident surveys consistently show that cleanliness is the #1 factor influencing satisfaction with amenities.

Pro Tip: Don't overlook the power of landscaping and aesthetic appeal in making amenities more inviting.

Checklist:

- **Basics:**
  - Cleanliness (first impressions!)
  - Functionality (equipment working, signage, lighting, etc.)
  - Safety (hazards, emergency signage if applicable)
  - Accessibility (considering diverse needs)
- **Budgetary Impact:**
  - Routine maintenance costs
  - Estimate long-term repair/replacement needs

Timeline:

- **Concurrent with previous section:** Walk-throughs with

checklists.
- **Upon resident feedback:** Prioritize areas residents highlight.

Action Steps

- Create prioritized action list (urgent repairs, cleaning upgrades, etc.)
- Research potential accessibility improvements, budgeting accordingly.

Strategic Planning For New Amenities: A Must-Do

While new amenities can be incredibly exciting, adding them shouldn't be an impulsive decision. A well-thought-out strategy is crucial to ensure any new additions align with your condominium community's long-term goals and financial health. Strategic planning helps you avoid costly mistakes, maximizes the potential benefits, and creates amenities that residents will truly value for years to come. Think of the following roadmap as your guide:

Budgetary Considerations

- **Assess Your Finances:** Begin by analyzing your reserves. Can you fund the amenity without dipping into essential funds? If not, carefully consider a special assessment, but be aware of how this may affect residents.
- **Long-term Outlook:** Calculate ongoing maintenance and upkeep costs beyond the initial price tag. Research how similar amenities affect property values in your area – is there a potential for a positive return on investment?

Pro Tip: During the budget process, set aside a small 'contingency fund' for unexpected amenity repairs.

Demographic Analysis

- **Know Your Residents:**
    - Age Groups: Will the amenity serve a wide range of ages (children, young professionals, retirees)?
    - Interests: Does it match resident hobbies and lifestyles?

- o   Get Feedback: Directly survey residents to gauge their interest and specific preferences.

Market Research

- **Scope Out the Competition:** What amenities do comparable condominiums offer? Can you fill a current gap and gain an edge?
- **Stay Current:** Research amenity trends to keep your community desirable and competitive.

Extra Tip: Consult local real estate professionals. They have unique insights into how a new amenity might attract buyers and how it compares to other communities in your market.

Fast Fact: Dog parks are one of the most requested amenities among condo buyers.

Pro Tip: Rotate a small selection of high-quality gym equipment periodically to keep things fresh and cater to different fitness goals.

Checklist:

- **Budget Analysis:**
  - o   Available reserves, special assessment potential
  - o   Long-term maintenance costs (include in the true cost calculation)
- **Demographics:**
  - o   Needs of different age groups, interests
  - o   Survey results from previous sections
- **Market Research:**
  - o   What do competitors offer? Identify gaps
  - o   Staying up-to-date on amenity trends

Timeline:

- **Weeks 1-2:** Financial analysis (may need professional consultation)
- **Weeks 2-4** Resident survey fine-tuning, distribution.

Resident input is crucial here.
- **Weeks 5-6:** Market research, board discussions with all the data gathered

Action Steps

- Narrow potential amenities based on budget + resident wants
- Research vendors IF a clear direction emerges

Amenity Management Best Practices

Amenity management isn't just about keeping things functional; it has a direct impact on the overall appeal and success of your condominium community. Effective amenity management safeguards your property values by making your community more desirable. It boosts resident happiness by providing spaces for leisure and connection. Additionally, well-managed amenities reduce the likelihood of disputes arising from unclear rules or neglected maintenance. Follow these best practices:

Rules and Regulations

- **Set Clear Expectations:** Draft and share rules outlining hours of operation, guest allowances (and potential fees), noise restrictions, any age limits for certain amenities, and reservation procedures, if applicable.

Maintenance and Upkeep

- **Stay Ahead of Issues:** Schedule regular cleaning and inspections. Prioritize preventative maintenance on equipment. Ensure your budget can handle repairs and replacements.
- **Gather Feedback:** Make it easy for residents to report maintenance concerns. Track repair history to spot patterns. Incorporate insights from professional vendors who inspect your amenities.

Professional Management

- **When Outsourcing Makes Sense:** Consider contracting out management for amenities that require specialized knowledge (think large pools, complex gyms), have costly or unpredictable upkeep needs, or place excessive time burdens on your board or staff.

- **Choose Wisely:** Do your homework on potential management companies. Check references, ask about their strategies, and ensure they feel like a good fit for your community.

Fast Fact: Smart technology integration (e.g., app-based reservation systems) can streamline amenity management and appeal to younger residents.

Pro Tip: Track repair history – recurring issues might signal the need for equipment replacement.

Checklist

- **Clear Rules:**
  - Hours, guest policies, noise restrictions, age limits
  - How are these communicated? (signage, website, etc.)
- **Proactive Maintenance:**
  - Regular schedules for every amenity type
  - System for resident reporting of issues
- **Professional Help:**
  - When to outsource? (expertise, time burden)

Timeline:

- **Immediate:** Review existing rules (gaps, outdated info)
- **Ongoing:** Regular maintenance reviews, refining processes
- **As needed:** Vendor research if outsourcing becomes viable

Action Steps:

- Update rules, improve communication to residents
- Optimize maintenance tracking (tools, staff assignments)

Enhancing The Lifestyle Experience

Amenities are a major selling point, but they also represent a promise to residents – a promise of a lifestyle beyond just a place to live. A thriving community delivers on that promise by offering ways to connect, socialize, and create lasting memories. Here's how to enhance the resident experience and maximize the value of your amenities.

Social Events & Community-Building

- **Cater to Everyone:** Offer a mix of large gatherings (holiday parties), smaller groups (book clubs, etc.), and casual meetups (by the pool).
- **Resident-Led Initiatives:** Encourage residents to propose and organize activities – this builds a sense of ownership.

Newsletters & Communication

- **The Community Hub:** Use newsletters (digital or print) for news, resident spotlights, and event promotion.
- **Amenity-Centric:** Include maintenance info, tips for respectful use, and reminders about amenity-related events.

Partnerships & Collaborations

- **Support Local:** Offer on-site classes (yoga, fitness) taught by local businesses. Negotiate resident discounts at nearby shops or services.
- **Win-Win Promotion:** Share community news in exchange for businesses promoting your amenities and events.

Amenity-Focused Communication

- **Transparency is Key:** Inform residents about maintenance, closures, or temporary rule changes.
- **Maximize Enjoyment:** Share tips for safe and optimal use of amenities.
- **Spread the Word:** Use newsletters, boards, and digital channels to promote events tied to your amenities.

Pro Tip: Create a "New Resident Welcome Packet" including information about amenities, usage guidelines, and event calendars.

Enhancing the Lifestyle Experience

Checklist/Action Steps:

- **Mix of events:** Cater to varied interests
- **Resident-led initiatives:** Provide support framework
- **Newsletter:** Regular updates, amenity focus, resident spotlights
- **Partnerships:** Scope out local businesses fitting resident needs
- **Communication is key:** Promote events, usage tips, etc.

Timeline: Timeline less rigid here, depends on your community

Beyond The Amenities: Planning For Long-Term Success

Adding new amenities or enhancing your existing ones has the potential to significantly boost resident satisfaction and increase your community's appeal. However, it's crucial to approach these decisions with careful planning. Beyond the immediate costs and logistical factors, there are essential considerations to ensure the long-term safety, financial protection, and overall well-being of your community. Here are some vital points to keep in mind:

Insurance and Liability

- **Be Thorough:** Ensure your policy covers all amenities for accidents, damage, or potential legal issues.
- **Stay Updated:** Work with your insurance provider to adjust coverage as your amenities change.
- **Seek Legal Advice:** Consult an attorney before implementing liability waivers for high-risk amenities.
- **Inform Residents:** Display clear signage with relevant insurance and liability information.

Checklist:

- **Comprehensive Coverage:**
    - Review policy with an insurance agent specializing in condominiums.
    - Ensure all current amenities are adequately covered.
- **Liability Waivers:**
    - Consult with the board's attorney for guidance on specific amenities and situations where waivers may be appropriate.

- **Signage:**
  - Display clear signage outlining relevant insurance and liability information where applicable.

Timeline:

- **Week 1-2:** Insurance policy review. Identify any gaps in coverage.
- **Week 3:** Consultation with an attorney regarding waivers.
- **Week 4:** Develop and implement signage strategy,

Action Steps

- Update insurance as needed immediately.
- Draft waiver language (with legal counsel). Determine signage placement.

Accessibility and Inclusivity

- **Aim Higher:** Go beyond simply meeting legal requirements (like ADA standards) to create a genuinely inclusive space.
- **Consider All Residents:** Design amenities with diverse abilities, ages, and sensitivities in mind.
- **Evaluate and Improve:** Identify any accessibility barriers in existing amenities and make upgrades a priority.
- **Prioritize Universal Design:** Whenever possible, incorporate universal design principles into new amenities or renovations.
- **Listen to Residents:** Proactively gather feedback from residents with disabilities to pinpoint their needs and find solutions.

Checklist:

- **Beyond Compliance:**
  - Research ADA guidelines. Familiarize yourself with universal design principles.
- **Resident Input:**

- Proactively seek feedback from residents with diverse needs. Consider a committee focused on accessibility issues.
- **Assessment:**
  - Evaluate existing amenities for barriers, potential improvements.

Timeline:

- **Week 1-2:** Research guidelines and design principles.
- **Weeks 2-4:** Outreach to residents for feedback, committee formation.
- **Weeks 5-6:** Amenity assessment, prioritize potential improvement areas.

Action Steps

- Identify immediate adjustments (signage, temporary fixes).
- Develop longer-term plan (budgeted upgrades, phased-in approach).

Sample Project Timeline: Pool Accessibility Improvement

- **Phase 1:** Consultation with accessibility expert, resident input, cost estimates.
- **Phase 2:** Secure funding (budget, special assessment if needed).
- **Phase 3:** Vendor selection, construction timeline.
- **Phase 4** Ongoing review, further improvement planning.

Important Note: Accessibility projects sometimes require professional guidance and may need longer timelines.

Fast Fact: Accessibility features, even when not legally required, can benefit a surprisingly large portion of residents, including seniors and families with young children.

Test Your Knowledge!

1. What are three key elements to include in an amenity maintenance checklist?
2. Name two ways to gather resident feedback on amenities.
3. What is the difference between proactive maintenance and reactive maintenance?
4. When considering a new amenity, why is it important to research comparable condominiums in your area?
5. List two benefits of partnering with local businesses for amenity-related services.
6. Why is accessibility an important factor, even when exceeding basic legal requirements?
7. What does "special assessment" mean in the context of funding amenities?
8. Give an example of a social event that encourages resident-led initiatives.
9. How can newsletters promote a sense of community beyond just sharing information?
10. What is one key consideration when ensuring insurance policies cover your amenities?

The answers are at the end of this chapter

Case Study: The "Small But Mighty" Condo (Rewritten)

Sarah, a young professional living in a cozy 50-unit condo building, loved the location but yearned for a greater sense of community. While neighbors were friendly, everyone seemed to rush in and out, lacking a place to linger. The courtyard, potentially the heart of the building, was bleak: a patch of uneven grass, a couple of chipped benches, and a sense of neglect.

Resident surveys confirmed her hunch: people craved connection but lacked inviting spaces. The board, though operating on a modest budget, decided to tackle this issue head-on. Seeking inspiration, they visited a nearby park, noting how simple elements created distinct "zones."

Back at their building, they got creative. Thrifty landscaping provided structure – a curved row of flowering bushes formed a "wall" separating a sunny patio from a quieter corner. Refurbished benches were complemented by a bistro table set for impromptu coffee chats. A winding gravel path beckoned towards a shaded nook, where a new bench nestled beside a soothing water fountain. Finally, a few potted herbs and colorful annuals added welcoming pops of color.

The transformation was remarkable. Suddenly, Sarah sipped her morning coffee amidst birdsong, nodding hellos to retirees watering the flowers. Lunch breaks meant sharing takeout on the patio with a chatty neighbor. The once-empty space even hosted a building-wide potluck, laughter echoing until dusk. The "Small But Mighty" condo had discovered something profound: thoughtful design, even on a tight budget, could cultivate a true sense of belonging.

What Could They Have Done Differently?

- **Involve Residents Earlier:** While surveys were used, engaging residents in the brainstorming phase could have sparked creative solutions and built ownership of the project.

Board Member Voice: Sarah (young professional board member): "Honestly, before, I saw the courtyard as a maintenance issue, not an opportunity. This project opened my eyes to how even small changes can transform people's experience of where they live."

Reader Reflection: Are there underutilized spaces in your community that could be reimagined with a similar approach?

Key Takeaways

- Don't underestimate the power of small, thoughtful improvements.
- Resident input is key: Surveys are useful, but even informal conversations can uncover valuable insights.
- "Zones" create purpose: Designate areas for socializing, quiet contemplation, etc., to cater to diverse needs.
- Budget-friendly options exist: Landscaping, repainting, and repurposed furniture can go a long way.

Case Study: The Revitalized Fitness Center

Oakwood Condominiums had a problem. Their fitness center, once a decent perk, had fallen into disrepair. The treadmill belts squeaked ominously, the weight machines seemed more like museum relics than workout equipment, and the overall vibe was more depressing than motivating. Residents, tired of the sad state of affairs, opted to pay for pricey gym memberships elsewhere, leaving Oakwood's amenity to gather dust.

When Alex became board president, he was determined to turn things around. A complete overhaul was financially impossible, but letting the gym languish wasn't an option either. He started with a resident survey, determined to pinpoint the biggest pain points. Cardio and free weights were the clear priorities – people wanted functional basics. Armed with this data, Alex presented a phased plan to the board: Replace the most outdated cardio machines first, then tackle the weight room in stages, spreading the investment over time.

The initial changes made a noticeable difference, but the gym still felt lackluster. That's when Alex had a stroke of inspiration. He proposed hiring a certified trainer, not for one-on-one sessions, but for group fitness classes and equipment orientations a few hours per week. This was the game-changer. Suddenly, residents who felt intimidated by the equipment had guidance. Group classes added a social element, making workouts fun. Soon, the gym buzzed with energy. People canceled those external memberships, saving money while actually getting healthier in their own building. Oakwood's revitalized fitness center became a source of pride, a selling point for prospective residents, and proof that smart investments can have a major impact.

What Could They Have Done Differently?

- **Acted Sooner:** Waiting for the problem to reach a crisis point meant resident frustration and lost value. Proactive maintenance and budgeting for gradual upgrades could have prevented such a drastic decline.
- **Involve Residents from the Start:** While the survey was a good step, early focus groups might have uncovered the desire for trainer-led classes, potentially accelerating the transformation.

Board Member Voice: Alex, Board President: "Honestly, we'd fallen into that "out of sight, out of mind" trap. The gym wasn't terrible, just...neglected. Seeing those survey results was a wake-up call."

Question for the Reader: Are there amenities in your community that are just "getting by" rather than truly serving residents?

Key Takeaways

- **Don't Let Amenities Stagnate:** Proactive assessments and resident feedback prevent small problems from becoming big ones.
- **Prioritize Function Over Flash:** Residents often value well-maintained basics over fancy features they don't use.
- **The Human Touch Matters:** Sometimes the biggest amenity upgrade is adding skilled staff for even limited hours.

Case Study: Embracing Accessibility In Luxury Living

Horizon Condominiums was the epitome of luxury living – gleaming towers, panoramic views, and a resort-style pool that was the envy of the neighborhood. But for residents like Emily, a young mother with a rambunctious toddler, and Mr. Johnson, a retired gentleman who relied on a walker, the pool area was more intimidating than inviting. The sleek, multi-level design prioritized aesthetics over accessibility. Emily longed for a safe way for her daughter to play in the water, while Mr. Johnson wished he could participate in the water aerobics classes he'd heard so much about.

Initially, the board hesitated to invest in accessibility upgrades. They prided themselves on the sleek, modern image of Horizon, and worried that renovations might detract from that aesthetic. However, a growing sense of unease nagged at them. Was true luxury about appearances, or about ensuring that all residents felt welcome and included?

Seeking guidance, they consulted with accessibility experts and formed a resident advisory group. The feedback was eye-opening. With thoughtful design, accessibility could be seamlessly integrated. Inspired, the board approved a plan that included a gently graduated pool entry, strategically placed handrails, and a designated area with ample deck space for strollers, wheelchairs, and those needing a little extra room.

The transformation was remarkable. Emily's daughter now delights in the shallow end, building sandcastles at the water's edge. Mr. Johnson confidently participates in water therapy classes, regaining strength and mobility. Word of Horizon's commitment to inclusivity spread, attracting new buyers who valued not just the breathtaking-taking views, but the equally compelling sense of community that embraced residents of all abilities. The investment proved that true luxury lies in creating a space where everyone feels they belong.

What Could They Have Done Differently?

- **Acted Sooner:** The board could have proactively addressed accessibility concerns during the initial design or in earlier renovations, preventing the need for costly retrofits.

Board Member Mindset Quote: "Honestly, we fell into the trap of thinking 'luxury' meant sleek and exclusive. It took hearing the personal stories of residents to realize we were excluding people unintentionally."

Question for the Reader: Are there areas in your community amenities where the design might be inadvertently creating barriers for certain residents?

Key Takeaways

- Accessibility isn't just about meeting legal requirements; it's about promoting genuine inclusion.
- Consulting experts and residents with disabilities is crucial for identifying and addressing accessibility issues.
- Embracing accessibility can positively impact your community's reputation and attract potential buyers.

Case Study: The Community Coffeehouse

Janice had always been the type to bake cookies for new neighbors on her old block. Moving to her condo felt like a step down – sure, it was sleek, with its granite countertops and stainless steel, but also a bit cold and impersonal. People kept to themselves, renters came and went, and the only time she saw familiar faces was in the elevator. Then, while grabbing some wilting chives for dinner from the sadly underused community herb garden, she bumped into Mark. He was a fellow dog owner she'd nod to while walking her terrier. Turns out, he was feeling the same disconnect.

An idea sparked. Sure, they didn't have a sprawling clubhouse or pool, but what about that depressing meeting room? It was always empty, with its plastic chairs and flickering fluorescent lights. But Janice saw potential — a cozy "coffeehouse" corner, mismatched armchairs scavenged from thrift shops, and a donated coffee maker. The smell of brewing coffee alone could change the atmosphere. She pitched the idea to the board, expecting at least some eye rolls. To her surprise, they agreed to a trial run, provided it was fully resident-run and cost-neutral.

The transformation was stunningly quick. Janice became a regular at flea markets, turning up treasures. Mark, surprisingly handy, repainted the walls a warm yellow. A simple bulletin board bloomed with flyers – resident-led book swaps, offers of dog-walking, a Friday "Happy Hour" (BYOB, but the conversation flowed). Janice became the unofficial barista, chatting with everyone, regulars and newcomers alike. Now, the room buzzes, laughter spills into hallways, and even the elevator isn't so awkwardly silent. Janice baked a batch of cookies – her condo building was finally starting to feel like a true home.

What Could They Have Done Differently?

- **Involve Residents Sooner:** Even before pitching the concept, Janice and Mark could have informally polled fellow residents to gauge interest and gather ideas to make the space more appealing.
- **Start Smaller:** Instead of overhauling the whole room, perhaps a trial "Coffee Cart" with basic supplies in a corner could have tested the concept before full commitment.

Board Member Mindset Quote: "Honestly, we were skeptical. Nice idea, but would people really use it? Seemed like a lot of work for something that might fizzle out." - (The Board Treasurer)

Question for the Reader: Does your building have any underused spaces that, with a little creativity and resident involvement, could become a new kind of community hub?

Key Takeaways

- **Connection Trumps Fancy Amenities:** Sometimes, the most impactful amenities are born from resident-led initiatives and build a sense of ownership.
- **Cost-Effective Transformation:** Big changes aren't always about big spending. Resourcefulness and a welcoming vibe go a long way.
- **The Board as Enabler:** Boards can play a powerful role by supporting resident-led ideas, even when skeptical, allowing true community spirit to emerge.

Case Study: The Tech-Forward Amenity Upgrade

Michael, a fast-paced marketing exec, loved the urban energy of Cityview Apartments. But when it came to working remotely and connecting with neighbors, the building fell short. Common spaces were generic, WiFi was spotty, and battling for a decent table at the overcrowded coffee shop down the street wasn't his idea of productivity. Driven to change things, he joined the condo board, where fellow residents echoed his frustrations.

His first mission: to make Cityview truly work-from-home friendly. Gone were the flickering fluorescent lights and unreliable internet. The board invested in blazing-fast WiFi throughout the building and transformed a neglected lounge into a bright co-working haven. Charging stations sprouted at sleek communal tables, ergonomic chairs replaced the dated sofas, and a fancy coffee machine became the new water cooler.

But Michael didn't stop there. Recognizing that his generation valued both tech and face-to-face connection, he spearheaded the development of an integrated app. Booking the newly renovated gym? Done. Reserving the rooftop terrace for his team's brainstorming session? A few taps. Spontaneous wine and cheese night with his floor neighbors? The app made it easy to organize.

The results were profound. Michael now breezed through his workday from the comfort of the common areas, feeling a sense of both focus and connection. Residents lingered longer after work, sparking conversations over high-end lattes. Cityview shed its impersonal vibe, becoming a place where tech-driven convenience encouraged genuine community – a selling point the board was quick to capitalize on, attracting even more young professionals seeking that elusive work/life integration.

What Could They Have Done Differently?

- **Early Resident Input:** While tech upgrades were clearly needed, surveying residents upfront on their specific needs (quiet zones vs. collaborative, app functions) could have refined the plan further.

Board Member Mindset Quote: "Honestly, we were stuck in the past. Fancy amenities meant a pool or maybe those movie theater rooms. It took someone like Michael to show us that 'amenity' nowadays meant making life easier and more connected for our kind of residents."

Question for the Reader: Does your building's technology support the way residents actually work and live, or is it time for an upgrade that adds real value?

Key Takeaways

- Tech-focused amenities can be a powerful differentiator, especially for attracting younger demographics.
- Digital tools shouldn't replace the need for well-designed common spaces that promote social interaction.
- Truly understanding your resident's lifestyle is key to identifying the tech upgrades that will actually be used.

Case Study: Partnering For Perks

Willow Creek Condominiums offered a suburban haven for busy families, but everyone felt something was missing. The kids longed for a pool to beat the summer heat, while parents craved a convenient workout space those hectic evenings. Building such amenities was beyond their budget. Board member Lisa, however, saw a hidden opportunity just down the road: their bustling neighborhood shopping center.

Lisa knew local businesses could benefit from the complex's numerous residents. With the board's approval, she approached the yoga studio struggling to fill their afternoon classes, the gym with unused treadmills during weekdays, and even the family-owned swim school seeking new students. Her pitch was simple: offer exclusive discounts to Willow Creek residents in exchange for guaranteed new customers.

The response was enthusiastic! Soon, residents brandished their building ID for reduced yoga class fees, easing the stress of long days. Kids splashed happily during their dedicated swim lesson slots, and moms treated themselves to discounted manicures at the salon. Word spread, and renting at Willow Creek became even more attractive. Turns out, the best amenity wasn't always something you had to build, but rather, a bridge to the community right outside your door.

What Could They Have Done Differently?

- **Broader Outreach:** While Lisa focused on businesses catering to their resident demographics, exploring partnerships with even more diverse vendors (pet services, restaurants, etc.) could have expanded benefits further.
- **Resident-Led Initiatives:** Encouraging residents to propose business partnerships based on their own

interests would promote a sense of ownership and tap into the community's knowledge of local offerings.

Board Member Mindset: Lisa: "Honestly, at first, I was fixated on what we didn't have. But then I realized our location was our hidden strength. We just needed to think beyond our own walls."

Question for the Reader: What existing resources are right within reach of your community? Could local partnerships enhance your residents' experience in unexpected ways?

Key Takeaways

- **Creative Solutions:** Sometimes, the best amenities don't require expensive construction.
- **Out-of-the-Box Thinking:** Your community's surroundings could hold untapped potential.
- **Win-Win Partnerships:** Local businesses often welcome mutually beneficial collaborations.

Test Your Knowledge! Answers

1. **Three key elements in a maintenance checklist:**

    - **Specific Equipment or Areas:** Detail parts to inspect (e.g., pool filters, gym equipment belts, playground surfaces).
    - **Action Items:** Cleaning, lubrication, testing, minor repairs.
    - **Frequency:** Schedule for daily, weekly, or monthly checks.

2. **Two ways to gather resident feedback:**

    - **Surveys:** Written or online, mix of open-ended questions and rating scales.
    - **Focus Groups:** Facilitated discussions to explore

opinions in depth.

3. **Proactive vs. Reactive Maintenance:**

   - **Proactive:** Regular inspections, preventative servicing, catching problems early.
   - **Reactive:** Addressing issues only after they break down, often leading to more costly repairs and resident inconvenience.

4. **Researching Comparable Condominiums:**

   - **Identify Gaps:** Discover what amenities your competitors offer that you're missing.
   - Stay Competitive: See what's considered standard or desirable in your market.

5. **Benefits of Partnering with Local Businesses:**

   - **Expertise:** Access specialized services without having to hire in-house staff.
   - **Resident perks:** Negotiate discounts for your community, adding value.

6. **Accessibility Beyond Legal Requirements:**

   - **Inclusivity:** Welcomes residents of all abilities, promoting a true sense of belonging.
   - **Wider Appeal:** Accessible design often benefits a broader range of people (e.g., parents with strollers, aging residents)

7. **Special Assessment:**

   - An additional fee levied on residents, specifically to fund a project or major expense (like a new amenity).

8. **Resident-Led Social Event Example:**

   - **Community Potluck:** Residents bring dishes to share, showcasing diversity and encouraging interaction.

9. **Newsletters Building Community:**

   - **Resident Spotlights:** Feature individuals/families, creating connections.
   - **Celebrate Successes:** Highlight resident achievements in the community or beyond.

10. **Insurance Considerations:**

    - **Specific Risks:** Ensure your coverage aligns with the potential hazards of each amenity (e.g., pool accidents, gym equipment injuries).

CHAPTER 11: THE BOARD-MANAGER PARTNERSHIP

Introduction

This chapter emphasizes the importance of your board's relationship with the entire management company, not just your community manager. While the manager is your primary contact, remember they have a whole team behind them. Understanding this broader structure is key for effective communication and collaboration.

Your community manager plays a crucial role in the day-to-day running of your condominium. They put your board's decisions into action, handle maintenance, manage finances, and resolve resident concerns. A skilled manager makes a huge difference in keeping your community running smoothly and maintaining resident satisfaction.

A strong board-management company partnership benefits everyone involved. It leads to better efficiency, proactive solutions, and a happier community. Conversely, a strained relationship leads to miscommunication, mistrust, and decisions that could negatively impact your community's progress.

Fast Fact: Resident satisfaction is often directly linked to their perception of the management company.

Pro Tip: When interviewing potential management companies, ask about their conflict resolution processes and communication strategies.

The Foundation Of A Successful Partnership

A successful partnership between the board and your management company isn't just about ticking boxes; it's about creating a foundation for a thriving community. When everyone understands their roles and responsibilities, it unlocks efficiency, minimizes misunderstandings, and allows both the board and the management company to focus on what they do best. Let's dive into the specific contributions of each party, and highlight the crucial areas where collaboration makes all the difference:

The Board's Authority

The board acts as the guiding force of the community. You're responsible for:

- Setting the overall direction and policies that shape resident life.
- Approving budgets and ensuring wise financial management of major expenses.
- Overseeing the management company's performance to ensure they meet expectations.

Fast Fact: HOA/condo boards are legally obligated to act as fiduciaries, meaning they must put the community's interests first.

The Management Company's Duties

Your management company is the engine that keeps your community running smoothly. Their core duties include:

- Putting the board's decisions into action, translating

your vision into reality.
- Handling routine maintenance and repairs, ensuring the property is always in good condition.
- Communicating effectively with residents and vendors, building a sense of transparency.
- Managing finances and collecting fees responsibly, safeguarding your community's assets.

Where Collaboration is Key

There are areas where a true partnership shines:
- Strategic planning and goal-setting: The board and management company must work together to define long-term goals.
- Addressing complex issues: When resident conflicts or major challenges arise, open communication and joint problem-solving are essential.

Shared Goals and Vision

When the board and management company are aligned, the whole community benefits. To achieve this:
- Hold joint workshops to define goals and priorities, ensuring both parties are on the same page.
- Include the management company in long-range planning discussions. Their expertise and insights are invaluable.
- Periodically check in and reaffirm your shared vision. This prevents misaligned efforts down the road.

Effective Communication

Strong communication is the lifeblood of your partnership. Here's how to make it work:
- Regular meetings: Schedule them consistently, with well-structured agendas for focused discussions.
- Agreed-upon reporting: Transparent reports on finances,

maintenance, and legal matters build trust.
- Best channels: Know when to use specific channels (email, in-person, portals) for efficient communication.
- Open dialogue: Create an atmosphere where respectful idea exchange is encouraged, and concerns are addressed quickly.

Additional Considerations

- Management Contract: This is your rulebook. Make sure roles are clear and include provisions for changes as your community evolves. Boards may need legal guidance.
- Board Liaison: Designating a single point of contact for the management company will prevent conflicting messages and keep everyone on track.

Fast Fact: The average tenure for a community association manager is less than 3 years. Building a strong relationship is key to continuity.

Pro Tip: During board transitions, prioritize a comprehensive handover meeting with both the outgoing and incoming board and the management company.

Pro Tip: Regularly invite your community manager to attend a portion of your board meetings for open updates and Q&A sessions.

Checklist: Assessing Your Current Relationship

- Is there open, regular communication?
- Do both the board and management company feel respected and heard?
- Are expectations clear on both sides?
- Is there a shared understanding of the community's goals?

Timeline: Building a Strong Foundation (If Needed)

- **Week 1:** Open communication channels. Schedule initial

meeting.
- **Weeks 2-4:** Discuss community goals, board expectations, and management company capabilities.
- **Month 1-2:** Draft initial expectations, responsibilities, and communication plan.
- **Ongoing:** Regularly review and refine as needed.

Action Steps

- Designate a board liaison as a primary point of contact.
- Include communication expectations in management contract.

Performance Evaluations: A Tool For Excellence

Performance evaluations are essential for a productive board-management company relationship – they work just like they do in any workplace! Here's how boards can leverage them:

Accountability & Improvement: Evaluations hold your management company accountable and highlight areas for improvement. This benefits your entire community.

Setting Clear Expectations: Use measurable indicators (KPIs) – resident satisfaction, financial targets, maintenance speed – to define success. Ensure your management company shares the board's vision. Some examples of KPI's:

Resident Satisfaction KPIs

- Survey Response Rate: Tracks resident engagement in feedback processes.
- Overall Satisfaction Scores: Measures general contentment with the community.
- Specific Area Ratings: Cleanliness, amenities, staff responsiveness, etc.
- Work Order Resolution Satisfaction: How happy are residents with maintenance outcomes.
- Renewal Rates: A strong indicator of long-term satisfaction.

Financial KPIs

- Budget Adherence: How well the management company stays within budget.
- Delinquency Rates: Percentage of residents late on fees.
- Collections Success Rate: Ability to collect overdue fees

effectively.
- Cost Savings: Did the management company find ways to save money on services?
- Return on Investments (If applicable): Performance of any community investments.

Maintenance & Operations KPIs

- Work Order Completion Time: How quickly maintenance requests are addressed.
- Preventive Maintenance Rate: Proactive vs. reactive maintenance balance.
- Emergency Response Time: Speed of handling urgent issues.
- Vendor Costs & Satisfaction: Are vendors reliable and cost-effective?
- Safety Incident Rate: Tracks any accidents or safety concerns on the property.

Additional KPI Considerations

- Community-Specific Goals: Tailor KPIs to your unique priorities (e.g., sustainability initiatives, event participation).
- Benchmarking: Compare KPIs to similar communities to gauge performance.

Cautionary Considerations for Board-Developed Management Evaluation Criteria:

Performance evaluations are essential, but it's crucial for boards to be mindful of factors that might be beyond the management company's control. Unfairly penalizing them for external circumstances can damage your partnership and hinder progress. Additionally, the evaluation process should be a chance for the board to reflect on its own performance. Let's discuss some key considerations to ensure your evaluation process is both fair and promotes a productive two-way dialogue for continuous improvement:

Factors Beyond Management Company Control:

- **Market Conditions:** Economic downturns can negatively impact resident satisfaction (e.g., job losses impacting fee payments).
- **External Regulations:** Changes in local laws or regulations outside the management company's control can affect operations (e.g., construction delays due to permit hold-ups).
- **Unforeseen Events:** Natural disasters, accidents, or equipment failures may impact service delivery.

Avoiding Unfair Evaluations:

- **Focus on Controllable Factors:** Evaluate based on the management company's ability to adapt and respond to challenges within their control.
- **Historical Context:** Consider trends and past performance to get a clearer picture.
- **Transparency with Residents:** Communicate any external factors impacting the community.

Self-Reflection and Two-Way Communication:

- **Board Responsibilities:** Include board performance criteria in the evaluation (e.g., meeting attendance, communication with residents, budget oversight).
- **Open-Ended Feedback:** Incorporate sections where both the board and management company can provide constructive criticism and suggestions for improvement.
- **Joint Goal Setting:** Use the evaluation as a springboard for collaborative goal setting for the coming year.
- **Debrief Meetings:** Schedule discussions after evaluations to discuss findings openly and plan improvement actions together.

Additional Tips:

- **Benchmarking:** Compare your KPIs to similar

communities to identify areas for improvement for both the board and management company.
- **External Review:** Consider using an independent consultant to facilitate the evaluation process and provide a neutral perspective.
- **Focus on Solutions:** Use the evaluation to identify challenges and work together to find solutions, strengthening a stronger partnership.

Remember: The goal of the evaluation should be to improve the overall performance of the community, not assign blame. By acknowledging areas where both the board and management company can improve, you can create a more productive and successful partnership.

The Evaluation Process:

A well-structured evaluation process is key to ensuring both fairness and actionable insights. By setting clear expectations, involving the right stakeholders, and formalizing procedures, you'll get the most value out of your management company evaluations. Here's how to create a robust process:

The Evaluation Process

- **Consistency is Key:** Annual or semi-annual evaluations establish a rhythm. Regularity helps track progress and identify potential issues early on.

- **Board's Responsibility:** The board ultimately owns the evaluation process. You'll set timelines, gather feedback, and determine outcomes based on the results.

- **Resident Voices:** Surveys or designated comment periods provide invaluable perspectives on how your management company is perceived by those they serve. Consider both broad satisfaction surveys and specific feedback on recent interactions (maintenance requests, etc.).

- **Formalize It:** Develop a clear evaluation form with specific criteria (based on your KPIs). A written record ensures consistency year-over-year and provides reference points for discussions with the management company.

Closing the Loop: Post-Evaluation Actions

A thorough evaluation is only the first step. To truly drive improvement, you need to turn insights into action. Here's how to ensure your evaluation process has a lasting positive impact:

- **Collaborative Debriefing:** Schedule a meeting with the management company to review the evaluation results. Avoid an accusatory tone, focusing instead on jointly identifying solutions and setting new goals.
- **Action Plan:** Together, outline a plan addressing areas for improvement. This should include:
  - Specific action items assigned to the management company.
  - Agreed-upon timelines for implementation.
  - Support provided by the board (training resources, budget approvals, etc.).
- **Follow-up & Progress Tracking:** Establish check-in points to track progress on the action plan. Did the management company attend the workshop? Are new communication protocols being followed?
- **Utilize the Plan Throughout the Year:** Reference the evaluation and action plan during regular meetings with the management company. This keeps improvement initiatives top-of-mind.
- **The Next Evaluation Cycle:** Document the changes and results achieved since the previous evaluation. This demonstrates the success of your collaborative efforts.

Key Takeaway: Performance evaluations are most effective when viewed as part of an ongoing cycle of improvement, not a one-and-done event.

From Evaluation to Elevation: Finding Growth Opportunities

While evaluations are a chance to address areas for improvement, it's equally important to celebrate your management company's strengths and unlock further potential. Here's how to use the evaluation to support their continuous development:

- **Emerging Trends:** Did the evaluation reveal strong adaptability or openness to change? Encourage proactive training on new technologies and industry best practices. This future-proofs your management company's skills.
- **Evolving Resident Needs:** Does your community's demographic shift, or are resident priorities evolving? Provide your management company with training to meet those changing needs (communication platforms, tailored events, etc.).
- **Manager's Passions:** Is your manager passionate about sustainability or streamlining processes? Nurture those interests with relevant training that benefits the entire community.
- **Leveraging Strengths:** Did particular areas earn top scores? Explore advanced training to turn those strengths into even greater advantages.

Transition to Action Planning

By identifying these growth opportunities, you lay the groundwork for the next crucial step: the collaborative debriefing and action plan development, where the board and management company turn insights into tangible improvements.

Types of Training to Consider

- **Conferences and Industry Events** for networking and exposure to new ideas.
- **Skill-Specific Workshops:** Conflict resolution, legal updates, maintenance best practices, etc.
- **Online Courses:** Convenient and flexible for busy management staff.
- **In-House Training:** Bring in experts for tailored sessions to your company's needs.

Additional Considerations:

- **Budget for Growth:** Allocate funds in your budget for management company development.
- **Track and Celebrate:** Document training as part of the performance review process, recognizing their dedication to improvement.

Checklist: Designing a Meaningful Evaluation

- What are the core performance areas to evaluate? (e.g., communication, financial management)
- Who participates in the evaluation? (Board members, residents, etc.)
- Will it use quantitative measures (surveys) or qualitative feedback (comments)?
- How will results guide improvement plans?

Timeline: Annual Performance Evaluation

- **Month 10-11:** Board designs evaluation process.
- **Month 12:** Evaluation conducted.
- **Month 1 (next year):** Board and manager review results together, set goals.
- **Ongoing:** Quarterly or semi-annual progress check-ins.

Action Steps:

- Create a standard evaluation form/process.

- Decide on timing and frequency that work for your board and manager.

Contract Negotiation

A clear and well-written management contract is crucial for a strong board-management company relationship. These contracts can be complex, so careful negotiation is a must. If you have an existing relationship with an attorney, consult them to ensure the contract protects your community's interests and that you understand all the terms.

Before negotiations, familiarize yourself with these key areas:

- **Compensation & Benefits:**
    - How the base management fee is structured.
    - Any additional fees for specific services.
    - Benefits provided to the management company.
- **Termination Clauses:**
    - Under what circumstances can either party end the agreement.
    - Required notice periods, potential penalties, and how disputes will be resolved.
- **Renewal Process:**
    - Does the contract renew automatically, or is renegotiation needed?
    - What are the timeframes for giving notice regarding renewal intentions?
    - Are there cost-of-living adjustments built into the contract?
- **Scope of Services & Performance Expectations:**
    - A detailed list of the management company's duties.
    - How performance will be measured (KPIs), and if exceeding goals can lead to bonuses.

Professional Guidance: Attorneys who focus on management contracts can help you understand industry standards and protect your community by ensuring the terms are favorable and avoid any negative loopholes.

Pro Tip: Set clear expectations in your management contract about meeting frequency, communication methods, and reporting requirements.

The Risks of Being Too Aggressive

Negotiating a management contract is all about finding the right balance. You need to be a strong advocate for your community, but don't view the management company as an adversary. Being too aggressive on price or terms can alienate potential partners and create problems down the line. Avoid these pitfalls:

1. **Risk of Focusing Only on the Bottom Line:** Forcing a management company to accept an unsustainably low fee will compromise their ability to serve you well. This could lead to...
   a. **High Turnover:** Underpaid staff may become demotivated and leave frequently, creating instability.
   b. **Understaffing:** The management company may take on too many communities per manager, leading to overworked staff and neglected tasks.
   c. **Insufficient Resources:** Cost-cutting could compromise technology, training, or office resources needed for quality service.
2. **Risk of Short-Sighted Savings:** Don't be lured in by unrealistic promises from a company desperate for your business. They may not be able to deliver what they promise, and this could spell future trouble. Watch out for companies with a history of client

turnover.

3. **Risk of Going in Unprepared:** If you don't know what your community truly needs, you might miss crucial details in the contract. This could lead to disappointment and unmet expectations.

Recommendations:

- **Do Your Homework:** Research industry standards for management fees.
- **Value Over Price:** Focus on getting quality service at a fair price, not just the cheapest option.
- **Define Your Needs:** Know exactly what you expect from the management company before negotiations begin.
- **Get Help:** Consult an attorney who understands management contracts.
- **Build a Partnership:** Seek a contract that benefits both your community and the management company for long-term success.

Remember!!!! A strong community thrives with a skilled and committed management company. While it's tempting to try to squeeze the lowest possible price, this strategy often backfires. By excluding high-performing companies right from the start, you're left with those desperate for business, willing to promise anything just to get the contract. This ultimately harms your community as these companies cut corners to stay afloat.

Boards that insist on rock-bottom pricing signal they don't see this as a true partnership. This drives away reputable management companies who understand that providing quality service has real costs. Trying to disguise your price obsession as a quest for 'value' won't fool anyone. High-performing management companies know their worth and won't compromise their reputation by working with boards focused exclusively on the bottom line.

The result? If you're unwilling to pay a fair price, the only companies willing to negotiate with you will likely be those with poor track records. They'll say whatever it takes to get the contract, only to struggle to fulfill their promises later. A good management company more than pays for itself in the long run. Focus on finding that fair price that ensures quality service, and you'll ultimately save your community money and headaches.

Checklist: Pre-Negotiation Prep

- Outline community priorities and non-negotiables.
- Review contracts from other communities (with legal assistance).
- Research management company reputations (industry groups, resident reviews).
- Assemble your negotiation team (board members, attorney, etc.).

Timeline: Simplified Contract Process

- **Weeks 1-2:** Board develops priorities
- **Weeks 3-4:** Request proposals
- **Weeks 5-8:** Interview candidates, check references
- **Weeks 9-12:** Negotiation and legal review
- **Week 13+:** Finalize and sign

Action Steps

- Start the process WELL before any current contract expires.
- Get legal advice specific to your state's HOA/condo laws.

Conflict Resolution

Successful communities understand that conflict isn't a sign of failure, but rather an opportunity for growth. They embrace conflict resolution as a normal part of the board-management company relationship, leading to stronger partnerships and better outcomes for residents. Here's how to minimize conflict, handle disagreements effectively, and address those who might hinder the process:

Proactive Measures

- **Clear Communication:** Talk regularly and honestly to avoid surprises.
- **Quick Action:** Discuss problems early, before they get worse.
- **Strong Relationships:** A little trust goes a long way when disagreements arise.

When Conflicts Arise

- **United Front:** Have rules for how your board handles internal disagreements. Don't look divided.
- **Point Person:** One board member handles most communication for smoother interactions.
- **Plan Ahead:** Agree on a step-by-step process if issues can't be resolved quickly (who talks to whom, when do you go to the next level, etc.)

Dealing with Disruptive Individuals

However, even the most proactive approach can be challenged by individuals with personal agendas. Some board members might approach disagreements with an "ax to grind," aiming to stir up conflict and rally support to push out the management company, rather than seeking solutions. This "us vs. them" narrative can be disruptive and ultimately counterproductive. Here's how to address such situations:

Addressing Toxic Board Members

While prevention is ideal, sometimes a board member's behavior toward the community's management company becomes disruptive and requires direct intervention. Here's how to address it:

- **Open but Private Conversation:** If feasible, have the board chair or other respected board members approach the disruptive member privately. Express concerns about the impact of their behavior on the board's work and its relationship with the management company. Offer ways to contribute more constructively, but be prepared that this approach might not be successful.

- **Counteracting Disruptive Behavior**

  During meetings, it's essential to have strategies in place to address toxic behavior and protect the board's collaborative process. Employ the following:

  - **Unified Response:** When the disruptive board member makes statements that don't reflect the board's position, other members should calmly say, "We appreciate your perspective, but that's not the board's consensus on this matter."
  - **Controlled Communication:** Emphasize the rule of having at least two board representatives present for any communications with the management company. This prevents misrepresentation of the board's stance.
  - **Detailed Documentation:** Keep thorough meeting minutes, highlighting instances where the problematic member misrepresents their opinion as

the board's official position.

Fast Fact: Board meeting minutes are considered legal documents. Accuracy is essential.

- **Procedural Control:** Use Robert's Rules of Order or a similar meeting structure to control the flow of the meeting. This can help limit rambling rants and maintain order.
- **Addressing Escalation:** If the toxic board member becomes uncivil and refuses to respect their colleagues, ask them to leave the meeting. This demonstrates that disruptive behavior won't be tolerated.

- **Review Your Governing Documents:** Check your bylaws or governing documents for potential mechanisms to censure or even remove a board member engaging in disruptive or harmful behavior.

Fast Fact: Many states have laws specifically governing community associations. Make sure your board and management company understand them.

- **Seek Legal Guidance:** If the situation significantly impacts the board's operation or there's concern about legal liability, consult with an attorney specializing in community association law for guidance.

Additional Tips
- **Get Help:** Mediators can guide tough talks, lawyers step in if legal matters are involved.
- **Write it Down:** Keep notes on disagreements for future reference.
- **Seek Solutions:** Focus on finding fixes everyone can agree on, not just who's at fault.
- **The Contract is Key:** Put conflict management steps right in your agreement with the management company.

Remember: The goal is to protect the community's interests

and maintain a productive working relationship with your management company. Stay focused on these objectives when addressing a toxic board member.

Pro Tip: Don't underestimate the power of informal communication. Build rapport with your community manager to facilitate smoother interactions when problems DO arise.

Checklist: Is Your Board Conflict-Ready?

- Do you have procedures for addressing internal board disagreements?
- Is there a designated point person for managing company communication?
- Are conflict escalation steps outlined (discussion, mediation, etc.)?
- Are meeting minutes accurate and detailed?

Timeline: Sample Conflict Resolution

- **Day 1:** Issue raised. Designated liaison communicates with the manager.
- **Days 2-5:** Initial attempts to resolve.
- **Day 6+:** If unresolved, escalate as per predetermined steps, with documentation throughout.

Action Steps

- Review governing documents for any conflict resolution provisions.
- Add conflict procedures to your management contract if not already present.

Optimizing The Board-Manager Partnership

Proactive boards recognize the value of a well-informed and tech-savvy community manager. Support your manager's success and enhance your board's efficiency with these strategies:

A Smarter Manager Benefits Everyone: Invest in your community manager's education – conferences, certifications, etc. – to stay on top of industry trends. Prioritize a demonstrated work ethic over any specific credential. Proactively include professional development provisions in your management contract.

Streamlining with Tech: Don't overload your manager with emails. Use portals for resident requests, board-only platforms for internal discussions, and collaborative tools to reduce back-and-forth messages. When choosing these tools, prioritize data security.

Checklist: Tech for Better Collaboration

- Does your community need a resident portal?
- Would a board-only platform improve internal communication?
- Have you explored document-sharing and approval tools?
- Do you have data security protocols in place?

Action Steps:

- Ask your manager for tech recommendations.
- Consult an IT advisor to assess data security needs.

Test Your Knowledge!

1. What's the first step to minimizing conflict between the board and the management company?
2. Name two situations where a mediator might be helpful in a board-management relationship.
3. Why is it important to have a designated point person on the board for communicating with the management company?
4. What's a key point to address in your management contract regarding conflict resolution?
5. List two things a board should document when there's a disagreement with the management company.
6. Why should a board be cautious about relying solely on email for communication with their community manager?
7. Give one example of how a board-only platform can improve collaboration.
8. Describe a potential negative consequence of a board member having a personal vendetta against the management company.
9. What's the difference between a manager attending a conference and obtaining a professional certification?
10. Besides conferences, name one way a manager can demonstrate commitment to professional development.

The answers are at the end of this chapter

Case Study: The Value Of Open Communication

Willow Creek HOA was haunted by a recurring nightmare. Every few years, their relationship with their management company would implode in a storm of accusations, misunderstandings, and frustrating delays. Each time, they'd vow to do better – only to watch the cycle repeat itself. It became a community joke, one tinged with genuine exasperation.

When Green Tree Management took over, the board was prepared for the worst but determined to try something new. Prioritizing communication, they took several proactive steps:

- **Monthly Check-Ins:** Regular meetings with the community manager weren't just for reporting; they became a space to discuss potential issues proactively.
- **Resident Visibility:** Inviting the manager to quarterly board meetings gave her a voice, built familiarity with residents, and demystified her role.
- **"No Surprises" Policy:** Board members were expected to funnel concerns through established channels, preventing unexpected curveballs for the manager.
- **Contract Clarity:** Communication expectations were written into their contract, ensuring everyone was on the same page.

The transformation was dramatic. Instead of animosity, there was a sense of partnership. Minor disagreements? Sure, but they were handled swiftly within the established communication framework. It wasn't just the board who noticed the change. Resident surveys revealed a dramatic increase in satisfaction with the community's overall management.

Five years later, Green Tree is still their trusted partner, a testament to the power of open communication. The key takeaway from Willow Creek isn't just having systems in place – it's the mindset shift. Both board and management company embraced communication as a preventive tool, not just a crisis management strategy. This commitment is what broke the cycle and cultivated a truly successful partnership.

What Could They Have Done Differently?

History had taught the Willow Creek board that "good intentions" weren't enough. Without clear systems, communication would inevitably fray. They focused on actionable steps, like the monthly check-ins and the "no surprises" policy, to turn their good intentions into reality.

Board Member Voice: "Honestly, we were tired of feeling like we were always in crisis mode. We wanted to be proactive, not just keep patching holes in a sinking ship." - Susan, Board President, Willow Creek HOA

Question for the Reader: Does your board have clear communication protocols in place *before* problems arise? Or do you tend to address things only after they've escalated?

Key Takeaways

- Open communication is preventative maintenance for the board-management company relationship.
- Good intentions alone don't fix problems. Boards need clear, actionable communication systems.
- Including communication expectations in your management contract sets clear standards for both parties.
- A proactive approach leads to increased resident satisfaction and a healthier community overall.

Case Study: Mediation Makes The Difference

Pleasant Hills Condo Association prided itself on a strong sense of community, but things took a turn. Disputes with their management company, Evergreen Property Solutions, began to multiply. It started small: a landscaping issue that snowballed, a misunderstanding about a repair budget, then growing frustration on both sides. The board felt like Evergreen wasn't listening, like their needs were always secondary. Meanwhile, Evergreen's community manager, Emily, felt she was constantly bombarded by demands with no appreciation for the complexities of her role.

Board meetings became tense. Emails turned pointed. Soon, a chill descended over what was once a cordial relationship. Work orders were delayed, communication slowed to a trickle, and residents began noticing the decline in service. Both sides were entrenched, blaming the other.

Sarah, the board president, realized this path wasn't sustainable. She'd heard about mediation for community association disputes and, despite initial skepticism, presented the idea to the board. While some balked at "giving in," others recognized the situation was harming the entire community. Sarah reached out to Evergreen's regional director, proposing mediation with a neutral third party. Reluctantly, but seeing the mounting issues, Evergreen agreed.

The mediation session was initially fraught with tension. However, with the facilitator's guidance, they slowly untangled the misunderstandings. The board realized the complexities of some of their requests, and Emily gained a clearer picture of the board's priorities. They discovered points where their communication protocols simply weren't working.

The outcome wasn't about who was "right." It was about finding solutions. They renegotiated the timeline for certain non-urgent projects, established an approval process for budget-impacting repairs, and instituted quarterly meetings with the mediator present for the first year.

The transformation wasn't overnight. Flare-ups still happened, but they now had a process to de-escalate them. More importantly, both sides felt invested in making the partnership work, leading to better communication, increased trust, and ultimately, a vastly improved living experience for Pleasant Hills' residents.

What Could They Have Done Differently?

- **Early intervention:** Had either side suggested a simple conversation to address initial frustrations, escalation may have been prevented.
- **Focus on solutions:** Rather than fixating on who was right or wrong, a solutions-focused approach could have yielded faster results.
- **Consider a third party:** An unbiased outsider (consultant or even respected resident) might have helped facilitate communication before things deteriorated.

Board Member Voice: Sarah, the board president: "Honestly, I was angry. We pay good money for management, and it felt like we were getting lip service. But looking back... we weren't communicating our priorities well either."

Question for the Reader: Are there simmering issues with your management company that could benefit from an outside perspective before they boil over?

Key Takeaways

- Don't underestimate the power of good-faith communication early on.
- A "we vs. them" mentality hinders finding solutions that benefit everyone.
- Mediation isn't admitting defeat; it's a tool for restoring a functional partnership.

Case Study: Trouble At The Top

Mr. Smith, board president of Oak Grove HOA, started out with valid concerns. Small things irked him about their community manager's responsiveness – a few delayed emails, a slightly dismissive tone at a meeting. However, his frustration ballooned into something disproportionate. He began publicly criticizing the manager during board meetings, his comments becoming increasingly pointed and personal. Worse, he took his complaints directly to residents, stirring up discontent and undermining the manager's authority.

Initially, other board members had some sympathy. There had been occasional hiccups in communication, after all. But Mr. Smith's relentless negativity shifted the dynamic. The barrage of emails directed at the manager bordered on harassment. When board members privately approached Mr. Smith, hoping to reason with him, they hit a wall. He argued he was just "holding them accountable," ignoring the damage he was inflicting on the board's unity and their working relationship with the management company.

The breaking point came when Mr. Smith threatened a lawsuit over a minor landscaping issue, without consulting the rest of the board. It became clear his vendetta had overtaken his fiduciary duty. The board consulted with legal counsel, who confirmed they had grounds to remove him. However, recognizing the potential for community division, they first offered Mr. Smith a way out: voluntary resignation under the guise of "personal reasons."

Though he initially blustered, the weight of the board's unified stance forced Mr. Smith to back down. He reluctantly resigned. While the situation was far from ideal, it removed the toxic element. The board made peace with the management company, apologized for the disruption, and refocused on their core mission. New board elections were held, with a renewed emphasis on teamwork and collaborative problem-solving.

What Could They Have Done Differently?

- **Early Intervention:** Address confrontational behavior during meetings immediately with reminders about respectful conduct.
- **Documentation:** Keep records of disruptive behavior to support stronger actions if needed.
- **Outside Perspective:** Consult an HOA attorney before issuing threats of removal to understand their legal rights and obligations.

Board Member Voice: "Initially, we sided with Mr. Smith. Some of his issues were valid. But his relentless negativity and undermining the manager crossed a line. We should've acted sooner."

Reader Reflection: Are there simmering tensions with an individual board member becoming disruptive? How can you maintain a unified front while addressing the issue in a way that protects the entire community?

Key Takeaways:

- Toxic board members hinder progress and damage the community's relationship with its management company.
- Prioritize respectful communication and adherence to procedures, even during difficult disagreements.
- Seek legal advice if disruptive behavior escalates, impacting the board's ability to function.

Case Study: The Power Of A Point Person

Sunshine Villas HOA wasn't just an HOA; it often felt like a hydra trying to communicate with its management company. Each board member, with the best of intentions, felt empowered to reach out individually. This meant their community manager, Sarah, was juggling multiple emails, calls, and even impromptu conversations in the community clubhouse.

Questions were redundant, instructions overlapped, and sometimes board members even contradicted each other. Sarah was dedicated, but this disorganized approach made her feel overwhelmed and unsure about how to prioritize tasks. The board, meanwhile, wondered why their requests weren't being addressed promptly. Morale was declining on both sides.

Then, during a particularly frustrating board meeting, they had a breakthrough. Susan, a newer board member, suggested, "What if we channeled everything through one person? We can still discuss issues as a board, but let's say I'm the primary contact with Sarah."

Initially, some members were hesitant. Didn't this take away their individual authority? But the more they discussed it, the more sense it made. They agreed on a trial period, rotating the point-person role every few months to ensure everyone had a turn.

The difference was night and day. Sarah now had a single, reliable source of information and could organize her workload better. Instead of multiple emails with the same question, she received one consolidated inquiry. This allowed her to give comprehensive answers, reducing the need for further back-and-forth.

The board also benefited. They got faster, clearer responses, and the potential for one member impulsively undermining another's instructions was drastically decreased. It instilled a sense of teamwork even outside of their formal meetings. Most importantly, their relationship with Sarah significantly improved. They began to truly function as a partnership rather than a group of well-meaning but scattered individuals.

What Could They Have Done Differently?

- **Implement Sooner:** This strategy could've been established from the beginning of the board's term to prevent initial chaotic communication.
- **Manager Input:** Involve the community manager in designing the system, ensuring it works for both their workflow and the board's needs.

Board Member Voice: "We all cared deeply, but our good intentions caused more problems than they solved. Having Sarah work with one main contact made her life, and ours, much easier!"

Reader Reflection: Does your board's communication with the management company feel efficient and effective? If not, what simple changes could streamline things for everyone?

Key Takeaways:

- A point-person system improves communication, reduces stress for the manager, and prevents mixed messages.
- Collaborate with your community manager on communication processes that work for everyone.

Case Study: Why Documentation Matters

Maplewood Estates HOA prided itself on a casual, trusting relationship with its management company, Lakeside Properties. "We don't need to write everything down," was a commonly voiced belief. However, this came back to haunt them when disagreements arose about the community's deteriorating landscaping.

The board insisted that lush, well-maintained common areas were part of their agreement with Lakeside. Yet, the contract itself was vague on specifics, and meeting minutes rarely detailed maintenance expectations. Lakeside maintained that major landscaping upgrades were beyond their agreed-upon duties and would incur extra charges.

What followed was a frustrating stalemate. The "he said, she said" arguments consumed board meetings, strained resident relationships, and made it impossible to resolve the actual landscaping issue. In desperation, the board sought legal counsel. The lawyers, while sympathetic, could do little without clear documentation to support Maplewood's position.

The situation was eventually settled, but at significant cost. Legal fees drained the HOA's budget, and the compromise on landscaping left residents disgruntled. The worst part? The board knew they'd been in the right, but their lack of documentation tied their hands.

This painful lesson triggered a complete overhaul of Maplewood Estates' approach. They hired a professional minute-taker for board meetings, and created templates to ensure key points were always captured: decisions made, action items assigned, and any discussions that could impact either the HOA's or the management company's responsibilities. This transformed their operations, ensuring that everyone was on the same page, and that the community was always protected.

What Could They Have Done Differently?

- **Contract Clarity:** Ensure meeting minutes thoroughly document key decisions, agreements, and changes to the management company's scope of work.
- **Central Repository:** Have an accessible system for storing minutes and other relevant documents.

Board Member Voice: "We honestly thought we were on the same page. Looking back, it was all too casual. This could've been avoided with better records."

Reader Reflection: How strong is your documentation system for board actions and communications with the Management Company? Could you easily reference key decisions if a dispute arose?

Key Takeaways:

- Meeting minutes serve as a vital record, protecting both the board and the management company.
- Invest time in accurate minutes – it's cheaper than legal battles due to ambiguity.

Case Study: Investing In The Manager – The Power Of Professional Growth

Rosewood Community Association had a competent

community manager, but things felt... stagnant. While the basics were done well, there was a lack of innovation, and resident satisfaction scores were plateaued. Recognizing this, the board took a proactive step. Instead of assuming their manager would seek out professional development independently, they allocated a yearly $1500 budget within their management contract dedicated to her growth.

This transformed their working relationship. The manager, Sarah, attended her first major industry conference. She returned brimming with ideas – a streamlined resident onboarding process inspired by another community, a tech tool she discovered for simplifying maintenance requests, and insights into emerging trends that prompted the board to revisit their long-term budget planning.

Next, Sarah pursued a targeted certification in financial management, an area where she felt less confident. This not only gave her practical knowledge but boosted her (and the board's) confidence in budget discussions. Seeing their investment pay off, the board was even more supportive of her professional development. Industry publications, webinars, even a local mentorship group, became part of Sarah's ongoing learning.

The most profound shift, however, was in Sarah herself. She felt deeply valued as a professional, not just an employee. This translated directly into her loyalty and dedication to Rosewood. Resident satisfaction surveys reflected this renewed energy, turnover in the management company's support staff decreased (often a sign of a happy manager), and Rosewood became known in local industry circles as a community that truly invested in its people.

What Could They Have Done Differently?

- **Set Expectations:** Have clear goals for the manager's professional growth and how it will be applied in the

community.
- **Ongoing Support:** Offer encouragement and flexibility, not just funding. Discuss ways to implement new knowledge or adapt new practices.

Board Member Voice: "Our initial thought was, 'Why does our management company need to fund this?' Now, we see our manager as an investment, not just a cost."

Reader Reflection: Do you view professional development as a perk or a strategic tool for community success? How does your current management contract reflect this?

Key Takeaways:

- Investing in your manager benefits the entire community through increased knowledge, innovation, and loyalty.
- Professional development should be a strategic partnership between the board and the manager.

Test Your Knowledge! Answers

1. **Open and Regular Communication:** Proactive communication prevents misunderstandings that lead to conflict.
2. **Mediation is helpful:**
   - When disagreements escalate despite good-faith communication efforts.
   - If the conflict involves potential legal violations or breaches of contract.
3. **Designated Point Person:** This keeps communication streamlined, prevents mixed messages, and avoids overwhelming the manager.
4. **Management Contract:** Outline a dispute resolution

process within the contract – steps for escalation, whether mediation is required, etc.
5. **Documentation:**
   o   Meeting minutes where the disagreement is discussed, noting who said what.
   o   Written communication (emails, letters) related to the issue.
6. **Email Shortcomings:**
   o   Tone can be easily misinterpreted, fueling frustration.
   o   Emails can overwhelm a manager's inbox, hindering efficient response.
7. **Board-Only Platforms:** Allow for private discussions, decision-making, and voting outside of lengthy email chains or in-person meetings.
8. **Personal Vendettas:** Can poison board dynamics, hinder solutions-focused problem-solving, and negatively impact the relationship with the entire management company.
9. **Conferences vs. Certification:**
   o   Conferences offer exposure to current trends and networking.
   o   Certifications demonstrate mastery of specific knowledge after rigorous testing.
10. **Professional Development Options:**
- Webinars or online courses
- Industry publications and newsletters
- Membership in professional organizations

CHAPTER 12: DATA-DRIVEN DECISION MAKING

Introduction

"Without data, you're just another person with an opinion."

W. EDWARDS DEMING

I've seen condo boards struggle with difficult decisions. One board was confronted with the choice to either replace rotten wood siding and exterior trim wood, but had a cash crunch and, going with its gut, chose to save money by painting over some of the lesser rotted areas, ignoring the painting contractor's warnings. This short-sighted decision led to the paint failing within months when it was originally intended to last seven years. That fateful decision turned out to be the worse of the two options from a cashflow standpoint because they had to circle back on the project and they had voided the painting contractor's warranty by ignoring the recommendation to replace all rotten wood.

In contrast, another community faced a similar dilemma with their asphalt. They carefully analyzed the immediate costs of repair versus a full replacement, but also factored in future expenses and performed a detailed financial analysis, used a discount rate to put the cash flows of the options into a like-for-like structure before voting on the path forward. This data-driven approach, supported by their management company, showed that proactive repairs would be more cost-effective in the long run. The board voted accordingly.

These cases demonstrate how data removes the guesswork and potential biases from decision-making. By using data strategically, boards can make choices that better serve their community's needs, improve resident satisfaction, and ensure financial stability.

Data: The Key To Informed Decisions

Data analysis is crucial for making sound decisions. It replaces guesswork with facts, allowing communities to take targeted action. Setting clear metric triggers takes this further – when those thresholds are reached, it automatically prompts action for efficient, timely responses. This data helps you spot trends, streamline operations, and improve resident satisfaction.

Remember, successful businesses don't rely on gut feelings; they use data to thrive long-term. Here's how your community can do the same:

- **Resident Surveys:** Get honest feedback about maintenance, amenities, and policies. Use this to improve resident life, prioritize projects that matter, and support budget requests with hard data.

- **Financial Reports:** Track every dollar meticulously. This underpins accurate budgeting, smart forecasting, cost-saving efforts, and strategic financial planning.

- **Maintenance Records:** Document repairs and costs. This allows proactive scheduling, helps predict when major assets need replacing, and reveals recurring problems for targeted solutions.

Fast Fact: Resident surveys have a much higher response rate when they are short, focused, and easy to complete.

Data Works Together

These datasets aren't isolated – they're interconnected:

- Resident surveys reveal maintenance needs.
- Maintenance data impacts long-term financial planning.
- Financial reports determine if resident-requested projects are feasible.

Understanding these links is vital for responsible boards. Actions taken in one area often affect others. Regular review of all your data (surveys, finances, maintenance) helps track progress, refine your approach, and demonstrate the impact of your decisions for the best possible resident experience.

Key Takeaways

- Ditch subjectivity, embrace data-driven decisions.
- Use metric triggers to automate action.
- Focus on resident surveys, financial reports, and maintenance records.
- See how these datasets form a cycle.
- Regularly review your data to assess progress and guide future choices.

Checklist: Is Your Board Data-Ready?

- Do we have a clear understanding of our community's goals and priorities?
- Do we know what types of data are most relevant to those goals?
- Do we have systems in place (or a plan to develop them) for collecting this data regularly?
- Is our board open to learning about data analysis and using it for decision-making?

Action Steps

- **Hold a board brainstorming session:** Discuss community goals and what data would track progress.
- **Identify existing data sources:** You might already have more data than you realize!

- **Start small:** Pick 2-3 key data points to track consistently as a pilot project.

Tools For Smart Data Collection

The right tools transform the data collection process. They make it easier, improve accuracy, and most importantly, encourage residents to get involved! Let's dive into the key types of tools you'll want to consider:

Survey Platforms

- **Meeting Residents on Their Turf:** To get the most meaningful responses, understand *how* your residents prefer to communicate. Some like email, others might prefer text-based surveys or even a community website portal. Adapting your approach ensures you gather the most representative data, not just a handful of scattered opinions.
- **Freebies for Basic Needs:** Need a quick, straightforward survey? Several free online platforms offer user-friendly interfaces that are easy to learn. A quick web search for "free survey tools" will point you in the right direction.
- **Upgrade When Needed:** If you have complex survey needs (like extensive question logic or in-depth analysis), exploring paid platforms opens up a wider range of powerful features. Invest some time in researching options, focusing on features that align best with your community's specific requirements.

Financial Software

- **Built for Condos:** Specialized accounting software understands the unique needs of condominiums and HOAs. These tools streamline processes and simplify tasks, saving you precious time and effort.

- **How to Find the Right Software:**
  - **Management Company Expertise:** If you have a management company, leverage their experience! They likely have preferred software ensuring compatibility and smooth collaboration.
  - **Online Resources:** Search online using keywords like "condominium accounting software" or "HOA management software." Prioritize options with features important to your community, such as bank integration, budgeting tools, and resident portals for easy bill pay.
  - **Read the Reviews:** Don't make a decision in a vacuum. Check independent review websites or industry publications to get real user feedback, helping you understand the pros and cons of different options.
- **Automate to Save Time:** Look for software that seamlessly connects to your bank accounts and assists with budget creation. These features are huge time-savers!

Maintenance Tracking

- **Spreadsheets for Starters:** Smaller communities might get by with spreadsheets to track basic repairs. But as your community grows, their limitations become apparent.
- **Dedicated Software: The Investment Pays Off:** Larger communities thrive with software specifically designed for work orders, scheduling, vendor management, and asset tracking. Here's what to look for:
  - **Tailored Features:** Prioritize solutions designed for the complexities of condos and HOAs.
  - **Workflow Management:** Opt for software that simplifies work order creation, scheduling, and vendor communication, making the whole process more efficient.
  - **Asset Tracking:** Choose platforms that

track equipment lifespan, repair frequencies, and replacement costs. This is essential for smart long-term budgeting.
- **Reporting Capabilities:** Seek out solutions with insightful trend reports to help you identify recurring issues and make data-backed decisions.

How to Find the Right Provider:

- **Industry Resources:** Websites and publications catering to the HOA/condominium industry often offer valuable recommendations and reviews.
- **Tap into Your Management Company's Network:** Your management company likely has established relationships with software providers.
- **Online Searches:** Targeted searches (e.g., "condominium maintenance management software" or "HOA asset tracking software") will reveal available options.

Other Must-Haves

- **Data Security is Paramount:** Resident privacy is non-negotiable. Only select tools with robust security measures that protect sensitive resident and financial information.
- **Easy to Use:** Make usability a priority. Choose software with intuitive interfaces and training resources available for both management and board members.

Bottom Line: Investing in the right tools may have an upfront cost, but the payoff is immense. You'll save time, improve data accuracy, experience greater resident engagement, and make smarter decisions – making it a priceless investment for any size community.

Checklist: Evaluating Data Collection Tools

- What types of data do we need to collect (financial, maintenance, resident feedback, etc.)?

- Does the tool integrate well with our existing systems (if any)?
- Is the tool user-friendly and accessible to our board members?
- Do we need training or support to use the tool effectively?
- Does the vendor have a good reputation and track record?

Sample Timeline: Implementing a Resident Survey Platform
- Week 1: Research and compare 3-4 survey platforms.
- Week 2: Request demos or free trials from top contenders.
- Week 3: Board discussion and selection of the platform.
- Week 4: Set up account, customize template surveys, train board members on use.
- Week 5: Launch first resident survey!

Action Steps:
- **If you don't have one:** Create a master list of your community's data sources.
- **Identify gaps:** Are there areas where you need better data? Prioritize these.

Analyzing Data For Smart Decision-Making

Gathering data is just the first step. To make truly informed choices, your board needs to analyze that data carefully. Let's dive into how to do that and the common pitfalls to watch out for.

Basic Calculations: Your Starting Toolkit

- **Averages:** Mean, median, and mode each tell a different part of the story about your dataset.
- **Percentages:** Expressing data as parts of a whole (like satisfaction rates or budget breakdowns) adds valuable context.
- **Trends Over Time:** Identify patterns – are costs rising, falling, or changing each year? This is crucial for future planning.

Understanding What the Numbers Tell You

- **Connect to Community Goals:** What do the numbers reveal about progress towards your community's priorities? Rising maintenance costs have implications for future budgets, temporary work orders need to be understood, etc.
- **Amenities Matter:** Resident surveys are invaluable for pinpointing where to focus improvement efforts. Prioritize what matters most to your community to get the best return on investment.

Pro Tip: Seek out dissenting opinions on your board. Diverse perspectives help combat groupthink and lead to better decisions.

Caution: Correlation vs. Causation

Don't assume that just because two things change together, one caused the other. Be wary of jumping to conclusions!

Why It's Important to Get This Right

Misinterpreting data leads to bad decisions. Here's why you need to be cautious:

- **Hidden Factors:** Don't get tunnel vision: there might be other variables influencing the data.
- **Coincidence Happens:** Sometimes patterns are just flukes, not meaningful trends.
- **It Might Be Backwards:** Sometimes what seemed like the effect is actually the cause!

Need More Proof?

To be confident about cause-and-effect, you typically need:

- **Logical Explanation:** Does it make sense that one thing would cause the other?
- **Experiments:** The gold standard is isolating factors to prove impact, but this isn't always practical in community management.
- **Expert Knowledge:** Does research or industry experience support a causal connection?

Key Takeaway: Question Everything!

Data is powerful, but it can be misleading. Scrutinize your findings – ask yourself:

- Are there other explanations for this?
- What would make me more certain about cause and effect?

Visualizations: Make Data Speak

- **Line graphs:** Perfect for showing trends

- **Bar charts:** Great for comparisons
- **Pie charts:** Highlight parts of a whole
- **Design Matters:** Keep visualizations simple and easy to read!

Pro Tip: Don't just present data, tell a story with it. Help residents visualize how it impacts their lives.

Example: The Case of the Declining Satisfaction Scores

- **Scenario:** A condo association's survey showed decreased amenity satisfaction.
- **The Mistake:** The board immediately blamed outdated pool and gym equipment, rushing into plans for expensive upgrades.

Where They Went Wrong

- **Ignoring Context:** They overlooked factors like fee increases, noise complaints, or cleanliness issues.
- **Jumping to Conclusions:** They didn't investigate the *true cause* of the dissatisfaction – maybe it wasn't the amenities themselves, but their hours or maintenance.
- **Possible Bias:** Perhaps some board members already wanted upgrades, and used the data to support their agenda.

Consequences

- **Wasted Money:** Potential for spending heavily on solutions that don't address the real problem.
- **Resident Frustration:** The underlying issues remain, potentially harming satisfaction further.
- **Loss of Trust:** Residents might see the board as hasty and mismanaging funds.

How to Avoid These Mistakes

- **Ask "Why?"** Never take data at face value. Dig deeper to understand what's driving the numbers.

- **Gather More Data:** Surveys are great, but supplement them with comment boxes, town halls, etc. for a richer picture.
- **Encourage Diverse Perspectives:** Seek out different opinions, both within the board and from qualified experts, to combat groupthink.

Checklist: Building Data Analysis Skills

- Are basic calculations (averages, percentages, etc.) familiar to most board members?
- Does anyone on the board have experience with data analysis or statistics?
- Are we open to utilizing software to help with more complex analysis?
- Are there online courses, workshops, or other resources available for board training?

Action Steps:

- **Start with the basics:** Free online tutorials can teach calculations, visualizations, etc.
- **Seek out 'plain language' resources:** Not all data training is aimed at business executives.
- **Consider a consultant:** For complex needs, initial expert help can be a good investment.

Using Data To Make Smart Decisions

Forget about relying on hunches! Data analysis is the key to making choices that truly benefit your community in the long run. It helps you avoid those gut-feeling decisions that can turn into expensive mistakes.

Project Prioritization: Where to Spend Your Money

- **Maintenance Records:** Look at past repairs to know what needs urgent attention and what problems might snowball if ignored. Proactive fixes prevent huge headaches later.
- **Reserve Studies:** Know when those big expenses (like a new roof) are coming up and make sure your reserve fund is ready. No financial surprises!
- **Resident Feedback:** What do residents *really* value? Surveys and conversations help you target upgrades that make the biggest impact on quality of life.

Justifying Expenses: Getting Residents on Board

- **Maintenance History:** Sometimes residents need to see the history of repeated problems to understand why a major fix is worth it, even if it seems costly upfront.
- **Vendor Quotes:** Being open about how you select contractors builds trust and shows you're careful with their money.
- **Long-Term Impact:** Explain how spending money *now* avoids even bigger costs or headaches down the road.

Fast Fact: Communities that prioritize proactive maintenance can save up to 30% on long-term repair costs.

Needs vs. Wants: Making the Tough Calls

- **Essentials First:** Safety and staying code compliant aren't optional. Fancy stuff can wait.
- **The Cost of "Nice to Haves":** If the budget is tight, be honest with residents about what projects might have to wait if they want something non-essential.
- **Resident Input:** Good surveys help tell the difference between what people truly need and what would simply be nice to have.

Budgeting: No More Surprises

- **Trend Analysis:** Know when your usual expenses spike and plan ahead so your budget isn't caught off-guard.
- **Inflation:** Don't let rising prices blindside you. Factor those into your budget, so you don't end up short next year.
- **Reserve Contributions:** Let data – not guesswork – determine how much your community should be setting aside for big replacements.

Pro Tip: Make a habit of regularly reviewing your community's reserve study to stay on top of future replacement costs.

Fast Fact: Communities with well-funded reserve accounts tend to have lower HOA fees in the long run.

Policy Changes: Do Them Smart

- **Pre-Policy Baseline:** Before changing rules, know the scale of the problem you're trying to solve (ex: how many parking complaints are there really?).
- **Resident Sentiment:** Surveys give you a heads-up about how residents feel about a change *before* you make it, avoiding surprises.
- **Think Ahead:** Could a well-meaning rule actually create new problems? Try to anticipate these.

Fast Fact: Clear communication about the "why" behind policy changes increases resident acceptance and reduces conflict.

Performance Tracking: Did it Work?

- **"Before and After":** Did that repair actually fix the complaints? Did the new policy solve the issue it was meant to?
- **Ongoing Monitoring:** Don't just make decisions and forget about them – use data to see if they were successful.
- **Be Flexible:** Be willing to change course if the data shows something isn't working, ego aside!

The Data Cycle

Decisions lead to actions, which give you new data, which then informs your next decisions...it goes on and on! Boards that embrace this cycle create the most resident-focused and financially healthy communities.

Checklist: Making a Data-Driven Decision

- Is the problem or opportunity clearly defined?
- What data do we have that relates to this decision?
- What additional data do we need, and how can we obtain it?
- Have we analyzed the data from multiple angles?
- Have we considered potential unintended consequences?
- How will we track whether our decision was successful?

Sample Timeline: Prioritizing Maintenance Projects

- Month 1: Detailed review of maintenance history and costs.
- Month 2: Inspection to assess the current condition of major assets.
- Month 3: Data analysis, prioritizing based on urgency, cost, and potential impact.
- Month 4: Develop project plan, obtain bids, present to residents for feedback and approval.

Data: Your Roadmap To A Thriving Community

In today's world, data-driven decision-making isn't just smart – it's essential for successful condominium management. Here's how it empowers your board:

- **Minimize Risk, Maximize Confidence:** Say goodbye to costly mistakes driven by hunches or incomplete information. Data provides the clarity you need to make informed choices.
- **Happy Residents, Strong Community:** Target investments towards the improvements and amenities that truly matter to your residents. This builds a sense of belonging and makes your community a desirable place to live.
- **Financial Security for the Long Haul:** Data translates into accurate budgets, timely reserve contributions, and wise spending decisions. Protect your community's financial future!
- **Trust: The Cornerstone of Good Governance:** When decisions are transparent and supported by data, residents know their interests are being well-served. This builds trust and cooperation.

Fast Fact: Did you know that 70% of condo owners feel their boards could do a better job with financial transparency?

Board Members: Step into the Data Age

Don't be intimidated! Here's how to harness the power of data:

- **Embrace the Learning Curve:** A wealth of resources and training on data analysis are available. Start with the

basics and build from there.
- **Tools of the Trade:** Resident surveys, financial software, and maintenance trackers put valuable insights at your fingertips. Use them consistently!
- **Expert Help is Out There:** Your management company, CPAs, and reserve study specialists offer valuable analysis and support. Tap into their knowledge.

Pro Tip: Build relationships with other condo boards in your area to share knowledge and best practices.

Important Reminder: It's Not Just Numbers

- **People Come First:** Data is a tool, not a dictator. Use it to prioritize the well-being and quality of life for your residents.
- **Keep Improving:** Data collection and analysis is a continuous journey. Use it to fine-tune your decisions and get even better results over time.

Pro Tip: Even small improvements in resident satisfaction can significantly increase property values.

The End Result?

Boards that commit to data-driven approaches create communities where residents are happy, investments are protected, and responsible, future-focused management is the standard. That's a win for everyone involved and a recipe for long-term success.

Test Your Knowledge!

1. Name three types of data that condo boards should regularly collect and analyze.
2. What's the difference between an average and a median, and when is each most useful?
3. Give an example of how resident surveys can guide project prioritization.
4. Why is it important to track trends in your maintenance costs over time?
5. What does "correlation vs. causation" mean, and why is it crucial for boards to understand?
6. How can vendor quotes build resident trust in the board's spending decisions?
7. Explain the importance of factoring inflation into your community's budgeting process.
8. Describe how a pre-policy baseline helps evaluate the effectiveness of policy changes.
9. Why should boards focus on the needs of the entire community, not just the loudest voices?
10. What is the cyclical nature of data-driven decision-making?

The answers are at the end of this chapter

Case Study: The Case Of The Unexpected Expense

Sunnyview Condominiums was the kind of community where everyone knew their neighbors and residents appreciated the predictability of their low HOA fees. Maintaining that affordability was a point of pride for the board. That's why, when a catastrophic water main break resulted in a repair bill exceeding $50,000, it sent shockwaves through the residents.

Whispers of financial mismanagement began to spread. Some residents, facing the potential specter of a special assessment, openly questioned if the board had cut corners on maintenance, leading to the crisis. Fortunately, the board wasn't caught unprepared. While the leak itself was unforeseeable, they had diligently prepared for the unexpected.

Over the years, they had regularly reviewed and updated their reserve study. They shared projections clearly showing that, while this expense was significant, the reserve fund was robust enough to handle it. The board also took the added step of transparency, providing maintenance records that detailed a long history of proactive plumbing inspections, upgrades where feasible, and a commitment to upkeep. This wasn't neglect, it was simply bad luck.

This data-driven approach had powerful effects:

- **Panic Subsided:** Faced with clear evidence of responsible planning, rumors of mismanagement fizzled out.
- **Trust Maintained:** Residents saw the board didn't hide from the situation but openly explained the "why" behind

the expense, reinforcing their trust.
- **Fee Increase Averted:** The healthy reserve fund meant residents weren't burdened with a sudden extra payment, maintaining the community's affordability.

The Sunnyview case highlights that even with the best intentions, unexpected events happen. Data-backed foresight, especially with reserve funds and maintenance records, is the key to weathering those storms. It protects the community financially and shows residents their board truly has their best interests at heart.

What Could They Have Done Differently? While the board ultimately handled the situation well, proactive communication about the importance of reserves could have eased resident shock even further. Regular budget updates highlighting reserve contributions build awareness that these funds exist for a reason.

Board Member Voice: "Honestly, we felt a bit smug at first, like 'See, we told you we were good stewards of your money!' But we quickly realized that even with data on our side, empathy and clear communication matter."

Reader Question: Does your community have a habit of only talking finances when there's a problem? How could proactive budget transparency change this?

Key Takeaways: Reserve studies aren't just a formality; they're a communication tool. Data alone won't ease resident anxiety if they don't understand the "why" behind board actions.

Case Study: Pool Or Playground? The Power Of Resident Feedback

Sunset Ridge Condominiums faced a classic community dilemma. Their amenities were limited, and a passionate group of residents lobbied for replacing the worn-out playground with a brand new pool. They argued it would increase property values and attract new buyers. On the other side, families with young children vehemently opposed the idea, stating the playground was crucial for their quality of life. Emotions ran high, and the board found itself at an impasse.

Previous boards at Sunset Ridge tended to make decisions based on intuition or prioritizing whoever voiced their opinions the loudest. But this board was determined to do things differently. They understood that data-driven decision-making was the key to a fair and informed choice.

A carefully designed resident survey was distributed, with both multiple-choice questions and space for open-ended comments. The questions were deliberately phrased to avoid bias, not assuming that *everyone* wanted a pool. The results were eye-opening:

- While a significant portion *did* support the pool idea, it wasn't the overwhelming majority the vocal pool proponents had suggested.
- Many residents expressed that even with a pool, they'd still want a safe, enjoyable play area for their children.
- A recurring theme in the comments was the desire for a more inviting atmosphere around the existing pool, with better shade and landscaping.

Armed with this data, the board saw a path forward. They worked on a compromise plan – a modest playground renovation with new equipment suitable for a wider age range, coupled with significantly upgrading the pool area's landscaping, seating, and shade structures. This addressed the needs of multiple groups within the community, while staying within a reasonable budget.

The outcome was overwhelmingly positive:

- The divisive "pool vs. playground" debate was diffused, replaced by a sense of collaboration.
- Residents felt genuinely heard by the board, strengthening trust.
- The targeted improvements led to a noticeable increase in the use *and* enjoyment of the community's amenities.

Sunset Ridge learned a valuable lesson: sometimes the best solution isn't about choosing one side over another, but about using data to find creative ways to address the underlying needs of your entire community.

What Could They Have Done Differently? It's wise to ask open-ended questions on surveys, not just "Which do you prefer?". This allows residents to voice alternative solutions the board may not have considered.

Board Member Voice: "We went into this with blinders on, thinking it was one or the other. The survey humbled us and showed the power of truly listening to our residents."

Reader Question: Is your board quick to frame problems as "either/or" choices? How can you leave room for resident-driven solutions?

Key Takeaways: Surveys are a starting point, not the whole decision. Prioritize resident needs, not just checking off a "data collection" box.

Case Study: The Curious Case Of The Rising Expenses

For the past three years, Oak Creek Condos had a nagging problem. Despite their best efforts, maintenance costs stubbornly crept upwards. Replacing the outdated landscaping? A little more expensive than expected. Fixing that recurring leak in the community room? The bill seemed surprisingly high. HVAC repairs, appliance replacements... it felt like a constant game of whack-a-mole, draining their budget.

The board members grew increasingly frustrated. They reviewed their budgets line by line, hunting for the big expense that must be the culprit, but nothing stood out dramatically. A sense of helplessness began to set in. Were rising costs just an inevitable reality of an aging community?

Then, board treasurer Lisa, inspired by a recent HOA conference seminar, had an idea. "What if we're not looking at the data the right way?", she proposed. Instead of just examining expense types, what if they added location data into the mix. The management company's software allowed them to easily tag work orders by unit or common area.

With renewed determination, they built a spreadsheet. Each row wasn't just "plumbing repair", it was "plumbing repair - Unit 203". The results were eye-opening. While repairs were scattered throughout the complex, a clear pattern emerged: a cluster of 20 older units accounted for nearly a third of all maintenance calls! Suddenly, they had a lead.

Further investigation revealed these units were nearing the

expected lifespan for original appliances, fixtures, and even internal plumbing. It wasn't that residents were careless, the infrastructure itself was reaching its breaking point. The board faced a choice: continue down the path of endless reactive repairs, or make a strategic shift.

Armed with data, they presented their findings to the community. While some residents initially balked at the idea of proactive replacements, the board explained how scattered repairs on failing systems would likely become even *more* costly over time. The clear data made their case. Instead of feeling like the board was chasing problems, Oak Creek Condos embarked on a targeted modernization plan, bringing long-term financial stability and peace of mind.

What Could They Have Done Differently? Regularly reviewing maintenance data could have caught this pattern sooner, potentially preventing some of those rising costs.

Board Member Voice: "We always looked at the total budget, not the details. Lesson learned: the devil IS in the details when it comes to controlling costs."

Reader Question: Does your board have a process for analyzing maintenance trends beyond the annual budget review?

Key Takeaways: Data isn't just for big decisions; routine analysis uncovers hidden cost drivers. Don't wait for expenses to become a crisis before digging deeper.

Case Study: The Parking Policy Problem

Greenview Condominiums had a headache that never seemed to go away: inadequate parking. For years, resident disputes over spaces were a constant source of frustration. Complaints about overnight guests unable to find spots, arguments over who had "rights" to convenient parking, and growing resentment filled board meetings. Past attempts at solutions felt like band-aids. A few extra visitor spaces did little, and a strict "one car per unit" rule proved impossible to enforce. The board was stuck.

This time, they resolved to tackle the problem with data, not just opinions. Here's what they did:

- **Quantifying the Problem:** Board members spent a week systematically documenting parking lot occupancy. They observed peak usage times (evenings and weekends), noted the typical number of empty spaces, and tracked which areas of the lot were most contested.
- **Cars vs. Units:** They discreetly surveyed the number of registered vehicles per unit. This revealed that the issue wasn't solely about too many cars, but also uneven distribution (some units had multiple vehicles, others none).
- **Resident Voices:** In a survey, they asked how severe residents felt the problem was, and crucially, for their ideas on solutions. Options ranged from permit systems, to timed visitor parking, to building a costly parking garage.

What the Data Revealed

- **Timing Matters:** Peak occupancy wasn't all day, every day. The crunch was primarily evenings and weekends.
- **It's Not Just Quantity:** While some units did exceed the average car ownership, making space for everyone wasn't realistically feasible.
- **Desire for Flexibility:** Residents were surprisingly split on solutions. Some wanted strict assignments, others prioritized visitor access, and most opposed the expense of major construction.

The Data-Driven Solution

The board realized a one-size-fits-all approach wouldn't work. They crafted a hybrid model:

- **Assigned Primary Spots:** Units received one guaranteed space near their building. Additional resident vehicles needed a permit for less convenient overflow lots.
- **Timed Visitor Passes:** Each unit was issued a set number of temporary passes per month, giving guests priority during peak hours.
- **Ongoing Assessment:** They pledged to revisit the system after six months, using further data to see if any tweaks were needed.

Outcome

Was it perfect? No. But the data-driven policy brought significant improvement. Knowing their primary car was secure calmed anxieties. Timed visitor spots eased the guest issue without sacrificing all resident convenience. Importantly, the process felt fairer because decisions weren't based on who yelled the loudest, but on the realities the data revealed.

What Could They Have Done Differently? Gathering occupancy data *before* past policy changes would have provided an even stronger baseline for comparison.

Board Member Voice: "In hindsight, we were flying blind, making decisions based on complaints, not real evidence of the problem's scale. Now we know better."

Reader Question: What problems in your community are addressed based on complaints rather than measured data?

Key Takeaways: A pre-policy baseline is essential for proving if your solution actually worked. Data collection should be ongoing, not just reactive.

Case Study: Ice Cream Vs. Sunburns: When Data Saves The Day

The board of Palm Breeze Condominiums loved providing a cool oasis for residents during the sweltering summer months. However, as temperatures soared, so did the community pool's maintenance costs. Initially, a simple explanation seemed obvious: more swimmers meant more sunscreen, lotions, and other contaminants in the water, requiring increased chemical treatments. The board's knee-jerk reaction was to consider restricting pool hours, hoping to reduce expenses.

Thankfully, cooler heads prevailed. One board member, remembering a recent discussion about data-informed decisions, suggested they dig deeper before inconveniencing residents. A review of detailed maintenance invoices shattered their initial assumption. While the *overall* cost was higher, the hourly rate for pool cleaning services hadn't changed. Instead, the culprit was a sharp increase in the price of chlorine and other pool chemicals during the peak summer season.

Data had saved the day in two ways:

1. **Prevented Misguided Action:** By identifying the true cause of increased costs, the board avoided wrongly restricting a popular amenity based on a faulty assumption. This maintained resident satisfaction and trust.

2. **Pointed Towards Solutions:** Knowing that market forces, not resident behavior, drove the price hike, the board shifted its focus. They researched bulk purchasing options and alternative chemical suppliers, potentially finding ways to mitigate the cost increase without sacrificing pool access.

What Could They Have Done Differently? Having a system to track other seasonal expenses could have made the correlation/causation issue clearer from the start.

Board Member Voice: "It was a good reminder that we can get tunnel vision. We had to step back and ask, 'What ELSE happens in summer that might impact this?'"

Reader Question: Does your board have a habit of seeking the fastest explanation, or do you encourage questioning assumptions?

Key Takeaways: Even simple problems warrant some critical thinking. Correlation is a clue to investigate further, not a definitive answer.

Case Study: The Power Of Visualization

Mountainview Condominiums faced an unavoidable reality: their aging roof needed a costly replacement. Faced with resident pushback, the board knew they needed a better way to communicate the necessity of this project. Past attempts to explain the situation using dense spreadsheets of budget figures had only created confusion and frustration. This time, they decided to let the data speak for itself – visually.

Working with their management company, the board developed three key visuals:

- **Bar Chart 1: The Rising Cost of Doing Nothing**
    - This chart showed the steadily increasing repair costs for the old roof over the past five years. Each bar represented a year, demonstrating a clear upward trend.
    - Importantly, it also projected a steeper increase in coming years if the roof wasn't replaced, as leaks and damage were likely to worsen.
- **Bar Chart 2: Investment vs. Band-Aid Fixes**
    - One bar showed the upfront cost of a new roof. The next bar, much taller, illustrated the *cumulative* cost of continued patchwork repairs over the expected lifespan of the new roof.
    - This drove home the point that the replacement, while initially more expensive, was the fiscally responsible choice long-term.
- **Line Graph: Reserve Fund Health**
    - This graph tracked the projected balance of the reserve fund over time. One line showed

- rapid depletion if the roof wasn't done, leaving the community financially vulnerable.
  - The second line showed the impact of the roof replacement followed by a slower, sustainable growth of the reserves, ensuring readiness for future expenses.

These visuals were presented at a community meeting alongside a short, plain-language explanation. The difference was striking. Instead of glazing over at numbers, residents could clearly see the financial story unfolding. Questions shifted from "Why is this so expensive?" to a more informed discussion about financing options and project timelines. The board's data-driven, visually focused approach built trust and ultimately secured the resident support needed to move forward with this essential project.

What Could They Have Done Differently? Presenting the visuals *alongside* a simplified budget could have been even more powerful. This directly ties the roof's impact on the overall financial health of the community.

Board Member Voice: "At first, we were afraid the charts would be too intimidating. But the visuals made the numbers come alive! It was a lightbulb moment for many residents."

Reader Question: Are there financial concepts your residents struggle to understand? Could visuals make a difference?

Key Takeaways: Visualizations make complex data accessible. Don't assume residents have the same financial fluency as the board.

Test Your Knowledge! Answers

1. **Three types of data:**
   - **Financial:** Income/expenses, budget, reserve fund balance, etc.
   - **Maintenance:** Repair history, frequency of issues, asset lifespans.
   - **Resident Feedback:** Surveys, satisfaction ratings, informal comments.
2. **Average vs. Median:**
   - **Average (Mean):** The sum of all values divided by the number of values. Sensitive to extreme outliers (very high/low numbers).
   - **Median:** The middle value when data is arranged in order. Better for datasets with outliers or skewed distributions.
3. **Survey Example:** A survey reveals the most desired amenities are a pool upgrade and improved gym equipment. The board prioritizes these projects to maximize resident satisfaction.
4. **Tracking Maintenance Costs:**
   - Identifies recurring problems that could signal a larger issue needing proactive attention.
   - Reveals seasonal spikes in spending, ensuring the budget is realistic.
5. **Correlation vs. Causation:**
   - **Correlation:** Two things change together (e.g., sunburns and ice cream sales both increase in summer).
   - **Causation:** One thing directly causes the other (e.g., heat causes sunburns).
   - **Boards must be careful:** Not to assume correlation means one thing caused the other.
6. **Vendor Quotes:**
   - **Transparency:** Shows residents the board did due diligence in selecting vendors.
   - **Trust:** Demonstrates responsible spending of

community funds.
7. **Inflation:**
   o Costs of goods/services rise over time. If not factored in, budgets will be insufficient.
   o Boards need to adjust budgets accordingly to avoid unexpected shortfalls.
8. **Pre-Policy Baseline:**
   o Measures the scale of a problem before the change (e.g., number of noise complaints).
   o Allows for comparison after the policy is implemented, showing if it was effective.
9. **Focus on the Entire Community:**
   o Boards have a duty to all residents, not just a vocal few.
   o Decisions based on the loudest voices may not address the true needs of the majority.
10. **Cyclical Nature:**
    o Decisions lead to actions.
    o Actions generate new data.
    o This data informs the next round of decisions, creating an ongoing cycle of improvement.

CHAPTER 13: COMMUNITY PSYCHOLOGY

Introduction

I once worked with a condo community in crisis. A high percentage of units were rentals, and the overall feeling among residents was bleak. Years of neglect had left people feeling isolated and frustrated. There were no community events to bring people together, and residents felt trapped rather than invested in their homes. To make matters worse, the board was struggling financially and lacked a clear direction. The old management company had focused solely on the bare minimum, completely ignoring the deeper needs of the community.

Imagine a place where everyone feels like they truly belong in their shared space. A board's job isn't just about the buildings, it's about the people inside them. That's where community psychology offers invaluable help. At its heart, it's about cultivating connection, empowerment, and a sense of ownership.

In a condo, this means residents who volunteer, respect the rules (and each other), and genuinely care about their neighbors' well-being. Since condo living involves shared spaces and decision-making, community psychology helps everyone navigate the unique challenges. Understanding group dynamics – how people interact, their roles, how decisions are made – is crucial for any board.

The result? Less conflict, better solutions, increased cooperation, and a sense of shared responsibility that makes the condo a truly enjoyable place to live for everyone.

Fast Fact: Small Wins Matter Celebrating small victories builds momentum and keeps both residents and the board motivated.

Beyond Formal Roles – Understanding Group Dynamics

Sure, you have titles on the board – President, Treasurer, etc. But you also play less official roles: the peacekeeper, the always-optimistic one, maybe even the resident skeptic. Understanding these roles is key because they shape how your board works together and interacts with the community. Don't get stuck in these roles – flexibility is important for a healthy group!

The Invisible Rulebook: Social Norms

Every community has unspoken rules – how loud is too loud, are dogs on leashes, how to share the pool area. These "norms" can be great. They make life smoother and create a sense of shared expectations. But, they can turn negative, making people feel excluded or preventing progress.

Fitting In: The Power of Conformity

Let's be honest, everyone wants to feel accepted. This pressure to 'fit in' impacts how decisions are made on the board and in the community at large. Conformity can create harmony... but it can also stifle creativity and much-needed debate. Watch out!

Danger: Groupthink Ahead!

If the need to agree becomes so strong that no one dares to disagree, that's groupthink. You might feel like everyone's on the same page, but critical thinking gets shut down. To prevent this, try playing devil's advocate or actively seek out diverse viewpoints from within the community.

Conflict Happens, Deal With It

Noise, rule-breaking, parking woes... conflict is a fact of life in a condo. How you handle it matters. Aim to collaborate (find solutions everyone can live with), compromise (each side gives a little), or even sometimes strategically avoid (when it's a minor annoyance). Boards that model constructive ways to tackle conflict create a healthier community overall.

Pro Tip: The Devil's Advocate Role Assign a rotating "devil's advocate" board member for big decisions. This helps combat groupthink.

Checklist:

- **Identify Existing Roles:** List the formal roles within your community (board members, committee heads, etc.) as well as any informal roles that frequently emerge (social organizer, unofficial tech-support, etc.).
- **Recognize Informal Leaders:** Pay attention to which residents others gravitate to for advice or help. These individuals often have strong influence within the community.
- **Map Group Dynamics:** Note how different groups interact: Is there collaboration among committees? Friction? Do certain informal groups dominate decision-making?

Timeline (Sample):

- **Week 1:** Focus on observation. Attend meetings or events, noting interactions and patterns.
- **Week 2:** Discreetly interview residents with different levels of involvement to get their perspectives on group dynamics.
- **Week 3:** Draft a preliminary analysis. Identify strengths, weaknesses, and potential areas for improvement.

Action Steps:

- **Share Insights:** Present your findings to the board in a way that's constructive, not accusatory.
- **Propose a Workshop:** Suggest a workshop on effective group dynamics tailored to your specific community.

Understanding What Drives Residents (And How To Respond)

Maslow's Pyramid: The Key to Understanding Needs

To be an effective board, you have to understand what makes residents tick. Maslow's hierarchy of needs helps here. Picture that pyramid: safety at the base, then belonging, then esteem. When these needs go unmet, you may see unexpected behaviors.

- **Safety Fears:** Someone who feels unsafe (whether the threat is real or not) might repeatedly report neighbors for normal activities like having a barbecue. These reports might seem excessive, but they're coming from a place of worry.
- **Seeking Connection:** A lonely resident could generate a lot of complaints, seeking attention and a sense of being part of things. I witnessed this firsthand – one resident seemed to call management over every little thing, creating an ongoing cycle.
- **Boosting Esteem:** Some residents strongly advocate for expensive upgrades, believing these additions will enhance their community's image (and their own standing). A new resident might insist on extravagant landscaping, even if it's beyond the budget.

Key Takeaway: When you understand these deeper needs, you can go beyond simply reacting to complaints or demands. Creating opportunities for residents to participate and feel a sense of ownership can help fulfill these needs in constructive ways.

Fast Fact: Social Time Isn't Just Fun Informal gatherings build the relationships that make conflict resolution easier down the line.

Communication: The Make-Or-Break Factor

How residents communicate drastically impacts conflict resolution. Consider these styles:

- **Aggressive:** Shouting at neighbors about noise, leaving angry notes about parking, dominating meetings.
- **Assertive:** Approaching noise concerns politely, discussing parking issues with the board, respectfully sharing opinions.
- **Passive:** Enduring noise without addressing it, reluctantly parking far away to avoid conflict, staying silent in meetings.

Why Assertiveness Matters

Boards should model assertiveness because it:

- **Sets the Tone:** Residents are more likely to adopt a civil, solution-focused approach when they see the board doing so.
- **Teaches by Example:** Many people need guidance on clear, constructive communication. The board can lead the way.
- **Prevents Escalation:** Assertive communication clarifies issues and de-escalates tense situations, stopping problems from becoming full-blown conflicts.
- **Builds Trust:** Residents trust boards that handle issues transparently and focus on solutions.

The Bystander Effect: A Community Challenge

In communities, it's easy to assume "someone else" will handle a problem. This bystander effect leads to:

- **Ignored Problems:** Rule violations, safety hazards, or a

neighbor in need might go unreported.
- **Apathy:** Residents feel their contributions don't matter, leading to disengagement.
- **Frustration:** The few who consistently step up feel overburdened and resentful.

Strategies to Counteract the Bystander Effect

- **Clear Reporting:** Make it easy to report issues with dedicated phone lines, online forms, etc.
- **Public Recognition:** Thank those who go the extra mile, showing that actions are noticed and valued.
- **Micro-Volunteering:** Offer small, specific roles to reduce barriers and encourage participation.
- **Direct Appeals:** The board can subtly address common issues without singling anyone out.
- **Build Community Spirit:** A connected community is more invested in each other's well-being.

Fast Fact: Participation Isn't Equal Some residents will always be more involved than others. The goal is to tip the scales towards a critical mass of engaged community members.

Important Note: Some residents will always be less engaged. The goal is to tip the scales towards a healthier community dynamic.

Understanding Difficult Personalities

It's important to remember that "difficult" is subjective. Here are some common types of challenging residents boards might encounter:

- **The Chronic Complainer:** Nothing is ever good enough, and they focus on negativity.
- **The Rule Obsessor:** Rigid and inflexible, they may report minor infractions with zeal, causing friction with neighbors.
- **The Narcissist:** They demand special treatment, lack

empathy, and may try to manipulate the board.
- **The Aggressor:** Prone to verbal attacks, threats, or attempts to intimidate the board or other residents.

Basic De-escalation Strategies
- **Stay Calm:** Don't take it personally, even if they attempt to provoke you. A calm demeanor helps diffuse situations.
- **Set Boundaries:** Be clear about what behavior is acceptable and unacceptable (no yelling, insults, etc.).
- **Redirect Towards Solutions:** Acknowledge their concern, but steer the conversation away from ranting and towards potential solutions.
- **Don't Reward Negative Behavior:** Don't cave in to demands made through threats or tantrums. This only reinforces the behavior.

Pro Tip: Avoid Negativity Spirals Don't let a single complainer dominate meetings. Acknowledge their concern, but pivot towards constructive solutions.

When to Seek External Support
- **Mediation:** A neutral third party can facilitate healthier communication and help find common ground, especially for ongoing disputes. Consider this before problems escalate.
- **Legal Advice:** Essential if a resident violates laws, persistently harasses others, or threatens the overall financial health of the condo. Don't wait until a situation becomes a legal liability.
- **Documentation is Key:** Have a system for documenting interactions with difficult residents. This builds a case if external support is needed.

Additional Tips
- **Have a Process:** The board should agree on protocols for handling difficult personalities in advance, preventing

chaotic or inconsistent responses.
- **Don't Isolate:** No one board member should shoulder the burden alone. Seek support from other board members or a management company.
- **Prioritize Community Well-being:** Difficult personalities can drain time and energy. Remember, your primary duty is the well-being of the community as a whole.

Checklist:

- **Resident Needs vs. Wants:** Brainstorm a list of basic needs (safety, cleanliness, etc.) as well as potential wants (social events, amenities, etc.).
- **Categorize Motivations:** Are residents primarily driven by self-interest, community spirit, a sense of duty, or something else?
- **Communication Preferences:** How do different segments of the community prefer to receive information (email, newsletter, app, etc.)?

Timeline (Sample):

- **Week 1-2:** Develop a short, clear resident survey encompassing needs, wants, and communication methods.
- **Weeks 3-4:** Distribute the survey widely, offering incentives for completion (small gift card raffle, etc.).
- **Week 5:** Analyze survey data. Look for trends, as well as any outlier opinions that may be important.

Action Steps:

- **Summarize Findings:** Create a visual infographic highlighting key data for easy digestion by the community.
- **Strategy Session:** Schedule a meeting to discuss how the board can better address resident needs and leverage different motivations.

Building A Positive Community Mindset: Together

A strong sense of belonging is a powerful force! Remember the feeling of moving into your own home, that sense of finally finding your place? Imagine if all your residents felt that sense of connection. Boards should actively work to create this feeling, and here's how:

- **Cultivate Connection:** Blend fun and practical events: potlucks, workshops, community clean-ups. Be inclusive – offer activities that appeal to diverse interests, ages, and accessibility needs.
- **Welcome Newcomers:** Pair new residents with established ones for a friendly face and helpful guidance. Shared spaces like cozy common areas, gardens, or even simple benches encourage casual interaction.
- **Define Your Purpose:** Use surveys to pinpoint what matters most to residents: beautification, safety, social events... Then host workshops where they help turn those priorities into clear, achievable goals. Collaborate on a vision statement that captures your community's ideals.
- **Keep Everyone Informed:** Share goals and progress through newsletters, bulletin boards, and website updates.
- **Listen and Empower:** Form resident committees based on interests: landscaping, events, budget review, etc. Hold open board meetings for questions and input. Provide feedback channels like suggestion boxes and online forms. Above all, be transparent – update residents on

decisions, challenges, and the board's solutions.
- **Celebrate Together!** Recognize victories big and small – completed projects, volunteer milestones, etc. Celebrate with newsletters, plaques, parties, or small gifts. Encourage residents to give each other 'shout-outs' on social media or a community appreciation board.

Pro Tip: Beyond the Formal Welcome Encourage existing residents to reach out to newcomers—it makes the official welcome feel more genuine.

Key Point: Enthusiasm is Infectious

Boards must lead with a positive mindset! Model the behavior you want to see: show enthusiasm, express gratitude, and residents will follow your example.

Fast Fact: The Rule of Seven In communication, people generally need to hear a message seven times before they fully internalize it.

Fast Fact: Surveys Get Specific Instead of asking "Do you like our landscaping?" try "On a scale of 1-5, how satisfied are you with our landscaping?"

Pro Tip: Appreciation is Public Thank volunteers not just privately, but in newsletters or at meetings. This encourages others to step up.

Checklist:

- **"Us" vs. "Them":** Is there a language divide between the board/management and general residents?
- **Identify Shared Values:** What common goals unite most of the community, regardless of their individual differences?
- **Obstacles to Mindset Change:** Consider potential sources of negativity – past conflicts, misinformation, apathy, etc.

Timeline (Sample - Ongoing Effort):

- **Monthly Focus:** Select a shared value to highlight each

month (respect, inclusivity, etc.). Weave that theme into communication and events.
- **Quarterly Review:** Assess the effectiveness of the mindset campaign. Are you seeing greater cooperation, decreased negativity? Adjust as needed.

Action Steps

- **Reframe Communication:** Emphasize partnership language ("we are working together...")
- **Celebrate Collective Wins:** Highlight any successes, big or small, that resulted from community-wide effort or collaboration.

Conclusion: The Heart Of A Thriving Condo Community

We've covered a lot of ground in this chapter:

- **Understanding Needs:** Maslow's hierarchy shows us that residents' actions are driven by basic needs for safety, belonging, and respect. Remember, what may seem strange to you likely holds meaning for them.
- **The Power of Community:** Community psychology offers tools to build strong connections, empower residents, and create a sense of ownership within your condo.
- **Healthy Group Dynamics:** Knowing how people communicate, the informal roles they take on, and avoiding 'groupthink' are key for a well-functioning board and positive community interactions.
- **Resolving Conflict:** Understanding different approaches to conflict resolution helps boards effectively mediate disputes and set a constructive example for everyone.

Actionable Steps:

- **Promote Belonging:** Welcome new residents, create inviting common spaces, and offer events that cater to everyone's interests.
- **Prioritize Communication:** Establish clear ways to report issues, offer channels for resident feedback, and always act with transparency to build trust.

Key Point: It's About People

Condo living is all about shared spaces and shared lives. Boards must focus on building relationships, not just managing buildings. This shift takes effort, but the payoff is huge.

Call to Action

Building a thriving community is an ongoing mission. Boards should regularly revisit these ideas and adjust their approach as needed. The result – a happier, more engaged community – is absolutely worth the investment.

Discover Your Communication Style – Key To A Harmonious Condo Board

How you communicate has a huge impact on your effectiveness as a board member. This quick quiz will help you identify your dominant communication style and areas where you could improve. Remember, a good board needs a mix of approaches to handle various situations effectively.

Instructions: Read each scenario and choose the response that most closely matches what you would realistically do.

1. **Scenario: A new resident has lots of improvement ideas, but they dominate discussions.** You would likely:
    - (A) Acknowledge their enthusiasm, but set boundaries for meeting participation to ensure everyone's voice is heard.
    - (B) Privately message them, suggesting other ways to share ideas without dominating the floor.
    - (C) Get visibly irritated during meetings, hoping they take the hint
2. **Scenario: Several residents disagree with how the board handled a situation.** You would likely:
    - (A) Schedule a meeting to hear concerns directly and explain the board's reasoning.
    - (B) Issue a written statement justifying the board's

actions.
- (C) Dismiss the criticism, feeling the board knows best.

3. **Scenario: You sense a board member is consistently unprepared for meetings.** You would:
    - (A) Have a private, supportive conversation offering resources and help.
    - (B) Hope they improve on their own without you saying anything.
    - (C) Openly express frustration during a meeting, embarrassing them.

4. **Scenario: A major project gets delayed due to unforeseen issues.** You communicate this to residents by:
    - (A) Sending a detailed update with the new timeline, acknowledging potential inconvenience.
    - (B) Posting a brief, matter-of-fact bulletin on the issue.
    - (C) Waiting to see if residents notice the delay before addressing it.

5. **Scenario:** A resident emails a lengthy complaint about noise from the unit above them. The email is filled with frustrated, somewhat dramatic language. You would likely:
    - (A) Reply immediately, validating their feelings and promising to investigate thoroughly.
    - (B) Draft a brief response acknowledging receipt, stating the board will look into it and provide an update by a specific date.
    - (C) Forward the email to another board member, expressing annoyance at the resident's tone.

6. **Scenario:** During a board meeting, there's disagreement on how to spend reserve funds. You strongly believe Option A is best, but others favor Option B. You would:
    - (A) Listen actively to others' reasoning, then clearly present your case for Option A, seeking common ground where possible.

- (B) Largely keep quiet, avoiding confrontation, but ultimately vote for your preferred option.
- (C) Push hard for Option A, dismissing concerns about Option B as uninformed.

7. **Scenario:** You notice a rule violation in a common area, but several other residents are present. You would likely:
    - (A) Directly address the resident(s) involved, reminding them of the rule in a friendly but firm way.
    - (B) Avoid intervening in the moment, but later submit a report about the violation.
    - (C) Ignore it, assuming someone else will likely deal with it.

Mostly As: Your style leans toward assertive – you balance directness with empathy and a solutions-oriented approach.

Mostly Bs: Your style is more passive – you avoid conflict and prefer formal processes.

Mostly Cs: Your style has aggressive tendencies – you prioritize your viewpoint and can be dismissive of others.

Reflection: No one style is best in all situations. This quiz is just a starting point! Consider where your typical style serves you well on the board, and where a different approach might be more effective.

Pro Tip: Board Self-Assessment Board members should periodically assess their own communication styles and areas for growth.

Test Your Knowledge!

1. What are the three basic levels of Maslow's hierarchy of needs, relevant to condo living?
2. Name two benefits of having specific resident committees (landscaping, social events, etc.).
3. What is the "bystander effect," and how can a board counteract it?
4. List three important elements of "assertive communication."
5. What's a key difference between "conforming" and "groupthink"?
6. Name two ways to informally welcome a new resident to your community.
7. Give an example of a SMART goal for a condo community.
8. Describe a situation where a board should consider using a mediator.
9. Why is celebrating even small successes important for community morale?
10. What's one advantage of having a mix of communication styles on a condo board?

The answers are at the end of this chapter

Case Study: When A Muffin Becomes A Mountain

For 15 years, Linda's presence at the monthly condo potluck dinners was defined by the sweet, blueberry-studded muffins she brought. They were a tradition, a gesture of generosity that warmed the room along with their fresh-baked aroma. Her joy came from the quiet smiles, the empty plates, knowing those small acts of baking nurtured a sense of community.

That's why her heart sank when Mrs. Peterson's email landed in her inbox. The accusation – that Linda had been seen hoarding her muffins rather than sharing – cut deep. These weren't just baked goods but symbols of Linda's long-standing goodwill, now twisted into a selfish act.

The board president's attempt at damage control felt even worse. A vague apology about a "misunderstanding" and a suggestion to "try something different" inflamed her further. It wasn't an apology at all, but a subtle confirmation of guilt. Linda's fingers hammered out an email battle with Mrs. Peterson, each salvo laced with fresh resentment.

The cozy potlucks became a warzone of silent side-eyes and whispered comments. The board, having initially swept the issue under the rug, discovered the problem had only grown in darkness. Linda's muffins were no longer the only source of contention. Every 'accidental' door slam by Mrs. Peterson sounded like an act of defiance. Every time Linda snagged the best visitor's parking spot, other residents muttered about entitlement.

The muffin, a symbol of community, had crumbled, revealing the layers of suspicion and long-simmering frustrations that lay beneath the surface of this seemingly peaceful condo community.

What Could They Have Done Differently?

- **Direct Address of the Issue:** The board could have stepped in immediately to address Mrs. Peterson's accusation directly with Linda, aiming to clarify whether it was a misunderstanding rather than an act of malice.
- **Empathetic Mediation:** The board could have played a more active role in mediating the situation between Linda and Mrs. Peterson, promoting communication and finding a path to resolution. This may have involved private conversations and emphasizing the importance of neighborly understanding.
- **Reminder of Shared Values:** The board could have used the initial incident to highlight the importance of kindness and community spirit within the condo, perhaps by organizing an event focused on neighborly appreciation.

Board of Directors Voice: "Honestly, it seemed like such a small thing at first – a misunderstanding over muffins. We never imagined it would blow up like this..."

Question for the Reader: Have you ever encountered a situation where a minor misunderstanding escalated into a larger conflict? How could you help de-escalate tensions and rebuild a sense of community in a similar scenario?

Key Takeaways

- **Don't Underestimate Small Issues:** Seemingly trivial complaints can signal deeper cracks in a community's harmony. Addressing them early is key to preventing wider conflicts.
- **The Power of Mediation:** A neutral third party, like a board member, can be crucial in facilitating communication and preventing personal resentment

from taking hold.
- **Community Values Matter:** Actively reinforcing positive shared values can create a foundation of goodwill, making people more likely to give each other the benefit of the doubt.

Case Study: When A Passion Project Becomes A Battleground

Mr. Green wasn't a flashy man. His hobbies were limited, but the pride he took in his balcony garden was immense. Every spring, that small concrete slab would explode with life. Tomato plants, their vines stretching towards the summer sun, clambered up makeshift trellises. Overflowing pots brimmed with fragrant herbs, and a few strawberry plants dangled temptingly over the railing, their ruby fruits like jewels.

This year, however, a shadow fell over Mr. Green's sanctuary. Muted grumblings turned into emails addressed to the building management: complaints about stray soil from watering, tomato vines brushing a little too close to someone's outdoor furniture. Feeling a sense of unease, Mr. Green waited, hoping the issue would resolve itself.

Instead, the building board responded. A formal letter landed in Mr. Green's mailbox, polite yet chilling. It requested he "tidy things up," to maintain a more cohesive "community aesthetic." Confusion gnawed at Mr. Green. Were there rules about plant height he didn't know about? What exactly qualified as the building's "aesthetic"? He had always received compliments on his garden from fellow residents, making the broad criticisms even more bewildering. A sense of injustice began to brew.

The next communication was far less diplomatic – a harshly-worded notice threatening fines if the garden wasn't drastically reduced. Now, Mr. Green felt truly cornered. His garden was his sanctuary, a sliver of the natural world he craved within the urban landscape. He mulled over the notice, anger rising like sap within him.

Driven by determination, he drafted a spirited petition, railing against the board's "overreach." This circulated among residents, igniting a whole new debate. Was Mr. Green's garden truly an eyesore, as some claimed? Or was the board being needlessly restrictive, trampling on a harmless passion project? The building thrummed with tension, the once-peaceful community abuzz with division.

What Could They Have Done Differently?

- **Clearer Communication:** The board could have initiated the conversation with Mr. Green directly, outlining their concerns and explaining the vaguely defined "community aesthetic." This open dialogue might have prevented escalation.
- **Proposing Solutions:** Instead of imposing demands, the board could have worked with Mr. Green to find solutions. Perhaps suggesting alternative trellising methods, or a compromise on the number of plants.
- **Seeking Resident Input:** The board could have considered the situation more broadly. Was there an issue with a lack of gardening guidelines overall, or was this an isolated case fueled by a few complaints?

Board of Directors Voice: "Look, we want a well-maintained building, a visual harmony. His... it was getting a bit wild. We figured a gentle nudge was all he needed."

Question for the Reader: How can you balance individual passions with the overall feel of your shared community? Are there ways to set clear guidelines that support residents' interests without leading to conflict?

Key Takeaways

- **Proactive communication is key:** Addressing issues early, with transparency and empathy, prevents them from spiraling into full-blown conflict.
- **Compromise and collaboration:** Working *with* people, collaborating on solutions together, creates more positive outcomes than a power struggle.
- **Clear guidelines benefit everyone:** Established rules about common spaces leave less room for misinterpretation and disputes.

Case Study: The Phantom Barking Dog

In the hushed stillness of the apartment complex, an unsettling mystery was unfolding. Each night, as residents drifted toward restless sleep, a piercing, high-pitched bark would shatter the peace. At first, it seemed like a random annoyance, but the relentless barking transformed into a source of mounting tension. Frustrated complaints poured into the management office, yet no culprit could be identified. This led to hushed whispers and simmering resentment among the residents.

With no clear source to blame, some residents turned their suspicions inward. Was it Mr. Johnson's terrier with the snaggletooth? Mrs. Patel's new excitable beagle? The tension escalated, and the once-friendly community edged towards hostility.

Desperation drove the board to call an emergency evening meeting. As residents crammed into the cramped community room, an apprehensive hush fell over the crowd. Then, a timid voice piped up. It was a new resident, Mrs. Williams, face flushed with embarrassment. She choked out an apology and sheepishly confessed that her recently adopted puppy was the source of the nightly disturbance.

Mrs. Williams explained the pup suffered from severe separation anxiety and that she was actively working with a trainer to address the issue. To her surprise, a wave of sympathy and understanding washed over the room. Residents who had been ready to point fingers instead offered advice and support, sharing tips on doggy daycares, calming techniques, and even the names of their own trusted trainers.

The phantom barking slowly subsided, replaced by the sounds of a community coming together. Mrs. Williams, once an anxious newcomer, found herself embraced and supported. The phantom barking incident had threatened to divide the residents but instead, it had unexpectedly illuminated a shared compassion and willingness to help, revealing the true heart of their apartment community.

What Could They Have Done Differently?

- **Proactive Notice:** The board could have put up a general notice earlier, acknowledging an issue and asking for help *identifying* the barking source, framing it as a community problem to solve.
- **Support, Not Accusation:** Management could have offered resources (trainers, helpful articles) alongside the complaint notices, showing understanding of how challenging dog behavior can be.
- **Emphasizing Community:** Regular newsletters or gatherings could have reinforced the idea of being a helpful neighbor, making it easier for someone like Mrs. Williams to come forward sooner.

Board of Directors Voice: "Honestly, we were getting desperate. We were ready to bring in some sound detection equipment, anything! It felt like someone was sabotaging the peace on purpose."

Question for the Reader: Have you ever been in a situation where an unidentified problem caused tension in your community? How could a more collaborative approach have changed the outcome?

Key Takeaways

- **Assumptions fuel conflict.** Without clear information, people fill in the blanks, often with negativity. Proactive,

transparent communication helps.
- **Shared problems need shared solutions.** Framing an issue as a community concern encourages people to contribute rather than feel attacked.
- **A little empathy goes a long way.** Understanding that disruptive behaviors often stem from a deeper source allows for a kinder, more helpful response.

Case Study: Great Idea, But How? When Community Funds Spark Conflict

A windfall of surplus funds hit Waterford Township, and with it came the age-old dilemma: how to best allocate them. Community board meetings quickly descended into noisy debates. The playground advocates, spearheaded by parents with young children, clashed with fitness enthusiasts pushing for a new gym facility. Meanwhile, a more pragmatic faction, led by fiscally-minded homeowners, emphasized the long-term necessity of roof repairs and a robust maintenance fund.

Amid the chaos, Sarah, a recently elected board member, brought a fresh perspective. "We're talking past each other," she observed. "Before any decisions, we need to understand what the majority of residents actually want." Her suggestion – a comprehensive community survey – wasn't intended as a binding vote, but a crucial first step in gauging priorities and shifting the focus away from personal agendas toward data-driven decision-making.

The survey offered a range of options while also allowing residents to voice new ideas. The results were eye-opening. While the major proposals had vocal support, other smaller-scale needs emerged: walking trails, community garden space, improved park benches. The board responded by organizing a public workshop. Cost estimates for each proposed project were presented, and residents were divided into small groups for discussion. This format encouraged greater understanding of the financial realities and encouraged a search for common ground.

Sarah's survey, followed by the workshop, changed the dynamic. Suddenly, compromise didn't seem so out of reach. The final decision reflected the community's diverse desires: a scaled-down but eagerly anticipated playground, a trial period for gym equipment rentals to test community usage, and a dedicated roof repair fund with a clear long-term maintenance plan.

What Could They Have Done Differently?

- **Proactive Needs Assessment:** A community survey could have been done even without the windfall. Understanding resident priorities beforehand would have streamlined the process and minimized initial conflict.
- **Earlier Cost Estimates:** Having cost estimates available for the most likely projects from the start would have injected a dose of reality into the initial debate.
- **Alternative Funding Exploration:** Some projects might have qualified for grants or partnerships (e.g., walking trails could be supported by health organizations).

Board of Directors Voice: "Honestly, everyone shouting their favorite project was getting us nowhere. We needed hard numbers and to hear from more than just the loudest voices."

Question for the Reader: How do you ensure the decision-making process in your community is fair and reflects the needs of the majority, not just a vocal minority?

Key Takeaways

- **Data-driven decisions:** Surveys and needs assessments

eliminate guesswork and ground discussions in shared reality.
- **Transparency builds trust:** Openly sharing cost estimates and financial realities promotes understanding and reduces suspicion.
- **Small wins matter:** Tackling less controversial, lower-cost needs alongside the big projects demonstrates responsiveness and keeps residents engaged.
- **Compromise is possible:** Structured workshops focusing on the practical aspects of implementation encourages collaboration over entrenched stances.

Case Study: When Personalities Clash – Transforming Dysfunction Into Dialogue

Board meetings at the Riverwood Community Association had devolved into a disheartening spectacle. Mrs. Johnson, a stickler for procedural minutiae, would derail discussions by pinpointing obscure rule infractions from past meetings. Conversely, Mr. Davis, a self-proclaimed visionary, scoffed at rules as obstacles to progress and relished long-winded speeches about sweeping changes impractical for the Association.

The remaining board members felt demoralized and ineffective. They appreciated both Mrs. Johnson's dedication to order and Mr. Davis's enthusiasm for innovation, but the constant clashing paralyzed the board's decision-making. Meetings went on for hours, with little accomplished beyond petty bickering.

Recognizing that inaction was harming the Association, the board president, Sarah Wilson, decided on a proactive approach. She understood that both Mrs. Johnson and Mr. Davis were driven by a genuine desire to serve their community but needed guidance on channeling their energies constructively.

Sarah scheduled one-on-one meetings with each of them. With Mrs. Johnson, she began by expressing gratitude for her attention to detail, followed by a gentle explanation of how her constant focus on past irregularities created a negative, accusatory atmosphere, hindering the board's ability to address current needs. Sarah suggested that Mrs. Johnson could utilize her meticulousness by volunteering to review and streamline the Association's bylaws for clarity.

In her meeting with Mr. Davis, Sarah acknowledged his passion and big-picture thinking. Yet, she also pointed out how his dismissive attitude towards rules and his tendency for impractical proposals discouraged other board members from truly engaging with his ideas. Sarah encouraged him to focus on identifying achievable goals that addressed the Association's pressing needs, offering to collaborate with him in developing actionable plans.

Remarkably, both Mrs. Johnson and Mr. Davis proved receptive to Sarah's feedback. Mrs. Johnson's barrage of accusatory emails diminished, and she enthusiastically took on the task of updating the bylaws – channeling her rule-oriented nature into a positive contribution. Mr. Davis, while still prone to the occasional grand idea, began grounding his proposals in more concrete terms and open dialogue with other board members.

The board meetings began to regain a sense of purposefulness. While the dynamic between Mrs. Johnson and Mr. Davis would never transform into one of warm camaraderie, the level of disruptive conflict subsided. Board members found it easier to collaborate, striking a healthy balance between maintaining order and pursuing feasible improvements.

What Could They Have Done Differently?

- **Early Intervention:** The board president, Sarah, could have stepped in sooner. Allowing the bickering to become the norm set a bad precedent for meetings.
- **Skill-Based Subcommittees:** The board could establish different committees based on individual strengths (detail-oriented tasks for Mrs. Johnson, visionary projects for Mr. Davis). This would provide a structured way to channel their energies.
- **Mediator:** In severe cases, an external facilitator or mediator could help with restructuring communication and teaching conflict resolution skills to the board members.

Board of Directors Voice: "Honestly, at first, their squabbles were kind of entertaining. But when it completely stopped us from making decisions... well, something had to change."

Question for the Reader: In your workplace or community groups, how do you balance strong personalities and differing work styles to achieve shared goals?

Key Takeaways

- **Don't let conflict fester:** Address disruptive behavior early to prevent it from becoming the accepted standard.
- **Utilize individual strengths:** Recognize that different personality types bring valuable skills. Channel these skills appropriately.
- **Conflict resolution is a skill:** Sometimes, teaching people how to work together effectively is as important as the actual work they're doing.
- **Leadership matters:** Proactive leaders who value both order and innovation can help navigate personality clashes and nurtures productive collaboration.

Case Study: From Apathy To Action – Revitalizing A Disengaged Community

A sense of stagnation had settled over the community. Resident turnout for events was consistently low, leaving the overworked homeowners' association board feeling increasingly discouraged. The board members recognized that the same old approaches weren't cutting it – they desperately needed a fresh infusion of energy.

That's when they decided to try something radically different: a volunteer appreciation BBQ. The atmosphere was deliberately informal, with a festive vibe replacing the usual rigid meeting format. Instead of focusing on problems, they emphasized sincere gratitude. Each volunteer received a personalized, thoughtful gift – not extravagant, but carefully chosen to show that their contributions were noticed and valued.

The BBQ itself was a success, but the board members knew the real impact would come from what happened next. They crafted a simple survey asking residents not to fixate on what was wrong, but to dream a little. What kind of events would they actually want to attend? Were there hidden passions or talents they'd like to share for the community's benefit?

The responses were like striking a hidden wellspring. One resident, it turned out, was an avid gardener willing to lead a beautification project. A retired teacher, previously shy about offering her services, expressed keen interest in organizing children's activities. A tech-savvy individual, long frustrated by the outdated community website, stepped forward to offer a complete overhaul.

This case study highlights the power of shifting from a problem-focused mindset to one of empowerment and appreciation. By acknowledging the hard work of existing volunteers, the board inadvertently tapped into a deeper pool of potential engagement. The survey was crucial – it demonstrated that the board genuinely cared about residents' desires and created a safe space for new ideas to flourish. This simple act of asking, "How would you like to contribute?" transformed apathy into enthusiastic community action.

What Could They Have Done Differently?

- **Earlier Outreach:** The board could have implemented proactive measures to identify disengagement earlier, such as regular surveys or informal resident "check-in" events. This would have prevented the sense of stagnation from deepening.
- **Diversify Communication:** Relying on traditional meeting formats might have excluded residents who prefer less formal interaction. The board could have used online forums, social media groups, or newsletters to reach different demographics within the community.

Board of Directors Voice: "Honestly, we were burned out. It felt like knocking on doors where nobody was home. This BBQ thing was a bit of a Hail Mary, to be frank."

Question for the Reader: Are there ways to recognize and appreciate the "quiet contributors" in your community – those who might not speak up at meetings but whose efforts are valuable nonetheless?

Key Takeaways

- **Appreciation fuels action:** Sincere acknowledgment of effort can reignite a passion for involvement, far more effectively than complaints or demands.

- **Listen, don't assume:** Don't decide what your community needs without asking them directly. Create accessible channels for residents to share their ideas and interests.
- **Empowerment over "fixing":** Instead of focusing exclusively on problems to solve, highlight opportunities for residents to contribute their skills and passions within the community.

Test Your Knowledge! Answers

1. **Maslow's Basics:** Safety (feeling secure in one's home), Belonging (feeling part of the community), and Esteem (pride in the community, self-respect as a resident).
2. **Why Committees?**
    - Distributes responsibility, preventing board burnout.
    - Taps into residents' specific skills and interests.
3. **Understanding the Bystander Effect:** This is when people assume someone else will handle a problem. Boards can counteract it with clear reporting systems, reminders of shared responsibility, and by publicly thanking those who do take action.
4. **Assertive Communication Elements:**
    - Direct and respectful
    - Focus on solutions, not just complaints
    - Active listening to understand others' viewpoints
5. **Conformity vs. Groupthink:** Conformity is about fitting in with social norms. Groupthink is when the desire for agreement leads to ignoring flaws in ideas or suppressing dissent.
6. **Informal Welcomes:**

- A friendly greeting from neighbors in common areas
    - A small welcome basket from existing residents
7. **SMART Goal Example:** "Within 6 months, increase resident participation in community events by 20% as measured by attendance records."
8. **When to Seek Mediation:**
    - Deeply entrenched disputes between residents
    - When the board is a direct party in the conflict
    - If legal threats are involved
9. **Celebrating Wins:**
    - Builds community pride and sense of accomplishment
    - Motivates further involvement and positive action
10. **Benefits of Diverse Communication Styles:** A mix of assertive, passive, and even the occasional 'devil's advocate' on a board ensures well-rounded decision-making and helps represent a broader range of resident perspectives.

CONCLUSION

The Launchpad: Embracing Your Role As A Leader

Think of this not as the conclusion of the book, but the launchpad for your journey as a knowledgeable, well-equipped board of directors member. Throughout this guide, you've explored the fundamental principles of condominium management, encountering both familiar and fresh concepts. The goal has always been to empower you as a board member, giving you the tools to lead your community with confidence and success. Let's recap some key takeaways and highlight the importance of proactive board leadership.

Beyond Problem-Solving: The Board's Strategic Role

Condominium board members hold a fiduciary duty to act in the best interest of the entire community. This shapes every decision, from budgets to maintenance. You must skillfully balance the needs of individuals with the overall well-being of the condominium, ensuring fairness, transparency, and swift conflict resolution.

Boards are not merely problem-solvers. You shape the community's future with long-term plans that secure its financial health, maintain the property, and create a desirable living environment. Remember, the board's authority is paramount. You are not beholden to the management company, attorneys, accountants, insurance brokers, residents, or any other entity.

Your residents trust you to provide strategic leadership. Manage third-party relationships, including your management company, to best serve your vision for the community. Focus on critical thinking and big-picture strategy – experts will handle the details so you don't have to.

Avoid micromanagement by staying focused on high-level goals. Optimize meeting schedules for maximum participation. Create a fulfilling board experience that consistently delivers on the promises you made when you joined.

Stay Ahead Of The Curve: Prioritize Board Education

Condominium management is constantly evolving. Laws change, technology advances, new best practices appear, and resident needs fluctuate. To stay ahead of the curve, prioritize continuous learning as a board member.

- **Get Training:** Seek out courses and workshops on governance, finances, conflict resolution, and areas specific to your community.
- **Stay Informed:** Read industry publications, websites, and association materials for the latest insights.
- **Leverage Your Vendors:** Your attorneys, management company, insurance agent, and CPA can be valuable sources of knowledge on current regulations and best practices.
- **Build a Network:** Connect with other boards locally and online. Share experiences and strategies – peer-to-peer learning is incredibly powerful.

Dynamic Leadership For Dynamic Communities

Your journey as a board member promises challenge, opportunity, and a diverse cast of characters. To thrive, embrace change, adapt your approach, and learn from every experience.

Consider the knowledge from this book your essential toolkit – use it as needed. Collaborate with fellow board members and promote open communication with residents. Teamwork and diverse perspectives are your greatest assets.

Always conduct yourself with professionalism, integrity, transparency, and respect. Follow established procedures and treat everyone with the courtesy you'd expect. Build strong relationships with those who support you; distance yourself from those who don't.

Focus on proactive leadership. Anticipate challenges, prioritize preventative maintenance, maintain financial reserves, and plan for the unexpected. Create a system that aligns with your community's needs and regulations, adapting as necessary.

A Final Word of Encouragement

Your dedication to your community is admirable! Your commitment to growth benefits everyone. Remember, you have a support network of fellow board members, residents, and professional advisors. Celebrate your achievements and the positive impact you have on your community.

Key Themes to Remember

- **Honest Assessment:** Realistically assess your

community's current situation and focus on positive change.
- **Long-Term Vision:** Make financial, maintenance, and partnership decisions with a long-term focus. Proactive strategies save time and money. Prioritize projects that improve the community. Set clear, multi-year goals.
- **Two-Way Communication:** Resident input is vital! Gather feedback and keep residents informed through surveys, town halls, forums, or newsletters. Strong communication builds trust and shared responsibility.

As your board leadership journey continues, embrace these principles. Take a specific, immediate action inspired by this book!

All the best on your journey!

ABOUT THE AUTHOR

Matthew Snyder, founder and leader of Managemax, draws on his extensive experience in community management. He wrote this book to share his experience and help boards navigate the complexities of community management. Having weathered Michigan's housing depression, managed foreclosure real estate sales for national clients, and has a proven record of advising boards and reviving struggling communities.

Driven by a commitment to excellence, he founded Managemax to revolutionize community management. The company combines technology, transparent communication, and proactive problem-solving to deliver innovative, client-focused solutions. Matthew's MBA from Carnegie Mellon University and CFA Charter exemplify Managemax's use of analytical rigor and human dynamics to deliver exceptional outcomes.

At Managemax, integrity, innovation, and client satisfaction guide every action. Learn more about how we empower communities at https://managemax.properties/

www.ingramcontent.com/pod-product-compliance
Lightning Source LLC
Chambersburg PA
CBHW050045230526
45470CB00004B/1409